ALSO BY BART D. EHRMAN

■ ■ ■

Heaven and Hell

The Triumph of Christianity

Jesus Before the Gospels

How Jesus Became God

The Other Gospels

The Bible: A Historical and Literary Introduction

Forgery and Counterforgery

Did Jesus Exist?

The Apocryphal Gospels: Texts and Translations

Forged

Jesus, Interrupted

God's Problem

The Lost Gospel of Judas Iscariot

Peter, Paul, and Mary Magdalene

Studies in the Textual Criticism of the New Testament

Misquoting Jesus

The Apostolic Fathers

Truth and Fiction in The Da Vinci Code

A Brief Introduction to the New Testament

After the New Testament

The New Testament: A Historical
Introduction to the Early Christian Writings

Christianity in Late Antiquity

Lost Christianities

Lost Scriptures

Jesus: Apocalyptic Prophet of the New Millennium

The Orthodox Corruption of Scripture

The Text of the Fourth Gospel in the Writings of Origen

Didymus the Blind and the Text of the Gospels

ARMAGEDDON

WHAT *the* BIBLE REALLY SAYS ABOUT *the* END

——— ...

BART D. EHRMAN

SIMON & SCHUSTER

New York   London   Toronto   Sydney   New Delhi

Simon & Schuster
1230 Avenue of the Americas
New York, NY 10020

First Simon & Schuster hardcover edition March 2023

SIMON & SCHUSTER and colophon are registered
trademarks of Simon & Schuster, Inc.

For information about special discounts for bulk purchases,
please contact Simon & Schuster Special Sales at 1-866-506-1949
or business@simonandschuster.com.

The Simon & Schuster Speakers Bureau can bring authors to
your live event. For more information or to book an event,
contact the Simon & Schuster Speakers Bureau at 1-866-248-3049
or visit our website at www.simonspeakers.com.

Interior design by Lewelin Polanco

Manufactured in the United States of America

10 9 8 7 6 5 4 3 2 1

Library of Congress Cataloging-in-Publication Data

Names: Ehrman, Bart D., author.
Title: Armageddon : what the Bible really says about the end /
    Bart D. Ehrman.
Description: First Simon & Schuster hardcover edition. | New York :
    Simon & Schuster, 2023. | Includes bibliographical references and index.
Identifiers: LCCN 2022043682 (print) | LCCN 2022043683 (ebook) |
    ISBN 9781982147990 | ISBN 9781982148010 (ebook)
Subjects: LCSH: Armageddon—Biblical teaching. | End of the world—
    Biblical teaching. | Bible—Prophecies—End of the world.
Classification: LCC BS649.A68 E37 2023 (print) | LCC BS649.A68 (ebook) |
    DDC 236/.9—dc23/eng/20221209
LC record available at https://lccn.loc.gov/2022043682
LC ebook record available at https://lccn.loc.gov/2022043683

ISBN 978-1-9821-4799-0
ISBN 978-1-9821-4801-0 (ebook)

To Roger Freet

Friend, Editor, and Agent Extraordinaire

Contents

Acknowledgments   xi

A Note on Quotations   xv

Preface   xvii

■ **ONE**   1
The End Is Near

■ **TWO**   23
The Most Mystifying Book of the Bible

■ **THREE**   49
A History of False Predictions

■ **FOUR**   75
Real-Life Consequences of the
Imminent Apocalypse

■ **FIVE**   109
How to Read the Book of Revelation

■ **SIX**   143
The Lamb Becomes a Lion:
Violence in the Book of Revelation

■ **SEVEN**   169
The Ideology of Dominance:
Wealth and Power in Revelation

■ **EIGHT**   195
The Apocalypse of John and the Gospel of Jesus

Notes   209

Index   237

Acknowledgments

The best thing about writing a book is finishing it, and the next best thing is being able to thank those who made it possible. I have incurred numerous debts during my research and writing, and here I am pleased to acknowledge them. Readers of my manuscript made helpful comments, helped me clarify my thoughts, and saved me from many mistakes. I can't thank them enough, so I'll thank them a lot.

First, I am grateful to the fellow scholars who generously gave of their time to help a colleague in need. They are all incredibly busy academics, and reading someone else's work was a much-appreciated act of supererogation.

- Stephen Andrews, Professor of American History, Indiana University of Bloomington
- Yaakov Ariel, Professor of American Religions, University of North Carolina at Chapel Hill
- Darrell Bock, Senior Research Professor of New Testament Studies, Dallas Theological Seminary
- Christopher Frilingos, Professor of Religious Studies, Michigan State University
- Robert Royalty, Professor of History and Religion, Wabash College
- Jeffrey Siker, Professor of New Testament, emeritus, Loyola Marymount University

- Judy Siker, Professor of New Testament, emerita, Loyola Marymount University
- James Tabor, Professor of Christian Origins, University of North Carolina at Charlotte

Because the book is meant for a broader audience, I asked a number of insightful non-scholars to read it as well. These are members of *The Bart Ehrman Blog*, a now ten-year venture that deals with issues connected with the New Testament and Early Christianity. The goals of the blog are to present scholarly views in language and terms laypeople can understand and in doing so to raise money for those in need. Blog members pay a small fee to join, and all the money goes directly to charities dealing with hunger, homelessness, and literacy.

I gave members of my blog the opportunity to read and comment on my manuscript in exchange for a set donation, and a number took me up on it. They made many helpful comments, and I'd like to thank them all: Rizwan Ahmed, Greg Bohlen, Dave Bohn, Luke Cartledge, Nathan Gordon, Kevin Grant, Jenise Huffman, Dan Kohanski, Jack Lange, John Merrick, Daniel Miller, Payman Nadimi, Diane Pittman, Cheryl Pletcher, Marc Sala, James Silva, Douglas Wadeson, Wannes Vanderheijden, and Jeff Williams.

My especial thanks go to three people without whom the book would never have happened. My brilliant wife and lifelong partner, Sarah Beckwith, the Katherine Everitt Gilbert Professor of English at Duke, remains the most insightful and scintillating dialogue partner I have ever known, and she willingly and even happily let me bounce ideas, good and bad, off her. Priscilla Painton, vice president and editorial director at Simon & Schuster, was enthusiastic about the project from the beginning and inordinately supportive every step along the way; this is our third book together and it has been a pleasure for the entire stretch. Megan Hogan, editor at Simon &

Schuster, deserves a special word of thanks. Megan took to my prose more seriously than any editor I have ever had, line by line, making this a much tighter, more compelling, and better written book. I have no clue how many hours, days, and weeks it took her. May her editorial tribe increase.

Finally, there is my agent, Roger Freet, the "constant" in my publishing endeavors for the past twenty years. Roger was first my editor at Harper for six books, and when he moved to his new life as a literary agent he brought me on board. When not working together on books we have become friends with a good deal in common: values, academic interests, and beverage preferences. My career would have been incalculably different without his guidance, support, and advocacy. And so, I have dedicated this book to him.

A Note on Quotations

Quotations of the Hebrew Bible are taken from the New Revised Standard Version; quotations of the New Testament are either my own translations or those of the NRSV.

Preface

Many early Christians opposed the book of Revelation and argued it should not be included in the New Testament. The author, they insisted, was not an apostle and the book presented unacceptable views of the future of earth and the people who will inherit it. In the end, of course, they lost the argument. Once the book was widely accepted as Scripture, the followers of Jesus had to figure out how to make sense of it.

Over the long course of Christian history, many readers of the Bible have opted simply not to delve into its mysteries. Even today, most find the book of Revelation bizarre and unapproachable. Those who do read it usually fall into two camps. Since the end of the nineteenth century, most evangelical Christians have taken the book as a blueprint for events soon to come. These readers are convinced that the book's prophecies are now, at last, being fulfilled. God has begun to intervene in history through a series of foreordained disasters. At a final confrontation of the powers of good and evil, the Battle of Armageddon, Christ will appear from heaven to destroy his enemies. But true believers in Jesus will survive and thrive in a glorious utopia—a city of gold with gates of pearl, from which they will rule the world for all time.

On the other side of the interpretive spectrum, liberal Christian scholars argue the book does not provide a literal description of divinely ordained catastrophes. It is instead a metaphorical narrative meant to provide a message of hope for those who suffer now, much as Christ himself suffered when he was among us. In this view, Revelation seeks to show that while evil is pervasive and misery rampant, the Ruler of all will eventually make right everything that is wrong. The book does not describe the imminent end of history as we know it; it celebrates God as the ultimate source of hope for all who follow him.

I have held both these views at different times in my life, and I now think they are both wrong.

I began my study of Revelation as a teenager in the mid-1970s. As a committed evangelical Christian, I considered every word of the Bible inspired and true, and I heartily embraced a literal reading of the prophecies of Revelation, convinced they showed beyond any doubt that Jesus was soon to return from heaven, and then there would be hell to pay, at least for those who, unlike me, were not true believers.

After some years, as I engaged in a more rigorous study of the Bible, I came to see the difficulties with this view and began to explore the book of Revelation from a more historical perspective. I realized why it was important to understand the work in its own context in relation to other ancient Jewish and Christian books collectively called "apocalypses." These are endlessly fascinating works that narrate visions of things to come in order to show how the awful realities of earth can be explained by the truths of heaven, with the goal of providing comfort.

This is how I taught the book when I began my university career, as a graphic but nonliteral proclamation of hope for those who are suffering. All will be well in the end. Good will triumph. God will prevail. And he will "wipe away every tear" (Revelation 21:4).

I eventually had to abandon this understanding of the book. It was difficult for me to do so, just as earlier in life it had been hard to give up on the idea that Revelation was predicting our future. In this book, I show why I think both views are flawed. In the first part, I explain how a "futuristic" understanding of the book as a blueprint for what is yet to come evolved and why this reading is almost certainly wrong—even though it continues to be the view of evangelical Christians and of American culture at large.

In the second part, I show why I also don't think Revelation provides a comforting message for the vast majority of those who suffer in this life. The overwhelming emphasis of Revelation is not about hope but about the wrath and vengeance of God against those who have incurred his displeasure. For the author of Revelation, that entails the vast majority of those who have ever lived, including, perhaps surprisingly, a number of committed Christians. The largest section of Revelation describes God inflicting horrible suffering on the planet: war, starvation, disease, drought, earthquake, torture, and death. The catastrophes end with the Battle of Armageddon, where Christ destroys all the armies of earth and calls on the scavengers of the sky to gorge themselves on their flesh. This is the climax of the history of earth.

But it is not the end of all things. After the slaughter there will be a final judgment, when God's faithful followers, his "slaves," will be saved; everyone else who has ever lived will be brought back to life and then thrown, while still alive, into a lake of burning sulfur. Afterward, God will reward his obedient slaves by giving them a glorious new city of gold with gates of pearl. That is indeed a happy ending for some, but not because God loves them deeply—at least the book never says so. The saved are God's minions who do what he demands. The love of God—for anyone or anything—is never mentioned in the book of Revelation, not once.

At the end of this book, I consider why Revelation was nearly excluded from the New Testament and ponder whether the ancient Christian opponents of the book may in fact have had some valid insights. In particular, I compare the views of its author, John of Patmos, with the teachings of Jesus. John certainly considered himself a follower of Jesus—a particularly ardent follower. But are his views actually consistent with those of his Lord? Would Jesus have accepted John's celebration of violence, quest for vengeance, passion for glory, and hope for world domination? Did he not instead urge his followers to pursue love, non-retaliation, poverty, and service?

Different readers, of course, will answer these questions differently. I would simply urge anyone who wants to pursue them to read, or reread, Revelation to see what it actually says. That is what I have tried to do here.

My book is not, however, meant simply to provide a better interpretation of the Apocalypse of John. I also explain how a literal reading has created disastrous problems, including personal and psychological damage of myriads around us: family members, friends, and neighbors. But there is more than that. The expectation—or, rather, hope—for imminent Armageddon has affected our world in ways you might not expect, involving carnage, US foreign policy, and the welfare of our planet.

There could scarcely be a better time to reflect on such matters. We live in apocalyptic times of massive starvation, population shifts, plague, global superpowers waging war, and, possibly most frightening of all, a burning planet. Parts of our Western cultural heritage that are driven by traditional apocalyptic thinking have encouraged fatalism and inaction in the face of our crises. We would do well, then, to reflect on the historical roots of these views.

ONE

The End Is Near

I was expecting some significant culture shock when I moved to North Carolina in 1988. I had spent ten years in New Jersey, four of them teaching at Rutgers University. It was a position I loved: teaching the New Testament to students who were curious but not, as a rule, particularly invested in the subject before taking the class. Most of my students were Roman Catholic, at least nominally; others were Jewish or secular. Not many were Bible-reading evangelicals. I was pretty sure things would be different in the South. The University of North Carolina at Chapel Hill was not known as a bastion of conservative thought, but it was, after all, in the Bible Belt. I braced myself, imagining that—as a former evangelical Christian myself—I knew what to expect. But the world is full of surprises.

I arrived in early August, and about a week after unpacking I received a call from a local newspaper. The reporter had heard I was a New Testament scholar and he had a pressing question: "Is it true that Jesus is returning in September?" My first thought was "Here we go."

The reporter was asking because there was a booklet in wide circulation by someone named Edgar Whisenant, who mounted numerous biblical arguments that the "rapture" would occur that year during the Jewish festival of Rosh Hashanah—just weeks away. There were some two million copies of the booklet in circulation.

For readers who do not know about the "rapture": for well over a century now, self-identified fundamentalists and other conservative evangelical Christians have maintained that Jesus is soon to return from heaven in order to take his followers out of the world.[1] They will be "snatched" up with him from earth to heaven—hence the term "rapture" (meaning "snatched up"). Jesus will remove them from the world so they can escape the coming "tribulation," a seven-year period of absolute misery in which the chief opponent of Christ, the Satan-inspired "Antichrist," assumes sole political power over all the nations of earth, while natural and military catastrophes occur one after the other. At the end of this period, when the world is about to blow itself into oblivion (in most scenarios since 1945 through a massive nuclear exchange), Jesus will return again, this time to put an end to the madness before all is lost. He will then bring a thousand-year period of peace on earth, to be followed by a last judgment and then a utopian kingdom for the saved, for all time.

Whisenant argued that the rapture was going to happen next month.

I assured the reporter that, well, no, this wasn't going to happen. He was a little disappointed, but I did tell him the good news: if I was wrong, either he wouldn't be around to worry about it or he would have lots to write about for the next seven years.

Since the end of the nineteenth century, most fundamentalist Christians have maintained that all this is taught in the Bible. That would have been news to Christians throughout most of the first nineteen hundred years of the church, who thought no such thing.

But starting especially in the 1890s, this view spread in popularity until it became the standard understanding of what was to happen here on planet earth, at least among Christians in North America and some parts of Europe. Today, a belief in the coming rapture is held by hundreds of millions of people—not just fundamentalists— all of whom believe it is simply what the Bible teaches, especially in its final book, the Apocalypse of John, also known as the book of Revelation. The author, who calls himself John, assures his readers that these events are "coming soon." But when?

Edgar Whisenant had narrowed the options down to September 11–13, 1988.

Almost no one had heard of Whisenant before he placed his booklet in circulation. He started out as a NASA rocket engineer, but he was less interested in propelling people into space than in knowing when God would take them there. To find the answer, Whisenant engaged in an intense investigation of the Bible. The hints he found were scattered in verses here and there throughout the Old and New Testaments: a verse from Daniel combined with one from Matthew, together with one from Zechariah, another from Romans, and, of course, a number of them from the visions of the book of Revelation. When Whisenant had assembled the requisite pieces of this divine jigsaw puzzle, he produced his small book, giving it a compelling title: *88 Reasons Why the Rapture Is in 1988.*[2]

Whisenant does indeed provide eighty-eight arguments for his prognostications, based mainly on the Bible but also on historical events and, well, "common sense." It would be tedious to discuss these at length (I can assure you), but a solitary example should give an idea. Matthew 24 shows Jesus speaking about what will happen at the end of time when the cosmic "Son of Man" arrives from heaven in judgment. His disciples, somewhat naturally, want to know when all this will happen, and so Jesus tells them: "Learn the parable from the fig tree. When its branch becomes tender and it puts forth leaves, you know that summer is near. So I tell you, when you see all these things happen, you know that he is near, at the gate. Truly I tell you, this generation will not pass away until all these things take place" (Matthew 24:32–34).

To explain the parable, Whisenant asks what the "fig tree" represents and points out that elsewhere in Scripture it is a symbol of the nation of Israel, expected to bear good fruit. In Jesus's saying, the tree has lain dormant through the winter—as if dead—but then comes back to life in spring and puts forth its leaves. When does the nation of Israel come back to life after a long period of dormancy? Israel was destroyed as a nation in the second century CE and did not become a sovereign state again until 1948.

Jesus declares: "This generation will not pass away before all these things take place." How long is a generation in the Bible? Forty years. And so, it is a matter of simple math: 1948 plus 40. Bingo! Jesus himself says he will return in 1988.

There are eighty-seven more of these arguments.[3]

Most people will find this kind of reasoning puzzling, or perhaps weirdly interesting. But Whisenant did not write his book for scoffers who could easily poke holes in his thinking. His predictions were for those who were inclined to be convinced. And many were. Not so much in New Jersey, but certainly in parts of the South. I had an undergraduate student that semester whose parents literally sold the farm.

It is not that there was unanimous fundamentalist support for Whisenant's convictions. Even conservative Christians often refuse to set a date for the rapture, and many of them pointed out to Whisenant that Jesus himself said that "no one knows the day or the hour" when the end will come, "not the angels in heaven nor even the Son" (Matthew 24:36). Whisenant, though, had a ready response. He agreed no one could know the day or the hour. He just knew the week.[4]

HAL LINDSEY AND THE
END OF THE WORLD

The Whisenant affair was new to me, but I had long been familiar with these lines of reasoning—even with the idea that Jesus would return around or even in 1988. That had been my own view for years. I had been brought up as a decidedly nonfundamentalist Episcopalian. But when I was fifteen, I had a "born-again" experience and became convinced that if I was going to be a "serious Christian," I would not do something pedestrian like go to a major university or liberal arts college. I decided to attend a fundamentalist Bible school. Someone suggested Moody Bible Institute in Chicago, so, in August 1973, there I went.

The summer before going, I studied the Bible as best I could. I knew there was an entrance exam at Moody, and I didn't want to seem like an idiot. But the book of Revelation scared me. I had glanced at it and had heard people talk about it, but it sounded so bizarre and puzzling that I wasn't sure I could handle it. The week before leaving for Chicago, I decided I had to bite the bullet, but it was to no avail: I couldn't make heads or tails of it.

My sense is that most readers are like that. It really is a mystifying book, and unless someone gives you a road map to explain how the author gets from point A to point B and tells you how to interpret the signs along the way, you'll get lost. After getting to Moody, I was given that map. I got the general lay of Revelation's land right off the bat—the book is quite popular among fundamentalist futurists—and in my second year I took a semester-long course on it. In addition, I had a private guide, recommended by millions of travelers before me: Hal Lindsey, whose book *The Late Great Planet Earth*, first published in 1970, became something of a second Bible for evangelicals around the country.[5]

Lindsey was a graduate of the fundamentalist Dallas Theological

Seminary—the school all we burgeoning fundamentalist intellectuals aspired to attend—and had become a spokesperson for the imminent end of the world. Unlike Whisenant, he was not on the fringes of American culture. On the contrary, *The Late Great Planet Earth* was the single bestselling work of nonfiction (using the term loosely) of the 1970s, a book later important to none other than President Ronald Reagan, Secretary of Defense Caspar Weinberger, and other members of Reagan's cabinet, who were convinced that the bombs were eventually going to fly. For people in power to think that mutual self-destruction has been foreordained in holy writ is not, obviously, a comforting thought.

Lindsey was not a number cruncher like Whisenant. He was a spinner of tales. He did believe that Jesus was returning by the end of the 1980s. Matthew 24:36 ("the fig tree puts forth its leaves") was determinative for him as well. But he was too canny to name a date. He was more interested in showing *how* it was all going to happen. Again, this involved a scrupulous examination of the Bible. It is not clear that Lindsey himself did much of the investigative legwork: while a student at the Dallas Theological Seminary he had taken classes with John Walvoord, famous in fundamentalist circles for his many books on biblical prophecies about the imminent end of the world. Some of Lindsey's classmates later claimed that he cribbed *The Late Great Planet Earth* from Walvoord's lectures.[6]

But Lindsey certainly had a flashy style of presentation, quite different from Walvoord's rather gloomy and ponderous prose. Lindsey was witty and clever and knew how to package the bad news. To us fundamentalists in the 1970s, his guide to the events soon to take place seemed not just plausible but virtually assured.

In Lindsey's account, the now-restored Israel was soon to assume control of the entire city of Jerusalem and, in the process, claim the Temple Mount entirely for itself. It would then level the Dome of the Rock, the Islamic shrine built over the site of the original temple, which had been destroyed in 70 CE. Israel would rebuild the temple, as predicted by the biblical prophets. This reassertion of Israel's religious and national rights would rouse opposition from the neighboring Arab states, compelling Israel to seek political and military assistance through an alliance with a newly formed ten-nation European Commonwealth. The leader of the Commonwealth would negotiate peace in the Middle East for three and a half years but would then show his true colors. He would enter the Jerusalem temple and, in the holy place itself, declare himself to be God. This would begin a reign of terror designed to beat the nations of earth into submission so that he himself, the Antichrist, could control the entire world's economy.

The Arab-African coalition would respond to this threat by invading Israel. Then the big guns would get involved. The Soviet Union, always eager to flex its expansionist muscles and keen to acquire the vast resources of the Middle East, would enter the fray with an amphibious and ground attack that would overwhelm the Arab-African alliance. The European Commonwealth would respond with a tactical nuclear strike, wiping out the Russian homeland. At this point, China would see its opportunity and, with a newly refurbished 200-million-soldier army, would converge on the Europeans in the final battle. (Lindsey did not spell out the involvement of the United States in all this; he vaguely links it with the European Commonwealth.) In desperation, both sides would release their nuclear arsenals and the human race would be on the brink of complete annihilation when . . . Jesus returned to end the nonsense.

For Hal Lindsey, this is what the Bible teaches. And it teaches it will all happen soon. But—and here is the big "but" that we Christians reveled in—believers in Jesus would see none of it happen. Immediately before this entire sequence of events begins, the followers of Jesus would be taken out of the world. They would be raptured.

For those of us inclined to subscribe to the infallibility of the prophetic writings of Scripture, these dismal projections were not speculations but judicious interpretations of God's holy word. Everyone had a choice. They could go directly to heaven at the first return of Jesus to enjoy the bliss of paradise, or they could stay down here to experience hell on earth.

Lindsey meant the book as an evangelistic tool. This was not an old-fashion revivalist evangelism in the dour mode of Jonathan Edwards's "Sinners in the Hands of an Angry God." This was a 1970s hip, blow-your-mind, futuristic evangelism. And it was highly effective . . . at least among those who were already fundamentalists. All of us bought it—literally. Millions of copies of *The Late Great Planet Earth* were sold (ten million by the end of the decade; twenty-eight million by the end of the 1990s).

THE RAPTURE IN SCRIPTURE?

What we had no idea of at the time—and what practically no one has any idea of still—is that the book of Revelation was almost never read this way throughout the course of Christian history. And yet almost everyone today thinks that Revelation provides a blueprint of what is to happen in the near future—at least those who think about it at all. There are, of course, some holdouts, even among conservative Christians, who maintain the book needs to be read another way. But the popular perception is that, whether absolutely right or terribly wrong, the book of Revelation tries to describe what is going to happen to us here in the twenty-first century.

Why does this seem to be the natural, commonsensical reading? Because the fundamentalists have won.[7] It is not that fundamentalists have won over the great bulk of society to the entire panoply of their religious views. The vast majority of the human race decidedly does not think the Bible is completely inerrant in everything it says, that the world was created in six days some six thousand years or so

ago, that there really was an Adam and Eve, and that . . . well, make
your list. But fundamentalists have succeeded in convincing everyone (or at least those who are remotely interested) that Revelation
describes what will happen in our own future, and probably soon.
Possibly starting next year, or, well, next Thursday.[8]

But here is a little-known factoid: The word "rapture" never appears in the Bible. Here's another: Even apart from the actual word,
the book of Revelation never says anything about the followers of
Jesus being taken out of the world before it all goes up in flames.
The idea of the rapture has not been taken from the Bible; it has
been *read into* the Bible.

Here is an even more interesting factoid: No one had even
thought of the idea of a "rapture" until the 1830s. Of the many,
many thousands of serious students of the Bible throughout Christian history who pored over every word—from leading early Christian scholars such as Irenaeus in the second century; to Tertullian
and Origen in the third; to Augustine in the fifth; to all the biblical scholars of the Middle Ages up to Aquinas; to the Reformation
greats Luther, Melanchthon, and Calvin; on to, well, everyone who
studied or simply read or even just heard passages from the Bible—
this idea of the rapture occurred to no one until John Nelson Darby
came up with the idea in the early 1800s (as we will discuss in chapter 3).

Even so, back in my fundamentalist days, I, too, was completely
certain the rapture was in the Bible, right there in black and white.
The key passage was 1 Thessalonians 4:13–18, a letter by the apostle
Paul to his converts in the city of Thessalonica, written to provide
assurance and comfort because they were worried about "those who
have fallen asleep." That's a euphemism in the Bible for "those who
have died." When Paul converted the Thessalonians, he had taught
them that the end of the present age was coming very soon: God was
about to bring a utopian world to the world, the glorious kingdom

of God. Now, some of the Thessalonians had died before this could happen, and the survivors were very upset: Had those who were no longer living lost out on their chance for the coming kingdom?

Paul writes to assure these people that they do not need to "grieve as the others who do not have hope" (that is, the non-Christians; 1 Thessalonians 4:13). When Jesus returns from heaven, the very first to be rewarded will be the believers who have already died. They will be raised up from their graves to meet Jesus on his way down; then those still living on earth will also rise up to meet him in the air.

That's the rapture, right? It sure seems to be if you read the passage with fundamentalist eyes:

> For we tell you this by a word of the Lord: we who are living, who are left until the coming of the Lord, will not go before those who sleep. For the Lord himself will descend from heaven with a cry, with the voice of an archangel, and with the trumpet of God—and the dead in Christ will rise first. Then we who are living, who remain, will be taken up together with them in the clouds, to meet the Lord in the air. And so we will always be with the Lord. (1 Thessalonians 4:15–18)

How can this not be referring to the rapture?

To begin with, it is important to read the passage, and all passages of the Bible, in context—a point I will be beating like a drum throughout this book. Paul certainly did believe Jesus would be returning from heaven and it would be soon. The key, though, is to understand Paul's explanation of what will actually occur at that second coming.

Throughout his writings Paul insists that Christ will return in judgment. Jesus was crushed by his enemies at the crucifixion, but he is coming back to annihilate them. His return will bring destruction to everyone who has not accepted the good news of his salvation. The "saved" will survive the onslaught and be rewarded with glorious bodies that will never again be hurt, sick, or die; they will then live forever with Christ in the coming kingdom (see 1 Corinthians 15 and 1 Thessalonians 1:9–10).

I want to pause here to discuss something seemingly small that will help us understand this passage, and every other passage in the Bible. Our Bibles today have chapter and verse divisions. These are extremely helpful, of course, since without them it is very hard indeed to tell someone where to find a passage. But the authors did not write in chapters and verses. One problem with our having them is that they make us think that the next chapter (or even verse) is changing the subject. But Paul would have written the first sentence of what is now 1 Thessalonians 5 right after the final sentence of what is now chapter 4 (quoted above) without skipping a beat. In these next words, he indicates that the coming of the Lord (4:13–18) will bring "sudden destruction" for those not expecting it (5:3). Christ will be like a "thief in the night" (5:4). This is not a reassuring image. The robber comes to harm, not to help. But the good news for Paul is that this harm will come only to those who are not among Jesus's followers; his faithful will survive the onslaught, "For God has not destined us for wrath but for salvation through our Lord Jesus Christ" (5:9).

So what does Paul mean in 4:17 when he says that Jesus's followers will "meet him in the air"? It can't be a "rapture" that removes his followers from the world before the long-term tribulation. Jesus is not coming to provide an escape for his followers but "sudden destruction" for his enemies. Then why are his followers floating up to meet him?

The Thessalonians, reading this letter in 50 CE, would have had no trouble understanding it. As scholars have long suggested, Paul's description of Jesus, the "Lord," coming to his "kingdom" uses an image familiar in antiquity. When a king or high-ranking official arrived for a visit to one of his cities, the citizens would know in advance he was coming and would prepare a banquet and festivities. When the long-awaited king and his entourage approached, the city would send out its leading figures to meet and greet him before escorting him back to their town with great fanfare.

For Paul in 1 Thessalonians, that's what it will be like when Jesus comes. He is the king coming to visit his own people, who will go out to greet him. In this case, though, he is not coming with his entourage on horses; he is coming with his angels from heaven to destroy his enemies. And so, to greet him, his followers—all of them, not just the leaders—will be taken "up" to "meet him in the air." But this escort will not *remain* in the air any more than, on earth, the king's welcoming committee would remain outside the city walls. They will accompany him back to earth, where he will enter his kingdom and rule forever, in a paradise provided to his chosen ones, now that all others have been suddenly destroyed.

There is no "rapture" here, no account of Jesus's followers being taken to heaven to escape a massive and prolonged tribulation on earth. The same is true of other passages used by fundamentalists who insist that the rapture is taught in Scripture. Another popular verse—we used to love this one—is Matthew 24:39–40:

> So too will be the coming of the Son of Man. Then two will be in the field; one will be taken and one will be left. Two women will be grinding meal together; one will be taken and one will be left. Keep awake therefore, for you do not know on what day your Lord is coming.

We took the verse out of context as a pretty obvious reference to the rapture, where some will be taken out of the world and others abandoned for long-term misery. If we had read it *in* context, however, we would have seen that this is the opposite of what Jesus was teaching. In the verses right before the passage (Matthew 24:38–39)

Jesus likens the coming of the Lord to what happened in "the days of Noah," when only Noah and his family were saved in the ark when the flood took away—that is, drowned—everyone else. In this passage, then, it is the people who are "taken" who are destroyed; those "left behind" are the ones who are saved.

Both Matthew and Paul warn their readers that they need to be alert because Jesus is coming soon. But how soon? When Paul talks about this coming day of judgment, he speaks about the reward that will come to Jesus's true followers, both those who have already died, who will be raised from the dead, and those who are still alive. Notice that Paul includes himself among the living at the time. When he speaks of the two groups, he refers to "those" who are dead and "we" who will still be alive. It's a point worth emphasizing. These New Testament authors who speak of Christ's return thought it was to happen in their own day.

MASS MARKETING THE RAPTURE

That's not what we believed back in my evangelical days. We had been told that passages like these referred to what would happen two millennia later, in *our* time. (Hey, it's all about us!) We needed to be ready. This was a message drummed into our heads through various media—not just "prophecy books," but Christian rock music, such as Larry Norman's ever popular "You've Been Left Behind," and Christian film, starting with *A Thief in the Night* in 1972, an unusually low-budget production about what would happen if you were not among those raptured and had to face the terrifying rule of the Antichrist. The movie was meant to scare the hell out of teenagers, and it was massively successful. Everyone I know who was a 1970s evangelical has stories about it, often about the horrible sense that came over them when, one day, they found themselves alone in the house and thought the rapture had just happened but they had missed it.

All this would seem terribly bizarre and irrelevant were it not for how commercially successful the subject remained in the decades that followed. The rapture is the theme of one of the bestselling book series in the history of publishing, the *Left Behind* novels by Timothy LaHaye and Jerry B. Jenkins. (As a fundamentalist prophecy spokesperson, LaHaye is the one usually credited with the idea for the series; Jenkins provided the writing skill.) Over the course of sixteen volumes (1995 to 2007) the pair narrate events on earth after true believers in Jesus (i.e., fellow conservative evangelicals) have been raptured out of it as those who realize their mistaken ways band together and wage battle with the Antichrist and his forces.

Literary scholars, needless to say, were no more impressed with the books than film critics were with *A Thief in the Night*. But the series was massively popular: when LaHaye died in 2016, eighty million copies had been sold. There were also three movies, a spin-off movie, and a reprisal starring Nicolas Cage. For many readers the books were page-turning stuff, and these people were not all fundamentalists, or even Christians. But the vast majority of them—studies have shown—not only turned the pages; they believed them. One important analysis by a scholar of contemporary religion, Amy Johnson Frykholm, suggests that most people who read the novels took them to be just as authoritative about what was soon to happen as the Bible itself. Readers didn't put it that way, of course. Instead, they said they thought that what they read in the novels was simply what the Bible itself says.[9]

IS IT ALL ABOUT US?

We are, then, talking about a wide-ranging cultural phenomenon. One fairly recent poll indicates that 79 percent of Christians in America believe Jesus will be returning to earth at some point. Another poll, taken in 2010, shows that 47 percent of the Christians in the country believe Jesus will return by 2050 (27 percent definitely and 20 percent probably). The vast majority of these people believe this is stated throughout the Bible itself, culminating in that great set of predictions in the book that brings the entire sacred canon of Scripture to a close, the Apocalypse of John.

I believe this view of Revelation, and indeed of the entire Bible, is simply wrong. In saying so, I am not suggesting anything novel or strange. Revelation was almost never read as a prediction of the near future for nearly two millennia. It certainly is not read that way among most historical scholars today. Revelation was not written to show what would happen in the twenty-first century. It was written by an author in the first century who was addressing readers of his own time with a message *they* needed to learn. This view of the book is certainly not as scintillating as the claim that a prophet two thousand years ago could see what would transpire at an end of the world that we ourselves will be experiencing. You mean God was *not* principally concerned about our generation from the very beginning? We aren't the culmination of the human race, the goal of all human history? How disappointing.

But even if Revelation is not predicting what will happen soon after the next presidential election, that does not mean we should relegate it to the trash heap of historical curiosities. On the contrary, it is a book that continues to be massively significant, even if for reasons people might not expect. To understand why, we will first need to see why the dominant futuristic readings of Revelation have not worked and never will work. In the next chapters, I will show how these kinds of futuristic readings originated and explore why (in every single case) they have proved to be wrong. That will naturally involve looking at what the book of Revelation actually does say and how it says it, matters surprisingly overlooked by many so-called experts on biblical prophecy. I will then show what scholars have long known about how the book is to be read and understood, and give a frank assessment of its major teachings and perspectives, especially what its author wants to say about God and his relation to both the world he created and the people who inhabit it. As we will see, it is a disturbing view.

STRANGE WAYS PEOPLE READ THE BIBLE

Before explaining why Revelation has never been successfully interpreted as a blueprint for the future—and why it never will be—I need to provide a broader overview of how people today read the Bible. Most people don't read the Bible the way they read other books, and "experts" in biblical prophecy certainly don't treat the Bible as a book at all.

There are, of course, numerous ways to read the Bible. Many people (most?) open the Bible to find answers to personal, pressing questions and to receive guidance. Such readers want direction. For them, since the Bible is the means by which God speaks to his followers, it can be used to provide almost mystical answers that would not be available through a simple reading. A very common technique is simply to open the Bible at random—either with a particular concern in mind or hoping to learn whatever God "wants to tell me today"— and to read the first passage that strikes your eye (or the passage you blindly place your finger on) to find out what it is saying to you.

That, of course, is not how you read *Jane Eyre* or *The Grapes of Wrath*. But the logic behind the approach is that the Bible is a different kind of book from every other, because God is speaking through it. In my view this is not reading the Bible as a book. It is using the Bible as a kind of Christian Ouija board. God directs your gaze or your finger to what he wants to tell you. You then interpret what you read in light of your concerns.

The professional prophecy writers like Hal Lindsey and Timothy LaHaye who appeal to Scripture as a guide to our imminent future do not take a Ouija board approach. On the contrary, they read the Bible very carefully, picking out subtleties that might be missed on a first or ninth reading. But in doing so they are looking for something. They are trying to find the pieces of a great puzzle, in fact the greatest puzzle of all: what will happen in the future. If the Bible is inspired and gives all the answers to the important questions of life, then this Big Answer must also be in its pages. For these readers, the Bible is like a great jigsaw puzzle, with one piece hidden in this place, one in another, and yet a third somewhere else. The way to use the Bible is to assemble the pieces to reveal the big picture, which until now no one has seen before.

It is relatively easy to observe prophecy writers ferreting out and arranging the pieces of their puzzle, having retrieved them from hither and yon. In one of his eighty-eight reasons, Edgar Whisenant reaches his date of 1988 by putting together Daniel 2:1, Leviticus 26:2, and Romans 11:25. On the same page, he appeals as well to the pieces provide by Matthew 13:39; Luke 21:24; Acts 3:21; and Zechariah 14:4. Lindsey also moves flawlessly over the entire expanse of Scripture, pulling out the requisite pieces from Ezekiel 38, Daniel 11, Joel 2, Matthew 24, and Revelation 11 all in one breath. These may be biblical books written over the course of many centuries by authors living in different areas, speaking different languages, addressing different audiences with different concerns, but for these fundamentalist readers, each writing may contain a vital missing piece to the Puzzle of the End.

In treating the Bible this way, Whisenant and Lindsey are not anomalies among the predictors of the imminent End of All Things. On my desk just now are a few books by another famous prophecy writer, Jack Van Impe, who spent a long career lecturing that the end was coming right away. In fact, he wrote basically the same book several times over, decades after first demonstrating from Scripture that the end was coming "any day now." A minute ago I opened one of Van Impe's books at random to see him prove this by splicing together Nahum 2:3; Isaiah 31:5; Deuteronomy 7:6–8; and 1 Chronicles 17:22.[10]

In graduate school we denigrated this approach to biblical "study" by calling it "proof-texting"—that is, finding "proofs" for your views by jumping from one text to another. This eschatological approach to proof-texting is particularly intriguing, as it is designed to assemble the pieces of the great puzzle of life hidden throughout the books of Scripture, even if each book is actually about something else altogether. It's a bit like finding Waldo in a Dickens novel.

The whole enterprise reminds me of a passage from the early church father Irenaeus (180 CE), who was attacking a group of Gnostic heretics for how they used Scripture. Irenaeus argues that since these Gnostics could not support their bizarre teachings about the creation of the world or the identity of Christ simply by appealing to the texts, they reassembled them. In a memorable image, Irenaeus says the heretics are like someone who takes a gorgeous mosaic of a gallant king and rearranges the stones so they now portray a mangy dog, claiming this is what the artist intended all along. Even more, they insist this *is* a portrait of the king. For Irenaeus, this is no way to treat a book (Irenaeus, *Against Heresies*, 1.8).

TREATING THE BIBLE LIKE A BOOK

Historical scholars could not agree more and so do not advise treating the Bible as either a Ouija board or a jigsaw puzzle. They argue that since the Bible is a book, you should read it as a book. Which of us reads by arbitrarily looking at a passage and seeing what guidance it offers, or taking bits and pieces and assembling them together? Is that how we should read *Pride and Prejudice* or *The Remains of the Day*? A Bible-believing Christian may respond by saying: Yes, but those books are not inspired by God. There is, however, a fairly obvious counterresponse: If God inspired a book, surely that means he wanted it to be read *as a book*. He certainly could have inspired a board game instead.

Indeed, the Bible is not a single book but an anthology of sixty-six books. If the Bible comes from God, he did not inspire a single author in a single time and place to write a single Bible; he inspired different authors with different backgrounds, different assumptions, and different views of the world. And we simply can't read books (at least if we want to understand them) without knowing at least something about the historical context in which they were written. Imagine reading *The Odyssey* or *The Divine Comedy* knowing nothing about the history of ancient Greece or medieval Italy. And we can't understand them without reading them from beginning to end. How can one possibly understand *On the Origin of Species* or *The Autobiography of Malcolm X* by randomly picking a sentence here or there to meditate on, or by taking lines scattered throughout and assembling them in the way one thinks best?

If you don't read a book the way books are written to be read, you'll be taking a mosaic and rearranging the pieces to show what you yourself want it to show. And that is precisely what modern prophecy writers do. This approach allows them to make bold claims about what will happen in our future, when, and where—without paying the least regard to the original meaning of the passages they apply to. That alone is one important reason why every biblical projection of when and how Jesus will return has been incontrovertibly proven to be flat-out wrong by the relentless march of history.

Most of us might think that, with egg on their face, such prophecy writers would never speak in public again. But that almost never happens.[11] When September 13, 1988, passed, what did Whisenant do? He wrote another book. In this one he explained that he had earlier made an unfortunate but slight miscalculation. He had forgotten there was no year 0. History moved from 1 BC to AD 1, so that the first decade had only nine years in it. That threw his calculations off by a year. So expect the rapture in 1989.[12]

So, too, when Hal Lindsey's prediction of the late 1980s didn't come true: he is still preaching his message today, over half a century later, telling us that the signs *now* are even more convincing than ever. That's the remarkable thing about signs of the imminent end: they are always there to be seen. As historian Norman Cohn pointed out about those who realized that the current news matched biblical predictions of what would happen near the end of the age: "Since the 'signs' included bad rulers, civil discord, war, drought, famine, plague, comets, sudden deaths of prominent persons and an increase in general sinfulness, there was never any difficulty about finding them."[13] It is important to note: Cohn was not talking about our Whisenants and Lindseys. He was talking about predictors of doom in the Middle Ages.[14] Some things never change.

Some end-time enthusiasts who make false prediction after false prediction eventually do give up. But it doesn't happen often. Prophecy scholar Harold Camping, for instance, made a very nice career out of predicting the end of the world. First, in 1992, he wrote a 551-page book filled with mathematical proofs explaining why Jesus would return for the rapture on September 6, 1994. When that didn't happen, he announced it would be September 29. Then October 11. Eventually he gave up on 1994 and in 2005 declared that it was now a certainty: the rapture would occur on May 21, 2011. This time, people outside his small coterie of followers took notice. His church and long-running Family Radio station invested $100 million in advertising—you could see the billboards on the highways—trying to convince people to repent before it was too late. He claimed that after the rapture, starting May 22, millions of people would die every day for five months. When nothing happened on May 21, Camping made a last-ditch effort, claiming the rapture would be October 21. Finally, on October 22, he quit. He had had enough. Many conservative Christians also hoping for the rapture had warned him: Jesus had said, "No one knows the day or the hour." Camping admitted he had been wrong and that he had sinned against God. He died two years later.[15]

THE RELEVANCE OF THE COMING APOCALYPSE

I don't hear about Christian prophets of doom and their millions of followers in my day-to-day life, even though I used to be one of them and am a scholar who deals with their texts. I expect most people on our planet don't hear or think about them much, either. But that does not mean such phenomena are in fact irrelevant. These seemingly bizarre predictions of the coming end are not only widely held but even more widely influential. As you will see in the pages to come, whether we know it or not, they affect our lives. Not only have they proved emotionally traumatic for millions of people in our world, they have had social and cultural effects, involving such things as US foreign policy and the welfare of our planet (think climate change).

For yet other reasons, and on a more personal level, I would also like us to think about what the book of Revelation really does say and why that matters. It may seem like an obscure book to spend any time thinking about, but the reality is, as a part of Christian Scripture, it is taken as inspired truth by billions of our fellow citizens of this planet. Even if it does not predict what will happen soon in our history together, it does try to present a "revelation" of sorts, a revelation—for many Christians—of the truth about God, humans, and the course of what's to come. But what kind of "truth" does it reveal?

Many people coming to the book of Revelation for the first time find its sweeping narrative disturbing. It is almost impossible to read the book without being struck by its sheer violence: it describes an apocalypse where God will vent his wrath against the world and everyone he opposes, bringing widespread misery and pain. The book recounts heaven-sent catastrophe after catastrophe: famine, epidemic, war and, in the end, a lake of fire for the majority of the human race.

What does one make of this narrative of divine violence and vengeance in a book of sacred Scripture? Is this a view of God that people should subscribe to? And is it consistent with the teaching of Jesus himself?

Before answering these questions, we need to consider what the book actually says.

TWO

The Most Mystifying Book of the Bible

There can be little question that the book of Revelation is the most mystifying book of the Bible. There are other contenders, of course, most certainly the book of Daniel, with its befuddling visions in chapters 7 through 12. Read them and you'll see. John, the author of Revelation, certainly read them, as they were a major source of inspiration for his own visionary expositions some two and a half centuries later. But he far exceeded his Danielic model: not stopping at six, he produced a full twenty-two chapters of narrative mystification. With Revelation we have a book so unusual, so bizarre, so loaded with symbols, images, and enigmas, that most people simply cannot get their heads around it, even if they try. That is not just the case with modern readers; the book has befuddled readers throughout the course of Christian history. For centuries, it was not widely read, and those who did read it admitted to finding it opaque at best. Even scribes were not particularly interested in copying it. We have far fewer manuscripts of Revelation than for any other book of comparable size in the New Testament.

Even top-of-the-line biblical scholars who labored long and hard over its meaning found it a frustrating task. Take Martin Luther (1483–1546), most famous, of course, for starting the Protestant Reformation and insisting that Scripture alone, not Catholic Church dogma and tradition, provided a basis for true Christian faith and practice. Luther was far more than a religious reformer. He was a true intellectual, a professor of theology and learned interpreter of the Bible. His German translation of the New Testament (1522) attained a revered status on German soil equivalent to that of the King James (1611) among Anglophones.

Despite Luther's insistence on the supreme authority of Scripture, or possibly because of it, he was not confident the book of Revelation belonged among the inspired writings of the New Testament. In his translation, he placed the book in an appendix.[1] His view of the book did fluctuate over the course of his long career: at times he used it to attack the Roman Catholic Church as the embodiment of evil. Like other reformers before him, Luther maintained the pope was the "Antichrist," the "beast" of the Apocalypse, whose number was 666.

Even so, Luther sometimes admitted that despite many long hours of study and reflection, he simply did not understand the book. He also did not think much of John's own exalted claims about its importance, including the statement he makes at the very outset: "Blessed is the one who reads out loud and those who hear the words of the prophecy [contained in this book], and who keep the things that are written in it. For the time is near" (Revelation 1:3). Luther's comment on the verse surely resonates with many readers today: "[The author says] they are to be blessed who keep what is written therein; and yet no one knows what that is."[2]

What Luther did understand about the book made him doubt its apostolic origin. In the Preface to Revelation, he explains:

> About this book of the Revelation of John, I leave every-
> one free to hold his own ideas, and would bind no man
> to my opinion or judgment: I say what I feel. I miss more
> than one thing in this book, and this makes me hold it to
> be neither apostolic nor prophetic. First, and foremost,
> the Apostles do not deal with visions, but prophesy in
> clear, plain words, as do Peter and Paul and Christ in the
> Gospel. . . . [But] I can in nothing detect that it [Revela-
> tion] was provided by the Holy Spirit.

Many people who begin reading the book feel the same, which is perhaps why they often never finish it. That is unfortunate, for the book is unusually intriguing and, in its way, powerful. As we have seen, though, the way to read it is not through a fundamental-ist approach that isolates statements scattered throughout its chap-ters and rearranges them like pieces of a great jigsaw puzzle to create a version of what is to happen soon. Biblical scholars have long emphasized the need to read literary works, even inspired works, as *texts* situated in specific *contexts*. Revelation is to be read from be-ginning to end, the way books are read, and it needs to be situated in its own historical setting. Once you do this, you'll recognize the hints the author himself gives to the meaning of his often bizarre symbols and see how they make sense in reference to issues of his own time.

Before we begin to explore what the book means, we have to know what it says. In this chapter I will provide a simple summary to show why there is nothing to be afraid of in the Apocalypse. I will not overburden you with a detailed, verse-by-verse, or even pas-sage-by-passage exposition. Instead, I will deal with the broad sweep of the action, concentrating on parts of the book that are especially key to its interpretation.[3]

THE BEGINNING OF THE END
(CHAPTER 1)

As is true for nearly all the writings of the New Testament, the book of Revelation begins with verses that help unpack the meaning of everything to come. Its very first word in the original Greek is "Apocalypse": "[The] apocalypse of Jesus Christ that God gave him to show his slaves the things that must happen soon, and he indicated it by sending it through his angel to his slave John" (1:1).

This is my own translation. Let me say here at the outset that Revelation is not difficult to read in Greek. The author is not at all sophisticated in his use of the language. Quite the contrary, his Greek is the worst of the entire New Testament. That itself is a rather low bar: the New Testament writings as a whole were notorious among the literati in the Roman world for their stylistic deficiencies. Some New Testament authors, of course, write better than others: the author of Hebrews is reasonably good; Luke can be. Not the John of Revelation. He is often clumsy and many times simply makes grammatical mistakes. The last time I taught an advanced Greek class for undergraduates in the classics department at UNC, I gave them an assignment to list all the grammatical peculiarities and actual errors just in the first two chapters of Revelation. There are some stunners.[4]

Scholars have various explanations for the bad grammar. One common view is that the author's native language was Hebrew or Aramaic. That would explain his unpleasant style and aberrant grammar. Other scholars, however, have shown there is no good evidence to suggest he was more accustomed to a Semitic language. And so some have claimed the author of Revelation was intentionally writing mysterious Greek to convey a mysterious message. This is an intriguing hypothesis, but the grammar is never especially mysterious, just awkward, bad, or sometimes simply wrong. Another interesting suggestion is that John decided to use "street lingo" to convey a countercultural message. But we don't have any other ancient Greek writings to show us what street lingo would even look like, and nothing in the text itself suggests John intentionally tried to replicate it.[5]

My view is more straightforward: John simply did not write well. Most people don't. It doesn't mean they are necessarily uneducated or unintelligent. We're all good at some things and not so good at others. And even if John's writing can be clumsy, it is usually not difficult to understand what he is trying to say.

Back to that first verse, in which the author introduces his book as an "apocalypse." The word means a "revealing" (hence the synonym "revelation") or an "unveiling" or a "disclosure." As we will see, among scholars the term has since taken on a technical meaning to refer to a literary genre. Like all genres (epics, short stories, limericks), apocalypses feature a number of shared characteristics: they describe highly symbolic visions given by God that "reveal" heavenly secrets that can make sense of (usually awful) earthly realities, and by doing so they show that, despite appearances, God is sovereign, and good will eventually triumph. (I will talk more about the genre of the apocalypse in chapter 5.)

John next indicates that the "revelation" he is about to recount did not come to him directly from God. It went through a number of intermediaries: God gave the message to Jesus Christ, who passed it along through his angel, who then delivered it to his slave John, to be given to his audience (1:1–2). Why is the message so heavily mediated? Because a revelation from God himself would be too exalted, too divine, to come directly to us peons. We, the later readers of the writer John, are getting the message fourth-hand (by reading what was written for someone else). Even so, we are surely to assume we are getting it reliably.

The term "slave," which John uses for himself, occurs frequently in the book of Revelation. It is a fraught term in our modern context, but even so it should not be translated as "servant." There is a different Greek word for that. John is not simply someone who chooses to serve God. He is his slave: purchased by God, owned by him, and bound to do what he tells him. All the followers of Jesus are slaves of God in Revelation (see 1:1; 2:20; 7:3; 10:7; 19:2, 5; 22:3, 6), but this is portrayed as a very good thing. You can be a slave to your passions, to your work, to your possessions, to the Devil. In the words of Bob Dylan, during his born-again phase, "You gotta serve somebody." In Revelation, the chosen serve God and him alone. And there is a clear upside to enslavement: in the end, God's entire slave force is allowed to live in the fantastic abode he provides and enjoy all its luxuries; everyone else will be ruthlessly destroyed.

John explains that the revelation he received involved a vision ("that he saw") about what "will take place soon" (1:2). He then names the intended recipients of his message: "the seven churches in Asia" (1:4). A few verses later he identifies these churches (1:11), and in chapters 2 and 3 he addresses a letter to each of them. These churches are in cities of the western part of Asia Minor (modern Turkey): Ephesus, Smyrna, Pergamum, Thyatira, Sardis, Philadelphia, and Laodicea. I need to stress this point: John was writing to seven groups of Christians that he personally knew, not to people living two thousand years later in North America. When he says he has seen a vision about what "will take place soon," he means "soon" for his actual readers. He does not mean "thousands of years from now."

John then gives some information about himself: he is the "brother" of these Christians and he shares their tribulation as he writes to them from the island of Patmos, off the west coast of Asia Minor. Since his readers knew him, he had no need to explain any further who he was. Later readers, however, have tried to figure out his identity. John was a common name in Jewish circles, and eventually became a name taken up by non-Jewish Christians. It is important to recognize that this John does not claim to be any particular John. He does not, for instance, claim to be the most famous John of all, the son of Zebedee, one of the twelve disciples of Jesus. Throughout his narrative, in fact, he indicates he was *not* a member of the original apostolic band. In chapter 4, for example, John sees twenty-four human "elders" surrounding the throne of God, worshipping him day and night. These are often understood to be the twelve patriarchs of Israel, representing the original people of God, and the twelve apostles of Jesus, representing the new people of God. If so, John is surely not seeing himself.

Some writers of the early church mention two prominent figures named John: Jesus's own disciple, who was taken to be the author of the Fourth Gospel, and the "Elder John," who wrote Revelation. These books have radically different writing styles (see chapter 8), making it unlikely they were written by the same person.[6]

Based on what our John says elsewhere in the book of Revelation, he appears to have been some kind of regional spiritual leader, a prophet. He indicates he is on the island of Patmos "because of the word of God and the testimony of Jesus" (v. 9). It has long been said that he was exiled there as a punishment for his Christian activities, but there is actually nothing in what he writes that requires this interpretation. Maybe the "testimony of Jesus" took him to Patmos because he was a missionary, or because he chose to go there for a time of meditation. It is true he does say that he is sharing "tribulation" with the Christians in the churches to which he writes, but that does not necessarily mean he is in exile. They and their leaders are sharing tribulation with *him* but are not in exile.

In any event, John is on Patmos, where he has his first vision, of Christ himself. John indicates this happened while he was "in the Spirit" on "the Lord's Day" (1:10). This is the first time in Christian literature that Sunday is called the Lord's day—named that because it is the day the Lord was raised from the dead. Being in the Spirit may indicate that he was deep in prayer or had even gone into a kind of trance. John hears a voice telling him to write letters to the seven churches and turns to "see the voice"—an odd expression (how do you see a voice?), but not unprecedented. On turning, he sees seven golden lampstands and "one like a son of man" walking among them. This is a clear reference to Christ, who in the early Christian tradition was identified as the "Son of Man," in reference to a passage found in John's visionary predecessor, Daniel (Daniel 7:13–14; see also Daniel 10:5–9).

The vision of Christ in 1:13–16 is quite stunning. Right off the bat we encounter an amazing array of images. He is clothed in a long robe with a large golden waistband; later in Revelation, this will be the attire of mighty angels who bring destruction on the earth (Revelation 15:6). His hair is white as wool or snow, showing he is ancient; his eyes are like a flame of fire, showing his piercing judgment. His feet are like fine bronze, showing his magnificence. His voice is like a rushing river or waterfall, showing the power of his speech. In his hand are seven stars, which I will explain later. And from his mouth comes a two-edged sword, an image used elsewhere in early Christian literature to denote the word of God (see Hebrews 4:12). His face shines with the brilliance of the sun.

John's response to this startling vision is what you might expect. He faints. Christ restores him with a touch and tells him there is no reason to be afraid. He, Christ, is the "first and the last" (a phrase later used of God himself), the one who is alive even though he died, who now has the power over Death and Hades, the realm of the dead. He instructs John to write to the seven churches to tell them "the things you have seen; the things that are; and the things that are about to take place after this" (v. 19). This is a key verse, which roughly organizes the Apocalypse into three uneven sections. What John has "seen" is the vision of Christ the Lord, the key to all the visions to come. The things "that are" refer to the current situations of the churches as described in the letters of chapters 2 and 3. The things "that are about to take place" are everything else in the book, all of chapters 4 through 22.

Christ then explains the meaning of John's opening vision. We will find something similar throughout the entire narrative: the author often uses divine characters, almost always (after this) an angel, to explain to the seer what he has seen. John is helping us readers by interpreting some of his key symbols. In this case, Christ indicates that the seven lampstands are the churches of Asia Minor and the seven stars in his hand are the angels over the churches (1:20). In other words, Christ is present in the midst of these churches (walking among them) and controls their guardian angels (holding them in his hand), at least for the time being. In the letters John writes to the churches, Christ threatens to remove their lampstands if they do not change their ways. That would not be good.

THE LETTERS TO THE SEVEN CHURCHES (CHAPTERS 2 AND 3)

Most readers find the letters written to the seven churches in chapters 2 and 3 a rather uninspiring beginning to the Apocalypse. Why do we need to read someone else's mail? Bring on the action!

But the letters are unusually important. John was told to write an account of his revelation to these seven specific churches and these letters show why the members of the churches need to listen. The letters indicate a range of circumstances the churches were experiencing, most of them difficult: a constant refrain in the letters, and elsewhere in the book, is that Jesus's followers need to "conquer" those things that are defeating them in their faith, whether false teachings, persecution, complacency, or anything else that draws their attention away from true and committed service to Christ.[7]

For a very long time, biblical scholars maintained that the main problem facing these churches was persecution by Roman authorities. From antiquity, many believed that the emperor at the time, Domitian (ruled 81–96 CE), ordered a great persecution of Christians that far exceeded the atrocities committed three decades earlier by his predecessor, Nero (64 CE). Today, however, scholars recognize there is no real evidence that Domitian took much notice of Christians. It is certainly possible that John *felt* the Roman authorities were hostile and *thought* they were murdering Christians left, right, and center; certainly, as we will see, he says so throughout this account. But the reality appears to have been quite different. There may have been local cases of opposition to Christians here and there throughout the empire, but there was no imperially sanctioned opposition.[8]

Why would John indicate there was? Throughout history— and still today—some religious groups have insisted, and believed, they have been violently opposed far more rigorously than in fact they were. Possibly John and his communities were like that. Some scholars have argued that he, and they, *perceived* persecution because they felt isolated and rejected, or because they made mountains out of molehills, or because thinking they were a persecuted minority helped strengthen their commitment and bonds.[9]

Even so, it is important to notice that when John addresses his churches in these opening letters, persecution is just one of the issues he raises. He is far more worried about false teachings and his followers' general lack of fervor. Christ has harsh words for the lax: those who remain lukewarm in their faith will be "spewed" out of his mouth (3:16).

John does mention opposition in his letters to two of the churches, but one case involves being blasphemed by Jews of the local synagogue (a "Synagogue of Satan"), rather than persecution by Roman authorities, and in this case he makes no reference to any physical violence (2:9). The other reference does indicate that pagans have persecuted the church, leading to a martyrdom (2:13), but it is hard to know the details. In any event, John does not say that any Roman officials were involved. On the whole, persecution does not appear to be his most pressing concern.

One of the most intriguing features of the letters of chapters 2 and 3 is that John does not compose them: he is merely serving as the secretary, taking dictation from Christ himself. This is the only place in the entire New Testament that Christ is said to "write" anything.[10] His words show he is not happy with his followers. We will later see, repeatedly, that he is *extremely* unhappy with the vast majority of the human race, who are not his followers—to a person, they will be sent to a horrendous death. But a lot of his followers are also in hot water (or, rather, bound for a lake of fire). When you read these letters, you cannot help being struck by the force of Christ's words. He shows no leniency to Christians who are morally lax or theologically adrift. He "hates" those (among his followers) who do not toe the line: accepting errant teachings, growing lazy in their commitment, accommodating themselves to outsiders, and being led astray by Satan no less than the pagans and Jews (see 2:6). If they do not repent and change their ways, Christ will judge them just as harshly as the rest of lost humanity.

The seven letters all follow the same basic sequence:

- First, Christ identifies himself by one of the images used elsewhere in the book, saying, for example, that he is the one who holds the seven stars and walks among the seven lampstands, or that he is the first and last, who came back to life from the dead.

- He then assesses the church's individual situation, both good and bad. In most cases, he focuses on the bad.
- He threatens the church community that he will respond harshly if they do not change their ways.
- And he extends a promise to those who return to his good graces.

Among the problems encountered in these churches, "false teaching" leaps out. I should note here that the false teachers are not outsiders trying to lead Christians astray. They are church leaders. John specifically attacks the "false teaching" that allows followers of Jesus to eat food offered to pagan idols and to practice fornication (2:14, 20). These issues were often linked in early Christian thinking: worshipping idols was thought to be intimately bound up with sexual immorality, on the assumption, apparently, that only reprobates would worship other gods (see Romans 1:18–32). Almost certainly, though, the church members under attack were not actively practicing paganism. More likely they were in a situation similar to that described by Paul some years earlier in 1 Corinthians 8 and 10, which deal with the problem of whether it is acceptable for Christians to eat meat that had been sacrificed to pagan gods.[11] How Paul and John each responds to this issue vividly illustrates their differences.

It is not completely clear in either context why Christians were inclined to eat meat that had been offered in sacrifice to pagan gods. Possibly the meat was sold at a discount, since, in theory, it had already been used once. Or possibly there was no real option for anyone wanting a piece of meat for a meal, since pagan priests were the local butchers. In any event, Paul indicates in his letter that the Christians who considered it acceptable to eat the meat did so because they thought the pagan gods did not actually exist. Idols were just wood or stone. If the gods didn't exist, they couldn't really have received sacrifices, so eating the meat didn't involve worshipping them. But others in Corinth—possibly people who were less educated and more superstitious—were convinced the pagan gods actually did exist—not because they were really gods but because they were demons. Eating the meat, then, involved participating in a demonic ritual, and that should be avoided at all costs.

Paul thought it was better not to eat the meat.[12] In Revelation, John is far more emphatic: eating meat offered to idols is an affront to Christ. In a letter to the church of Thyatira, Christ attacks a woman prophet he calls "Jezebel," an allusion to the notorious queen of Israel who led the people of God astray (1 Kings 16:31; 2 Kings 9:22). This Jezebel is said to be a church leader who "teaches and deceives my slaves to commit sexual immorality and to eat food offered to idols" (2:20). That is, she has taken the position on idol meat found among some of the prominent members of Paul's church in Corinth: Paul advises against the practice but does not roundly condemn it. In Revelation 2, Christ indicates he has already given Jezebel a chance to repent—in other words, to stop condoning the practice of eating meat purchased from a pagan temple—but she has refused. And so he indicates her judgment:

> See, I will throw her onto a bed, and those who commit
> adultery with her I will throw into a great affliction, if
> they do not repent from her deeds. And I will kill her
> children. (2:22)

Now, that's a verse I never learned in Sunday school. Some translators translate "bed" as "sickbed" (that is, Christ will make her ill), but that is reading something into the verse that isn't there. It is just the Greek word for "bed." And what happens on the bed is not that Jezebel gets sick. She has illicit sex with others. After Christ has thrown her there. This is not a pretty image, but it gets worse.

Those who fornicate with her will be greatly afflicted (we don't know how—is it connected with the sex?). And most startling of all, Christ will kill her children.

The passage is obviously symbolic, but it is not pleasant symbolism. And it is worth remembering: the passage is referring to a leading prophetess in a Christian church. John presumably calls her Jezebel because in his judgment she is the female embodiment·of evil who leads others into grotesque sin. Those who get into bed with her are those who join her in rank immorality (eating meat sacrificed to an idol). And her children are the fruit she bears—the people she convinces to join in as well. Christ will kill them. That probably means that they will be condemned in the coming judgment, but John may mean it literally as a threat in the present. We do have examples of God killing those among his followers he is not pleased with, not just in the Old Testament (for example, Numbers 16:1–35), but also in the book of Acts (5:1–11) and the writings of Paul (1 Corinthians 11:27–30). The latter instance, interestingly, also involves a case of inappropriate dining practices (misconduct at the Lord's supper).

In short, the letters of chapters 2 and 3 set the context for the entire Apocalypse. Christ is in charge. He considers Jews to be Satan-worshipping enemies of his people. Christians must avoid pagan associations. Those who are lax in their faith are in danger of losing their salvation. Christ hates Christians who do not adhere to correct teachings about how to live, so much so that he threatens them with a judgment that will be without mercy. But those who are obedient, faithful, and passionate about their faith—who in the end "conquer"—will be gloriously rewarded. There are clear dividing lines here between "us," the committed Christians who follow the truth, and "them," non-Christian and Christian alike. "They" are in big trouble.

THE THRONE ROOM OF GOD AND THE LAMB
(CHAPTERS 4 AND 5)

Chapter 4 is where the real action begins, or at least begins to begin. It opens with a striking episode. As soon as the prophet has finished writing his letters, he looks and sees a door in the sky, and a voice tells him to come up. John is again "in the spirit" and he arrives in heaven to a gloriously terrifying scene. He is in the throne room of God himself (4:1–6). On his throne, God appears like brightly colored jewels and his throne is surrounded by a rainbow with thunder and lightning shooting out (for a comparable vision, see Ezekiel 1:22–25).[13] Around the throne are four living creatures with eyes all over their bodies; apart from the eyes, they look like a lion, an ox, a human, and an eagle (4:6–8). Apparently, these represent the four zoological categories: a wild animal, a domestic animal, a human, and a bird (see Ezekiel 1:4–14). That matters because these creatures spend every minute, day and night, worshipping the one on the throne. In other words, they reveal that the entire order of living existence has been created to bow in eternal adoration before its creator.

There are also twenty-four human "elders" sitting on their own thrones around the throne of God (4:4, 9–11). As I suggested before, these may represent the twelve patriarchs of Israel and the twelve apostles of Jesus.[14] They, too, worship God constantly and "forever and ever," and they (periodically?) cast their crowns before him, declaring he alone is worthy of all glory, honor, and power. The vision thus begins with the absolute Sovereignty of the Almighty Creator God, who rules in heaven, dwelling in mind-boggling majesty, worshipped by those he has made.

Even though God's appearance is described as jewellike, he apparently has body parts. Chapter 5 begins by indicating that he is holding a scroll in his right hand. A scroll, of course, was the standard form of an ancient book. This one is "sealed with seven seals" (5:1). In the ancient world, an official communication would be sent out with a wax seal, marked with the signet ring of the sender. The communication could be opened only by the one to whom it was addressed or, if need be, by someone with equal or superior authority. That is the key to what happens next.

An angel calls out to ask if anyone in heaven or on earth has the authority to break the seals and see what is in the book. No one can do so and the prophet begins to weep (5:2–4).[15] One of the twenty-four elders tells John not to weep, because there is one with the authority to break the seals—that is, with authority equal to that of God. It is "the Lion from the tribe of Judah, the Root of David," the one who "has conquered" (5:5). This is coded language, of course, but in this case the code is not difficult to break. These are messianic terms from the Old Testament (Genesis 49:9–10; Isaiah 11:1, 10). The messiah was to come from the tribe of Judah, a patriarch likened to a lion, and to be the son of David. The "Lion" will obviously be Christ, who in his opening words to the prophet in chapter 1 had already emphasized that he is the one who has "conquered" death (Revelation 1:18).

When John looks for the Lion, however, he instead sees a "Lamb standing as one who was slaughtered" (5:6). In the Christian tradition, Jesus is identified as "the lamb of God who takes away the sins of the world" (John 1:29, 35).[16] A lion? A lamb? This is one of the first instances of intentionally mixed metaphors in Revelation. Readers should not take any of the images too literally and argue that John cannot be seeing a lion if it is a lamb. Christ is both the ferocious lion and the slaughtered lamb.

Many commentators have argued that since John expects the Lion but sees the Lamb, Christ does not conquer with forceful violence like a lion but by passive nonresistance like the "lamb who was slain." On those grounds, they argue that the book of Revelation is all about nonviolent resistance leading to ultimate triumph. That is a hopeful thought, but I do not see how the book can actually be read this way, for reasons I'll be discussing at length in chapter 6.

The Lamb takes the scroll from the hand of God, and all the creatures and elders around the throne worship him, much as they worship God, forever and ever. The Lamb is worthy to break the seals of the mysterious scroll and he begins to do so. The scroll appears to contain God's directives for the fate of planet earth. Now the disasters begin.

THE HEAVEN-SENT DISASTERS
(CHAPTERS 6–16)

Each time the Lamb breaks one of the seals, a new catastrophe hits the earth. First come the famous "four horsemen of the Apocalypse" (6:1–8). The first appears on a white horse and wields a bow with which he conquers, possibly signifying foreign (barbarian) invasions. The next rides a red horse and causes people to slaughter one another; that is, he prompts domestic bloodshed. Then there is one on a black horse who creates massive food shortages and starvation. Finally one appears on a pale green horse and is Death itself, with Hades following, having the authority to destroy an entire fourth of the world's population. The extent of the violence should give us pause: if this horseman—and he alone—were to appear tomorrow, he would slaughter nearly two billion people. The numbers would be far different in John's day, but the proportions are the same. These people would be killed suddenly, as decreed by God and initiated by the Lamb.

The fifth seal reveals a group of Christians who were executed, not by God but by their earthly enemies. They plead with God for revenge against their persecutors and are told it will come soon.

Then comes the most horrific seal of all, the sixth. When the

Lamb breaks this seal, cosmic chaos erupts: there is a massive earthquake, the sun turns black, the moon turns red as blood, the stars fall from the sky, the sky vanishes, and—well, you would think the world is over now with the collapse of the universe, right? Wrong. We're only in chapter 6.

How can the destruction continue for another fourteen chapters? For many centuries—since, in fact, our very first Christian commentator on Revelation, Victorinus of Pettau, around 280 CE—careful interpreters have realized that Revelation cannot be read as a straightforward chronological description of what is to take place.[17] With its many descriptions of wars, natural disasters, retribution, bloodshed, and death to come, the narrative is not showing an actual sequence of events but is instead repeating itself in different terms and various ways to emphasize a point: at the end, all hell is going to break out, until God brings it all to a crashing halt with the destruction of his enemies.

After the sixth seal we have a one-chapter hiatus, in which followers of God are separated from the rest of humankind, in two major groupings. First there are 144,000 Jews, twelve thousand from each of the twelve tribes of Israel, who are "sealed" with the "seal of the living God" (7:1–8). Since these Jews receive God's own seal, they will be saved, fulfilling God's promises to the Jewish people that they are the chosen ones. Or at least 144,000 of them are.

The second group constitutes a countless multitude from all nations, tribes, peoples, and languages—that is, non-Jews (7:13–17). They are already in heaven and worship before the throne of God. These people are identified as those who have "washed their robes . . . in the blood of the Lamb" (7:14). Are they Christian martyrs? It may be difficult for a historian to imagine that a Christian author in the year 95 could think there had already been countless thousands of Christian martyrs, but religious leaders experiencing opposition often exaggerate the situation, as is easily documented throughout the Christian tradition of the first few centuries.[18] Another alternative is that these multitudes are saved because the *Lamb* shed his blood, not because they shed theirs. They were persecuted ("the great ordeal") but have been saved because of Christ's atonement.

When Christ breaks the seventh seal, it does not lead to catastrophe (8:1). Instead, there is silence in heaven for a half hour; then we are introduced to seven angels, each of whom has a trumpet. John has structured his narrative of repetitive catastrophes by making the disasters of the seven seals conclude with disasters brought by seven angelic trumpet blasts; the trumpeting then concludes with seven disasters brought by seven bowls of God's wrath poured by angels onto the earth. Thus we have three sequences: the last of the seven seals contains the seven trumpets, the last of which contains the seven bowls of wrath. Seven, of course, is the perfect number in the Bible; three has also been hugely significant in Christian tradition. Here we have a threefold cycle of seven disasters each. Altogether the cycle takes eleven chapters (chapters 6 through 16), with several interludes that describe other key events, including two of particular significance.[19]

The first is the appearance in chapter 13 of God's archenemy on earth, "the beast of the sea" (13:1). This horrifying sea monster comes ashore and is empowered by Satan to assume complete control of the earth. The creature is often identified by readers as the "Antichrist," although that term is not used in Revelation. Still, it is certainly apt. This is Christ's opposite, a ruler of the human race who is wicked, seemingly all-powerful, and violently opposed to Christ's followers (13:1–18). Its number is 666. Following the sea beast is another beast, which rises up from the earth and is elsewhere called the "false prophet" (13:11–17; 16:13). Its purpose is to make the inhabitants of earth worship the first beast, persuading them by performing great miracles. Those it convinces—everyone but the followers of Jesus—must receive a "mark" on their right hand or forehead. Without this "mark of the beast," no one can buy or sell anything (13:17). In other words, the beast of the sea exercises a complete monopoly over the economy of the earth. We will be examining these beasts more fully in a later chapter.

The second interlude (14:14–20) involves a series of disasters, war, and bloodshed brought not by a seal, trumpet, or bowl of wrath but by the "one like a son of man" (Christ), along with an accompanying angel. The imagery used to describe the onslaught is terrifying. These two heavenly reapers use "sickles" to harvest the earth—that is, to cut down their enemies, who are likened to grapes for "the wine press of the wrath of God." The "harvest" of this slaughter is then "trodden" and we are told that "blood flowed from the wine press up to the horses' bridles, for two hundred miles" (14:20).

After these interludes, we return to the third set of seven disasters. The seven angels each pour out a bowl of God's wrath, one after the other (16:1–21), thus bringing the heaven-sent pain, misery, and slaughter to an end . . . for the time being. It is quite a climax: with the sixth bowl of wrath, demonic forces gather the kings of the entire world together to do battle against Christ. They come to the place called "Armageddon," a Hebrew word meaning "the mountains of Megiddo." Megiddo was a city in central Israel, outside of which a number of significant battles were fought in the Old Testament (see Judges 5:19; 2 Kings 23:29–30). Here, in the heart of Israel, is where the Final Battle will occur.

THE FALL OF BABYLON (CHAPTERS 17–20)

At this conclusion of the cycles of earthly disasters, an unusually memorable scene occurs as the prophet is taken into the wilderness in chapter 17 to see a horrifying woman, clothed with fine raiment and many jewels, sitting on a scarlet beast with seven heads and ten horns. She is "drunk with the blood of the saints and the blood of the witnesses to Jesus, and has a name written on her head: 'Babylon the great, mother of whores and of the abominations on earth'" (17:1–6).[20] The prophet is flabbergasted by the sight and understandably wants to know who or what this is. The angel explains, and yet interpreters have still had a field day arguing over the identity of this "Whore of Babylon." These disagreements are almost entirely unnecessary, though: the angel more or less gives the game away (17:9–18). The whore is called "Babylon," the name of the city of the archenemies of the people of God in the Old Testament, the city that conquered Judah in 586 BCE, destroying Jerusalem and burning the temple to the ground. The whore is also a "great city," and she, too, is portrayed as the ultimate enemy of God and his people alike, only in John's own day. We will discuss her identity in chapter 3.[21]

Whoever she is, in chapter 18, "Babylon" is overthrown through heavenly intervention, leading to much mourning by the kings of earth, as well as by rich merchants and sea traders, who have done business with the great city (committed "fornication" with the whore; see 18:9). Now they have lost their finest customer and will lose all their wealth. By contrast, in chapter 19, all of heaven rejoices that the whore has been destroyed, for now the "Lamb and his bride" will celebrate their glorious union. The bride, of course, is the church, who will "be clothed with bright and pure linen" (19:8), in contrast to the garishly clad whore. All the chosen will be invited to the "wedding banquet," but first there is more business to attend to.

Christ appears from heaven on a white horse with all his armies to do battle with the beast and its earthly forces in the "Battle of Armageddon" (16:14–16). It is no contest. The beast and its prophet (the beast of the earth) are quickly defeated and thrown alive into a lake of burning sulfur. Their armies are destroyed and become fodder for the birds (19:11–21).

Now that the earthly enemy of God has been disposed of, the supernatural force that empowered it needs to be dealt with. In a somewhat surprising twist, Satan is not destroyed immediately. Instead, he is seized by an angel, put in chains, and thrown into a bottomless pit for a thousand years (20:1–3). Then comes a scene of judgment, but not for everyone. Those who had refused the "mark of the beast"—that is, the followers of Jesus who had been martyred—are brought back to life to rule on earth with Christ for a thousand years. This is called the "first resurrection" (20:4–6). It is worth noting: those brought back to life for this "millennium" (literally meaning "thousand years") are only the Christian martyrs, not all the saints.

When the thousand years are over, Satan is released from his prison and once more makes war on the saints (20:7–9). It is a short-lived affair. The Devil is defeated, captured, and thrown into the lake of fire, where the beast and his prophet have already been bobbing for ten centuries.

Then comes the denouement of this extended period of revenge and justice, the "Great White Throne Judgment." All the dead—everyone who has ever lived—are restored to life and made to stand before the throne of God. A number of "books" are opened, along with a solitary book, the Book of Life. The fact that there is only one Book of Life and numerous other books, presumably of "death," suggests that the majority of the dead who have been raised are about to receive a very bad verdict. And they do. Everyone whose name is not in the Book of Life is thrown into the lake of fire with the beast, the prophet, and the Devil (20:13). The difference is that the humans are said to experience a "second death." That is, the fire actually destroys them. They are gone, annihilated, while the wicked supernatural beings, who are immortal, are tormented forever.

Last of all, Death and Hades themselves are thrown into the lake of fire, another indication that the dead have been annihilated.

Hades, the realm of the dead, can be destroyed since there are no more people to die or to go there.[22]

THE NEW HEAVENS, EARTH, AND JERUSALEM (CHAPTERS 21–22)

Throughout his narrative, John has described untold pain, misery, and suffering, but his book ends on a happy note, at least for the followers of Jesus who have survived. The universe as humans have known it—"the first heaven and first earth"—is taken away and God brings in a new one. This "new Jerusalem" will be the eternal home for the people of God, corresponding, though in much glorified fashion, to the original Jerusalem, the site of God's king, his temple, and his people. Those who enter this new city will feel no more sorrow: God will "wipe away every tear from their eyes and there will be no more death, suffering, weeping or pain" (21:4). They have "conquered" and now will inherit God's gifts. They and no one else: all other inhabitants of earth, we are told again, have been tossed into the lake of fire.

The new Jerusalem is a marvel to behold. It is said to be a 12,000 "stadia" cube—that is, about 1,500 miles long, wide, and high (21:16). Its length would be from about New York City to Oklahoma City, its width from Miami to Toronto, and its height, well, 1,500 miles. We are never told why it needs to be so high. (Many levels? Amazing skyscrapers? Just on principle?) The city is made of "pure gold" (21:18). It has twelve foundations made of precious stones, and twelve gates (Just twelve? For a city 1,500 miles on each side?), each featuring a single pearl. The street (singular!) of the city is pure gold (21:21). There is no temple in the city—none is needed. God and his Lamb are worshipped directly. And there is no need for light. The glory of God provides all the light needed and the Lamb is the lamp (21:22).

Then, in one of the many glorious perplexities of the book, we are told the other nations on earth will walk by the light of the city. Kings of other lands will bring their resources into it and no one who "practices abomination or lying" will be allowed to enter, "only those who are written in the Lamb's book of life" (21:24–27). The attentive reader (or even the inattentive one) will naturally wonder: *What* "other nations," "kings," and "sinners"? Weren't they all just destroyed?

That particular mystery continues in chapter 22, where we are told that the tree of life in the middle of the street of the city will bring "healing for the nations" and that the slaves of God (the saints) will worship him and "rule as kings forever" (22:2, 5). But rule whom? Who else is there? We are then told that outside the city of God are the "dogs, sorcerers, sexually immoral, murderers, idolaters, and liars" (22:15). But how did they escape the final judgment and the lake of fire? The book of Revelation is nothing if not puzzling.

The book ends with the prophet assuring his readers that everything he says is true and that anyone who alters anything in his book will suffer the divine catastrophes described in its pages (22:18–19). This is a very interesting—though widely misunderstood—verse. It does not mean that the reader must accept everything said in the book on pain of death (in the lake of fire). It is a curse formula similar to those found in other ancient writings, telling scribes who later copy the book not to make any alterations or mistakes. For anyone who does, it's the burning sulfur.

John certainly believes that what he has described in this mysterious narrative is to happen soon. In the final chapter alone he indicates that these things "must take place soon" (22:6); Jesus himself says, "I am coming soon" (22:7); Jesus again assures his readers, "I am coming soon" (22:12), and then yet again says, "I am coming soon" (22:20). John urges him on: "Amen. Come Lord Jesus!"

(22:20). For John, Jesus was not coming two thousand years later to rapture his followers out of this world. He was coming in judgment in John's own near future. Those who opposed him would be horribly destroyed, while his followers would enter into a glorious city made of gold, where they would enjoy peace, joy, and security in the worship of God forever. And God would wipe away every tear.

This is what the author says. I think he really meant it. But in what sense?

■ ■ ■

THREE

A History of
False Predictions

Whatever one makes of the bizarre symbolism of the Apocalypse of John, a relatively straightforward reading suggests that the author believed the world was soon to come to a rather climactic end. God would assert his wrath on this planet, bringing worldwide anguish and destruction. Even so, for most of Christian history, the book was not understood as a description of what was literally about to happen. After an initial burst of enthusiastic expectation focused on the imminent end of the world, most Christians apparently changed their minds. Possibly they were prompted by the inexorable march of history: the end didn't come, and the easiest explanation was that it was never really expected to come. That affected how Christians read the book of Revelation.

Throughout Christian history the dominant view was one espoused by Augustine (350–430 CE), the most influential theologian of Christian history. Augustine insisted that the "future" millennium described in Revelation—when Jesus and his followers would rule on earth—was not a literal event but a metaphor for what was already being experienced in the life of the church. We will explore Augustine's views later, but for now it is enough to observe that this great giant of a Christian intellectual sent the "futurist" understanding of Revelation into long-term hibernation. It reemerged only occasionally over the centuries, until it was born again in the 1800s and began to spread its message of an imminent end with all the fervor of the newly converted. Before we get to that, we should consider how the book of Revelation was understood by John's earliest readers.

THE EARLIEST INTERPRETATIONS OF REVELATION

We have no record of how the book of Revelation was read by its intended audience, the Christians of the seven churches of Asia Minor, but they likely would have understood most of the bizarre symbolism with relative ease. John had been among them as a preacher, possibly for years; they were presumably well acquainted with his views before he sent them the Apocalypse. They also shared his cultural context, which would have made unpacking the mysteries of the text—including the identity of the "beast of the sea" and the "Whore of Babylon"—much simpler. There are also good reasons for thinking they took John at his word that the end of the world was near. John certainly repeated often enough that Jesus would be returning soon, and he gives no hint he didn't mean it.

Whatever the first readers of the book believed, it is relatively clear that the earliest Christian readers we do know about seem to have understood that Revelation predicted the future appearance of a glorious and tactile utopia for the saints. Later church fathers would attack this view as materialistic and unsophisticated. They called those who subscribed to it "chiliasts," from the Greek word *chilias*, which means "one thousand." Chiliasts believed an actual thousand-year reign of Christ and his saints was soon to appear here on earth.

Church fathers found this literalist view of future glory troubling because they maintained salvation was a spiritual affair, not one of bodily pleasure in a luxurious kingdom of God. But chiliasts disdained this rather ascetic perspective. One of our earliest Christian writers to support a more sensualist view of the coming kingdom is the church father Papias (ca. 60–140 CE), who claims to be passing along the teachings of the apostles who had heard them from Jesus. Papias was a bishop of the church of Hierapolis in Phrygia (in modern Turkey) who wrote a five-volume work, *Expositions of the Sayings of the Lord*, that, to our eternal regret, no longer survives. We are not sure what this book was actually about: Was it a lengthy collection of the teachings of Jesus? A commentary that interpreted those teachings? An account of Jesus's activities as well? A discussion of Old Testament prophecies about the coming of Jesus? All of the above?[1]

We know about Papias's work only through references to it by later church fathers, especially the heresiologist (heresy hunter) Irenaeus (180 CE), who shared Papias's chiliast views, and Eusebius, the great church historian (ca. 300 CE), who vehemently opposed them. It may be that later scribes didn't copy Papias's book because they, like Eusebius, considered him misguided. But Eusebius indicates that, for a time, Papias successfully spread his ideas.

Judging from what we know about his teachings, it is easy to see why later Christian thinkers opposed them. Here is one of Papias's offending statements that happens to survive, an account of the glories of the age to come, which he said he learned from the followers of Jesus's disciple John:

> The elders who saw John, the disciple of the Lord, remembered hearing him say how the Lord used to teach about

those times, saying: "The days are coming when vines will come forth, each with ten thousand boughs; and on a single bough will be ten thousand branches. And indeed, on a single branch will be ten thousand shoots and on every shoot ten thousand clusters; and in every cluster will be ten thousand grapes, and every grape, when pressed, will yield twenty-five measures of wine. And when any of the saints grabs hold of a cluster, another will cry out, "I am better, take me; bless the Lord through me."

Now, *that* is a lot of wine. There will be plenty of food options as well:

So too a grain of wheat will produce ten thousand heads and every head will have ten thousand grains and every grain will yield ten pounds of pure, exceptionally fine flour. So too the remaining fruits and seeds and vegetation will produce in similar proportions. And all the animals who eat this food drawn from the earth will come to be at peace and harmony with one another, yielding in complete submission to humans. (Irenaeus, *Against Heresies*, 5.33.3–4)

This materialistic portrayal of the millennium generated an antagonistic response from Papias's later critics, who opposed the pleasures of the flesh as ungodly. Eusebius panned him with a rather frank snub: "He was remarkably unintelligent" (*Church History*, 3.39.19–2). Even so, for centuries a number of Christians continued to expect this glorious kingdom to arrive.

One of the first on record to *oppose* the idea of an imminent end of all things was a well-known church leader, Hippolytus of

Rome, who around 200 CE provided an actual date for the end of the world, apparently to circumvent the idea that it would be anytime soon.

To make sense of Hippolytus's dating of doomsday, we need to understand why there have long been Christians who thought the world would last six thousand years. The first Christian text to support the idea is the Epistle of Barnabas, which dates to around 135 CE. Some early church leaders considered the epistle part of the canon of Scripture, although we should be thankful that it wasn't ultimately included: it is far more vitriolic in its attacks on Jews than anything in the eventual New Testament.[2] The letter, whose real author was anonymous, argues that Jews follow a false religion. In his view, when God gave the Israelites the Law of Moses, they missed the point completely, thinking the laws were meant to be followed literally rather than to convey important spiritual truths. When the Law says not to eat pork, for example, Barnabas argues this means that the true followers of God should not behave like swine, which grunt loudly when hungry but stay silent when well-fed. People are not to be like that, praying desperately to God only when in need. They are to pray at all times, even when life is good and they are satisfied (Barnabas 10.3).

The passage relevant for understanding the time span of creation comes in Barnabas's interpretation of what it means to observe the Sabbath. He argues that Jews are wrong to think they are supposed, or allowed, to take a day off from work every week. (What are they, lazy?) It is instead a reference to what God himself did, "In the beginning." In Genesis 1, God created the world in six days, and then on the seventh he rested. This shows the seventh day is a Sabbath, the day of God's rest. God's creation thus lasts six days. The Bible elsewhere states that "with the Lord, a day is as a thousand years and a thousand years as one day" (2 Peter 3:8; see Psalms 90:4). And so, when God instructs his people to "observe" the Sabbath, he means they should realize that the world will last six thousand years before the "day" of rest, the earthly millennium (Barnabas 15.1–5). Armed with that kind of logic, when should the world come to an end? If you know when the world started, you can easily crunch the numbers. This is where our third-century Hippolytus comes in.[3]

Hippolytus wrote a number of commentaries on books of the Bible, including one that no longer survives on the Apocalypse of John and another that does survive, but only in fragments, on the book of Daniel. Daniel, as we have seen, served as an inspiration for the Apocalypse. Among the surviving fragments of Hippolytus's Daniel commentary is a discussion of the awe-inspiring visions of Daniel 2 and 7. Because these accounts appear to talk about the end of history, Hippolytus wants to explain when this will be. He argues that the world was created 5,500 years before Christ's birth. If the world is to last six thousand years (here Hippolytus relies on the tradition found in Barnabas), then it will end around 500 CE, when the Antichrist arises and persecutes the saints. Hippolytus wrote his commentary in about 204 CE, and the point he is making is a bit subtle: the end will not come right away. The world will last another nearly three hundred years, so there is no need for his readers to panic.[4]

You might well wonder how Hippolytus came up with 5500 BCE for the date of creation. It was through a clever interpretation of a seemingly unrelated set of texts, the most fascinating of which is a passage in the Old Testament that describes how God instructed Moses to build the Ark of the Covenant to house the Ten Commandments (Exodus 25:1–16). Moses is told to make the ark out of imperishable wood and to overlay it with gold both inside and out. Hippolytus finds that description significant: the ark, which encases the Word of God, is a symbol for the body of Christ, imperishable and precious, as if of gold. God specifies the dimensions of the ark: it is to be two and a half cubits by one and a half by another one and a half. (A cubit is about eighteen inches.) So it is simple math: the container of the Word of God is 2.5 + 1.5 + 1.5. These measurements add up to 5.5. This shows that God ordered his Word to be embodied 5,500 years after the creation of the world.

The argument may seem far-fetched, but it is the kind of reasoning meant to appeal to people who are ready to be persuaded, not to skeptics. By showing Jesus was born 5,500 years after creation, Hippolytus could ward off Christian predictors of imminent doom, who were causing some consternation in their communities of faith. At least his dating could silence them for 290 years or so. By then, it would be someone else's problem.[5]

The Christians who, like Hippolytus, did not think the end was imminent continued to believe that Revelation and other Scriptures did predict the *future* of the world. That is certainly true of the first commentary on Revelation that survives, written some decades after Hippolytus by Victorinus, the late third-century bishop of Pettau (modern Ptuj in Slovenia).[6] The commentary is brief and makes no attempt to explain every passage, let alone every verse. But the comments are nonetheless striking, and in some ways remarkably prescient. Victorinus takes a historical approach to the Apocalypse, arguing that the book needs to be understood in light of John's own historical context. He identifies the "Babylon" of Revelation as the city of Rome and the beast as Nero, identifications that, as we will see, scholars continue to hold. He also realizes that the cycles of catastrophes in the book cannot be a chronological listing of what will happen in linear fashion; they are repetitions made for effect, to emphasize just how disastrous the end will be.

At the same time, Victorinus's commentary is not historical through and through. While he argues that the seven seals of the scroll broken by the Lamb represent the teachings of the Old Testament—because the full meaning of Scripture could not be understood by anyone before Christ appeared to explain the ancient texts—they also represent the future course of history, when God enters into judgment of the world at the end of time. And so Victorinus continued to subscribe to a futuristic interpretation of Revelation.

APOCALYPSE NOT NOW BUT LATER

Augustine was without a doubt the greatest theologian of the early church and he had little difficulty putting his thoughts into writing. His surviving works take up eight volumes of over five hundred pages each in the standard edition of the Post-Nicene Fathers, comprising over five million words.[7] Among all his doctrinal treatises, anti-heretical works, expositions of Scripture, and letters, two works stand out as classics: the autobiographical account of his conversion, *The Confessions*, and his twenty-two-volume theology of history, *The City of God*. Augustine sets this history of God's people in contrast with that of the followers of the false gods of Rome, concluding his work with a three-chapter discussion of the end of all things and the fate of all humans after death (*City of God*, chapters 20–22).

The book arose as a response to the fall of Rome, which was sacked by the Visigoths under their king Alaric in 410 CE, the first successful assault on the Eternal City in eight hundred years. Some Christians saw this not just as a massive imperial tragedy but also as a sign that the End was near. As Augustine points out in one of his sermons, some Christians had declared: "Behold, from Adam all the years have passed and behold, the 6,000 years are completed. . . . Now comes the day of judgment" (*Sermon*, 113.8).

Augustine did not think so and went to great lengths to explain why in Book 20 of the *City of God*, largely through an exposition of the ending of Revelation and its description of the millennium. If you recall, Revelation indicates that after the final catastrophes and the fall of Babylon, the devil will be bound and cast into the bottomless pit (20:1–3). The Christian martyrs will then be raised from the dead and will rule the earth with Christ for a thousand years (20:4–6). After that the Devil will be set free for a short time, before being defeated and hurled into the lake of fire for his eternal residence. All the dead will then be raised to face judgment: most of them destroyed in the fiery lake, others allowed entrance into the glorious city of God (20:7–15).

Revelation, then, speaks of two resurrections: one of the martyrs of Christ who will rule the nations during the millennium and the other later, when all will be assigned their ultimate destination. Many Christians in Augustine's day believed the first resurrection was imminent; Christ would soon intervene to bind Satan and usher in a thousand-year period of peace and prosperity.

Augustine objected to this futuristic interpretation, in part because it entailed a chiliastic view of great material abundance. As a proponent of an ascetic life, Augustine rejected the millennial excesses so anticipated by some fellow Christians, writing:

> I myself, too, once held this opinion. But, as they assert that those who then rise again shall enjoy the leisure of immoderate carnal banquets, furnished with an amount of meat and drink such as not only to shock the feeling of the temperate, but even to surpass the measure of credulity itself, such assertions can be believed only by the carnal. (*City of God*, 20.7)[8]

Augustine argued that literal interpretations of John's words completely miss the point. John mentions two resurrections that are radically different from each other. In Augustine's view, the first is a spiritual resurrection; only the second is physical. Moreover, the first resurrection has already happened: the church is already experiencing the millennium.[9]

In support of his view, Augustine points out that Revelation indicates Christ will reign on earth during the millennium. But for Augustine he has already been doing so since his death and resurrection: Christ rules in the here and now, through his followers in the church. This period is designated by God as a millennium because in Scripture a "thousand years" indicates the "fullness of time"— that is, a lengthy period to last until the end of the world.

In Augustine's view, Christians will continue to reign supreme until the very end. Not even Satan can harm them, for he has been cast into the "bottomless pit," which is the abyss of the "wicked whose hearts are unfathomably deep in malignity against the Church of God" (*City of God*, 20.7). That is the Devil's only residence, since he holds no sway among Christians. At the end of time he will again be loosed on the world, but only for a brief while. Then the End will come with the judgment of all and the destruction of evil. But that is still a long way off.

This interpretation may seem counterintuitive to readers today who do not at all see the absence of devilish activity, even in the church. But because of Augustine's immense status it quickly became the dominant understanding of Revelation and remained so until relatively modern times. There were always, of course, other interpretations on the margins of the Christian church, predictions that the end was coming soon. But these predictions were consistently proved false by the passing of time, and so Augustine's view lived on for many centuries.[10]

A NEW VISION OF THE COMING KINGDOM: JOACHIM OF FIORE

One of the most significant shifts in Christian thinking about the Apocalypse away from the Augustinian view came over seven centuries later in the reflections of the medieval Italian monk, theologian, and mystic Joachim of Fiore (1135–1202 CE).[11] Joachim was born in Calabria and became a monk in the Benedictine (and then later Cistercian) monastery of Corazzo. In 1177 he was made the abbot, but he preferred the contemplative life to monastic administration. Sometime in the 1180s, Joachim had a series of visions that unlocked for him the meaning of the Bible and the course of all human history.

Theologians had long appealed to the mystical meaning of Scripture, going behind the literal meaning of the text to uncover deeper truths. What was different in Joachim's case was he argued that these truths were not only about the nature of the divine and the significance of the past: they were also about the future. Joachim believed God had revealed to him how the entire history of the world was meant to unfold, from the very beginning to the very end, based on all of Scripture, but especially the book of Revelation.

Joachim's insight was that God imprinted his own character on the world. Since God was a Trinity, history was to unfold in a succession of three ages, the age of the Father, of the Son, and of the Spirit. The first age, of the Father, was the period of law and servitude; God gave his law to show his chosen people how they were to relate to him. That age lasted until the life of Christ, whose death and resurrection brought in the second age, characterized by grace and submission. The final age, the age of the Spirit, was yet to come. It was to be characterized by the direct and immediate knowledge of God. For Joachim that would be heaven on earth. God's chosen people would live in ecstatic and devout contemplation of God. This, in effect, was the life of a Cistercian monk writ large. At the end of this third age, the Antichrist would briefly arise, but his evil influence would be put down and the final judgment would come.

Joachim did not set a precise date for the end of the current age, the age of the Son, but he did note that the first age is roughly dated in the New Testament. The Gospel of Matthew begins by giving the genealogy of the messiah starting with Abraham, the father of the Jews (the beginning of the first age), up to Jesus himself (the beginning of the second). Altogether, Matthew gives forty-two generations (Matthew 1:17–18). On the assumption that a biblical generation lasts thirty years, Joachim crunched the numbers. The age of the Father (from Abraham to Jesus) lasted 1,260 years. And the second? Joachim was writing his views around 1200 CE. Whenever the end of the age was coming, it would be soon.

After Joachim's death, his writings were taken up by a group of Franciscan monks who made his predictions more specific.[12] These "Spiritual Franciscans," who were devoted to the principles of voluntary poverty and removal from all worldly concerns, began to promote Joachim's claims that the end of the second age was not far off and that it would be followed by a blessed period of direct contemplation of God, with no interference from the petty concerns of the world. In the 1240s and 1250s, these Franciscans revived interest in Joachim's writings and in some cases began propagating forgeries in his name. Most important for our purposes, they began to insist on doing the math. If the first age lasted 1,260 years, so, too, would the second. The age began with the birth of Jesus and so would end in 1260 CE.

As propagated by the Franciscans, Joachim's concept of the three ages made a significant impact on Christian thinking, but it never became the majority view—possibly because of its vision of what the age of the Spirit would involve. Most rank-and-file Christians throughout history have never been especially interested in an eternal contemplative life. On the other hand, given the harsh realities of life for the vast majority of medieval Christians, surely most did not think they were living the millennial existence in the here and now, either, which had been Augustine's view. We have little reliable evidence for what most people thought throughout that period. Still, it is not hard to imagine that most people, barely able to eke out a living, would have had no objections to the older chiliast view: a paradise would soon arrive, bringing breathtaking abundance and luxury.

Even so, it was yet another five hundred years before a fully developed eschatology began to catch on—a "theology of the end-times"—that could provide hope for those suffering through the miserable exigencies of life. In European Christianity, it did not surface until there were reasons for thinking the world really was coming to an end. This terrifying thought led to a reinterpretation of the meaning of the book of Revelation.

THE RISE OF FUTURISTIC UNDERSTANDINGS OF REVELATION

One of the most monumental upheavals of the French Revolution occurred not in the realms of social history or political theory but in Christian theology. Granted, this upheaval didn't change the map of Europe or the course of democracy, but it nonetheless affected millions of people and continues to do so today.

As Ernest Sandeen, a modern historian of Christian fundamentalism, has shown, the unprecedented violence of the Reign of Terror was seen to be so catastrophic by some British Christians that devout church members could not help but think the horrors of the Apocalypse had come upon them. That would mean, of course, that what had been the traditional understanding of John's Revelation from the time of Augustine was completely wrong: the book was not describing what had already happened during the course of Christian history. Based on a more straightforward reading, the book really did appear to predict what was yet to come.[13]

This was not the first time that a more literal reading of Revelation had popped up. You will recall that Protestant Christians, going back to Luther himself, had identified the beast of the sea—which rules the earth, blasphemes God, and persecutes the saints—as the pope.

In Revelation, the beast's reign would last forty-two months, which, for some interpreters, became 1,260 years (with a "day," in this interpretation, meaning a year). In the 1790s some Anglican theologians calculated that the papacy as an institution assumed full power over the church in 538 CE under Pope Vigilius. If the beast was to rule 1,260 years, then his demise would come in 1798. As it turns out, that was the date Napoleon's chief of staff, Louis-Alexandre Berthier, invaded the Vatican, banished Pope Pius VI from office, imprisoned him, and established the Roman Republic. This was the "mortal wound" that Revelation predicted the beast would receive (Revelation 13:3).

In that very year one English commentator made the apocalyptic connection explicit:

> Is not the *Papal power* at Rome, which was once so terrible, and so domineering, at an end? But let us pause a little. Was not *this* End, in other parts of the Holy Prophecies, foretold to be *at the END of 1,260 years?* . . . And now let us see;—hear;—and understand. THIS IS THE YEAR 1798. And just 1,260 years ago, in the very beginning of the year 538, *Besiliarius* put an end to the Empire and Dominion of the Goths, at Rome.[14]

In other words, the end was nigh.

CHRISTIAN ZIONISM AND FUTURISTIC READINGS OF THE BIBLE

The apocalyptic implications of events in Europe happened to coincide with a seemingly unrelated development within British Christianity, a renewed interest in the fate of the nation of Israel based on biblical prophecies. As odd as it might seem, the combination of these two developments—a renewed sense that the end had begun and an interest in the fate of the Jewish people—led ultimately to the formation of biblical fundamentalism and, more recently, the apocalyptic expectations of the *Left Behind* series.[15]

The Christian interest in the modern state of Israel, most strongly expressed today among American evangelicals, has its roots in the first decades of nineteenth-century England, in a serendipitous course of events involving a little-known figure named Lewis Way (1772–1840).[16] Way was an impoverished barrister who had trouble finding clients. In October 1799, a wealthy and unrelated sixty-seven-year-old John Way was visiting his solicitor when he happened to notice Lewis Way's name painted on an office door. He decided to go in to meet this fellow who shared his somewhat unusual name.

The two Ways converged and they established an immediate friendship. Both were evangelical Christians and serious about their faith. Lewis started visiting his affluent namesake at his home, and as their mutual affection increased, John began providing Lewis with financial support.

John Way died in August 1804, leaving no children or other satisfactory heir. After providing a tidy sum for his wife, he bequeathed the rest of his estate to Lewis. The estate was worth £300,000 (around $42 million today). As one might expect, there were a number of news stories about Lewis Way's surprising bit of good fortune. One British newspaper, the *Leeds Mercury*, commented: "Where there's a Will, there's a Way."[17]

Lewis Way almost immediately used his inheritance to purchase an estate in West Sussex with a thousand acres of parkland and a forest designed by Capability Brown. He then spent six years restoring the home and becoming a philanthropist. Then another serendipity happened, once again of relevance to the future of apocalyptic thought and again seemingly unrelated.

In 1811, now a man of leisure, Way was riding with a friend through the countryside of Devon when he came upon a very odd sixteen-sided building called A La Ronde.[18] It had been designed as a residence for two wealthy cousins, Jane and Mary Parminter. The interior consisted of an octagonal hall opened to a sixty-foot-high ceiling, with three floors of rooms around the perimeter. The eight rooms on the ground floor were connected not with doors but with sliding panels so that one could walk through the circuit without entering the hall. The walls were decorated with shells and feathers. More important for our story was an unusual feature on the grounds, a line of oak trees standing beside a chapel. Lewis Way learned that when Jane Parminter had died just that year, she left a will that included a codicil: "These oaks shall remain standing, and the hand of man shall not be raised against them till Israel returns and is restored to the Land of Promise."[19]

These oak trees piqued Way's curiosity, changed the course of his life, and in the end affected the religious beliefs of millions of people, impacting international affairs down to our day.

For years, evangelical Christians had been convinced that Scripture predicted Jews were to return to the Holy Land to reestablish themselves there as a sovereign state. After all, the Old Testament prophet Jeremiah had reported God's words to the people of Judah: "I will restore your fortunes and gather you from all the nations and all the places where I have driven you . . . and I will bring you back to the place from which I sent you to exile" (Jeremiah 29:14). If the end was near, as indicated by the events in France, then the eschatological restoration of Israel must be at hand. Between 1796 and 1800, this view was advanced in fifty-some books published in Britain. Many evangelicals were thrilled when Napoleon's army invaded Palestine in 1799, declaring that Jews were "the rightful heirs" of the land. As one commentator put it in 1812, "We *know* that the latter times approach, and that the Jews *must* and *will* be restored; these things greatly animate us in exertion and enliven our hearts in labor."[20]

It was at just this time that Lewis Way, moved by the oak grove on the grounds of A La Ronde, decided to commit his time and resources to the cause of Jewish restoration. He quickly became involved with the London Society for Promoting Christianity among the Jews, an aptly named missionary society, which he transformed through his financial support and leadership. This was not a marginal group of religious fanatics: the society enjoyed the patronage of the Duke of Kent, third son of George III. Way transformed his estate into a college for the training of missionaries to the Jews. In the widely held evangelical view at the time, the "conversion of the Jews" would go hand in hand with divine restoration of Israel.

For years, Way used his wealth and influence wisely. A highly placed relative in the Foreign Office helped to arrange a meeting with Alexander I, emperor of Russia, to plan political strategies to establish Israel as a sovereign state. Alexander himself was a committed Christian who believed that Israel must be restored to fulfill prophecy. But to Way's chagrin, political crises intervened and both Alexander and the nations of Europe went on to other priorities.

Still, even though a political enactment of end-times prophecy did not come about, the new fervor for the return of Israel, combined with the widening belief that world events signaled the End was near, contributed to the rise of an entirely new school of eschatological thought that dominates conservative evangelical Christianity and its interpretation of Revelation still today. It is called dispensational premillennialism.

THE RISE OF DISPENSATIONAL PREMILLENNIALISM

The term "premillennialism" requires some explaining. In the eighteenth century, many British and American Protestants had started to move beyond Augustine's "historicist" approach to Revelation, which claimed that most of the events of the book had been fulfilled and that the millennium, Christ's reign on earth, was happening now. They instead adopted a "futuristic" approach, arguing that the book was predicting what was yet to come, and that the millennium could be expected at the end of the age.

In the American colonies, most futuristic Christian thinkers believed the millennium would arrive through human progress rather than direct divine intervention. New scientific discoveries, new technologies, and the worldwide spread of the Christian faith showed that humans were en route to achieving their potential, making this world a better place in the present and a utopian one in the future. This view eventually came to be known as "postmillennialism," since it posited that Christ would return only after the future millennial age had run its course.

This view was advocated most influentially by the great eighteenth-century Christian philosopher, theologian, and revivalist Jonathan Edwards (1703–1758). Edwards may be best known today for his intentionally terrifying sermon "Sinners in the Hands of an Angry God," but he was not your run-of-the-mill fire-and-brimstone preacher. Studious as a boy, he entered Yale College at the age of thirteen and received an advanced education in science and philosophy before going into ministry. As a Calvinist theologian and a high-profile preacher, he brought evangelical Christianity to the fore during the Great Awakening in the 1740s, prior to becoming the third president of Princeton University (then the College of New Jersey) near the end of his life.

Based on his understanding of human progress, American greatness, and Scripture, Edwards championed the view that the world was moving toward the glorious millennium, an idea that was to become exceedingly popular in the States and stayed that way until the early twentieth century. In the words of one American preacher in 1846, directed to a presumably somewhat incredulous British audience:

Allow me to say, that, in America, the state of society is without parallel in universal history. With all our mixtures, there is a leaven of heaven there; there is goodness there; there is excellent principle there. I really believe that God has got America within anchorage, and that upon that arena he intends to display his prodigies for the millennium.[21]

Already, though, an alternative view had appeared in some evangelical circles in Britain, a view that explicitly rejected such optimism and endorsed its opposite: an entirely pessimistic view of the immediate future of the human race. The view began in a small and inauspicious corner of Christendom, appearing like a tiny mustard seed that was eventually to grow into an enormous bush.

In 1830 a former Anglican priest from Ireland, John Nelson Darby (1800–1882), established a new religious community in Plymouth, England, which, as a consequence, became known as the Plymouth Brethren. This was a strict, pious, back-to-the-New-Testament group with an aversion to "professional clergy" and an insistence on the literal interpretation of the Bible. Though it spread throughout Britain and the United States, it never became one of the large denominations. In one sense, however, it became massively important: Darby advanced one of the most influential religious ideas of modern times, the idea that Christ would return twice, once before God inflicted the catastrophes described in the book of Revelation and then again afterward, when Christ would set up his millennial kingdom.

This, then, was a "premillennial" view, in which Jesus first returns *before* the millennium. Darby situated these two returns of Christ in a broader vision of God's plan for the history of salvation, which included a number of distinct periods of human history. Within each period people interacted with him differently, according to guidelines he established in light of ongoing events. These discrete periods of history were called "dispensations," and so Darby's system came to be known as dispensational premillennialism.

The idea of dividing history into discrete periods in which people worshipped and obeyed God differently had been around at least since Joachim of Fiore. But Darby's view was far more complex and, he would have argued, far more attentive to the entire biblical record of God's interactions with humans from the beginning.

Darby determined the length and character of each dispensation through an exceedingly careful evaluation of the scriptural narrative. The most popular form of his system posits seven dispensations and actually makes good sense of the sweep of "biblical history." At least it did to me when I was attending a Plymouth Brethren church and learning the truth of dispensationalism at Moody Bible Institute, a bastion of fundamentalist dispensational thought since its founding by evangelist Dwight Lyman Moody in 1886.

Our Bible of choice at Moody was the Scofield Reference Bible. The book was originally published in 1909 and quickly became the bestselling study Bible in the English-speaking world and probably the bestselling book of any kind published in America by Oxford University Press in the first half of the twentieth century.[22] From 1917 to 1967 it was a standard text for fundamentalists.

The Scofield Bible was originally produced by Cyrus I. Scofield, who came from Tennessee, fought in the Civil War under Robert E. Lee, became a state legislator in Kansas, and eventually, in 1879, converted to a very conservative form of Christianity.[23] He later became pastor of the Moody Church in Northfield, Massachusetts. Scofield realized there could be a way to spread a conservative evangelical view of the Bible by incorporating it into an edition of the Bible itself. His "Reference Bible" was one of the first of its kind, an edition of the King James Version that went beyond translation to provide introductions to each of the books, explanations of key biblical passages, footnotes to explain cross-references, maps, charts, and so on, all to guide readers in their reading and incorporating conservative evangelical views. Study Bibles are common today, with a wide variety to choose from, but they were unheard-of before the rise of fundamentalism.[24] Of particular importance for our purposes: Scofield's notes incorporated—and therefore propagated—Darby's understanding of the seven dispensations.[25] Readers who found a dispensational view in their Scofield Bible did not take it to be an unusual theory; it was part of the Bible itself. With so many conservative Protestant Christians reading the Scofield edition, its dispensational views became standard among evangelicals.

These were the seven dispensations:

1. *Innocence.* Extending from Adam to the expulsion from the Garden. In this brief opening period, humans lived in paradise with no real requirements for following God except the one command not to eat the fruit from the tree of the knowledge of good and evil. But Adam and Eve could not comply even with something that simple, leading to:

2. *Conscience.* From the expulsion from Eden to the flood. During this period God required people to rely on their conscience for guidance; now they knew the difference between good and evil and needed to act accordingly. That, too, did not go well. Apart from one man, Noah, the entire world became corrupt, so God destroyed the lot of them with the flood. Then came:

3. *Human Government.* From the flood to Abraham, the father of the chosen ones. After the flood, God commanded Noah to institute laws to govern human activity.

Anyone who murdered another, for instance, was to have their own life taken away. That, too, did not work, so God then went another preordained route:

4. *Promise*. From Abraham to Moses. When the postdiluvian population proved incapable of recognizing God and worshipping him appropriately, he implemented the next phase by making one part of the human race his own people, through whom, eventually, he would save the others. He called Abraham and promised him both a homeland and descendants to fill it. There were righteous people throughout this dispensation, but not many; God was using the period as a lead-in to the events that would bring ultimate salvation.

5. *Law*. From Moses to Christ. When the descendants of Abraham found themselves in serious trouble, enslaved as a people in Egypt, God intervened to deliver them under Moses at the exodus. He then gave Moses his Law to guide his people in social interactions and worship. Unfortunately, once more, humans proved incapable of obeying God's commandments and needed some other way of salvation, leading to:

6. *The Church* (or *Grace*). From Christ to the end of history as we know it. God sent Christ to deliver his recalcitrant people, and in fact all people on earth. Salvation now comes not by following one's conscience, trusting a promise, or trying to keep God's law, but by believing in the redemption brought by the death and resurrection of Jesus. This salvation comes to anyone who believes. But it, too, is not the end of the story:

7. *Kingdom*. Since many people do not accept the free gift of salvation and continue to live in sin, God will bring his plan to an end when he cleanses the earth in judgment,

removing all evil from the world. Those who refuse to obey him will be condemned in the coming onslaught and sent to eternal punishment; those who believe in his son the messiah will be rewarded with the millennial kingdom and then the New Jerusalem.

And so the system tracks the relationship of God and his people through a number of periods with different divinely given systems of order and governance until the very end.[26]

THE INVENTION OF THE RAPTURE

Darby's system of dispensations included one innovation that is especially relevant to our discussion. He and his small group of dispensational premillennialists disagreed with other Christians who claimed that advances in culture and the spread of Christianity painted a rosy picture for what lay ahead. They were pessimistic that things would get worse and worse until literally all hell broke out. After all, the Apocalypse of John was principally about disasters to come, and none of its predictions had been fulfilled yet. Unimaginable catastrophes were soon to transpire that would wipe out enormous swaths of the earth's population and natural resources. It would be a time of incredible suffering for everyone on the planet.

And so, in 1833, Darby pronounced his new idea: The followers of Jesus would not be here to experience these catastrophes. There would be a "rapture" before the coming tribulation. Thus, Christ would not come back just once, after the Battle of Armageddon, to set up his kingdom (Revelation 19:11–21), but twice: the "second" coming was therefore a second and third coming. First, Christ would return in the air for his followers, to escort them to heaven for a period of bliss.[27] Following this rapture, the world would descend into chaos and the Antichrist would arise. Some people would convert to Christ in this period and eventually be saved, but only after suffering through the most horrendous misery the world has ever seen. The tribulation would last for seven years. Then Christ would return again to bring an end to it all, destroying his enemies and bringing in his millennial kingdom.

Darby labeled his new insight—the first of the two second comings—the "secret" rapture. It was a secret because no one knew when it would happen. Christ himself said, "No one knows about that day or hour, not the angels in heaven, not even the Son, but only the Father" (Matthew 24:36). Still, Scripture affirms repeatedly that it would be coming "soon." Since it still hadn't happened, the biblical writers obviously did not mean it would come soon in their own day; their prophecies were for people living in our time, or in the near future. So be prepared, or look forward to hell on earth.

THE DISPENSATIONAL TAKEOVER

There were debates within Darby's Plymouth Brethren community about certain aspects of his views—principally the scriptural support for the "secret rapture"—leading to a split in 1845.[28] Over time, those who were convinced the rapture was scriptural won more advocates, and the view began to spread. Variants emerged. Some came to think the rapture would occur not before the tribulation but afterward; yet others argued that the rapture would come precisely halfway through the tribulation. These obviously were important issues for the individuals concerned: How much will I need to suffer? They also had broader social implications: Do I start stockpiling weapons to protect my family and food to help us survive?

Despite its spread, the dispensational view encountered real difficulties among many Christians, even evangelicals. In the end, it was less popular in Great Britain than in America, where its popularity was boosted by a series of conferences held in Niagara, New

York, in the 1890s, organized and attended by leading evangelical teachers who were concerned about the direction of both the world and the church. Science had begun to pose a clear and certain threat to traditional Christian claims, with biologists propounding Darwinism and geologists estimating the actual age of the earth. Even many religion scholars were being seduced, especially by biblical scholars in Germany, who were practicing "historical criticism," treating the Bible as if it were like any other book: finding contradictions, claiming historical errors, doubting the authorship of some of the writings, disputing its truth claims.

In response, the conservative theologians at the Niagara conferences doubled down on their literal views of Scripture. This is when modern formulations of the doctrine of biblical "inerrancy" arose: every word of the Bible was inspired by God and literally true, whether a statement about doctrine, history, or science. Anyone who said otherwise—who disputed a six-day creation, a real Adam and Eve, a worldwide flood, a tower of Babel, or anything else the Bible said—was not a genuine Christian and was in danger of eternal damnation.[29] As the decades passed, dispensational premillennialism emerged from the margins to become a central tenet of evangelical Christianity.

Dispensationalists insisted they alone took the literal teachings of biblical prophecy seriously, especially the book of Revelation. Since nothing John of Patmos predicted had happened yet, it all must be still to come. This literalist reading was aided by a widespread collapse of optimism about human progress. The bright possibilities of the future lay at the foundation of *post*millennial views: the world was moving toward millennial bliss through advances of civilization, the improvement of human culture, and the hopeful developments of technology. Those sanguine views were obliterated in the trenches of World War I. It may be hard to imagine that the invention of the machine gun would have affected biblical hermeneutics, but it certainly did. Any optimism in the West that remained after the armistice was more or less swallowed up by the Great Depression and then spit out by yet another world war that ended with the unleashing of atomic bombs. Then came the Cold War, nuclear proliferation, and the never-before-imagined possibility that we might destroy ourselves and our planet simply by the way we lived on it. How was postmillennial optimism to escape this onslaught of historical reality? Jesus had better come back soon, or there would be no one left to save.

It is no surprise that so many evangelical Christians today are dispensational premillennialists. It is not that anyone is interested in Darby and his innovations. Most evangelicals could not define a dispensation if you threatened them with seven years of tribulation. But as a rule they embrace the basic idea: Even though all hell will soon break out, there is hope for believers. Jesus will return to rescue his people from the horrors ahead. No one knows exactly when, so we all must be ready.

Anyone outside the evangelical fold who finds this view risible should not write it off. It deserves our attention if for no other reason than that it affects our world. The idea that the end is near has destroyed lives, shaped nations, and interfered with efforts to avoid planetary ruin. We'll explore how in the next chapter.

FOUR

Real-Life Consequences of the Imminent Apocalypse

The expectation that the End Is Near has never done anyone much good, except perhaps the prophecy authors who have made fame and fortune writing about it. On a personal level, the failure of one's expectations to materialize has usually led to bad, very bad, or disastrous results. But the effects of these beliefs are rarely purely individual. They are almost always communal, sometimes national, or even international. Now, in most recent times, they have become significant for the fate of humanity.

I cannot do full justice to the dangerous consequences of these beliefs in the space of one chapter, but I do want to illustrate the point with four case studies from American religion in particular.

THE GREAT DISAPPOINTMENT

I have already discussed the failed predictions of some of the modern date setters: prophecy writers who calculated the day, the week, or at least the decade when Jesus would return. Most predictors of the imminent end, however, refuse to be so precise. The value of imprecision, of course, is that it makes a prediction unfalsifiable. You can't say someone is wrong about the date if they don't give you one, and to say it is "soon" could mean most anything if you believe that "with the Lord a day is as a thousand years and a thousand years as one day" (2 Peter 3:8). In that case, if Jesus is coming back in, say, three days, we can start looking for him around 5023 CE.

The modern tendency for hedging one's bets, at least in America, is linked to a particular historical event, a disastrously wrong prediction of a precise date that shattered lives. American historians refer to it as the "Great Disappointment."[1] It involved the predictions of a small-time farmer from upstate New York named William Miller. Miller was not the kind of person anyone would expect to play a role in current affairs. He grew up in obscurity, with no advanced education and no ambitions for public attention. He had been raised in a religious household but became disillusioned with his faith while fighting in the War of 1812. After the war, plagued by doubts, he began studying the Bible, trying to understand the mysteries of life. He was particularly drawn to Scripture's most mysterious texts, the book of Revelation and the book of Daniel, the two apocalypses that appear to describe the future.

Miller was one of those lay readers who became intimately familiar with these texts down to their very precise detail, working to grasp their deeper meaning. After two years of study, his eyes were opened and he realized the ultimate plan of God: "I was thus brought, in 1818, at the close of my two years' study of the Scriptures, to the solemn conclusion, that in about twenty-five years from that time all the affairs of our present state would be wound up."[2] That is, he realized the world would end around 1843. He spent the next twenty-five years working out the details and starting a movement that grew to tens of thousands of believers.

Miller had reached his conclusion before Darby, overseas, came up with the idea of a rapture, and so did not hold to anything like a dispensationalist view. He thought Jesus was coming in judgment on the earth, not to remove his followers before the horrors arrived. Unlike Edgar Whisenant, he did not need "88 Reasons" for thinking so, although he did have several, none of them more important than his reading of the vision described in Daniel 8.

The vision involves two animals: a ram with two horns that rampages the nations of earth with reckless abandon, followed by a goat with a single horn that ruthlessly destroys the ram and creates even more havoc. At the height of its power, the single horn is broken, replaced by four other horns, which are then succeeded by a "little" horn, which is worst of all, opposing in particular the people of God, interrupting their worship, and defiling the sanctuary (Daniel 8:1–14).

Many readers even from ancient times recognized the symbolic significance of this vision. Daniel, who allegedly lived in the sixth century BCE, during the reign of the Babylonian empire, saw the course of future events. The animals represented two empires that would ravage the earth after Babylonia: the two-horned ram representing the joint empire of the Medes and the Persians, which would be destroyed by the goat with a single horn, representing Greece and its single leader, Alexander the Great. When Alexander died as a young man in 323 BCE, his empire was divided among his four generals, represented by the four horns; the "little horn" was a disastrous later ruler who proved especially dangerous for the people of Israel.[3]

Miller knew that all the things "predicted" in this vision had in fact come true—with the world empires of Medo-Persia and Greece. But he was particularly intrigued by what was supposed to transpire after the little horn did its foul deeds. What would it mean that the temple would be defiled for "two thousand three hundred evenings and mornings" and then be "restored to its rightful state" (Daniel 8:14)?

To make sense of this—that is, to assemble the biblical jigsaw puzzle—Miller turned to other passages of Scripture. First, he looked to the next vision of Daniel in the following chapter, where the angel Gabriel reveals to Daniel that "seventy weeks are decreed for your people and your holy city: to finish the transgression to put an end to sin, to atone for iniquity, to bring in everlasting righteousness, . . . and to anoint a most holy place" (Daniel 9:24). Since Miller knew that the temple (the "most holy place") had already been destroyed in Daniel's day by the Babylonians, he believed that the angel was giving the prophet a precise indication of how long the Jewish people had to stop sinning, receive atonement for their sins, and become righteous again in connection with a *new* temple that was yet to be built.

Miller was a firm believer in the principle that a "day" in prophetic language refers to a "year" in real time. Based on this passage from Daniel, he therefore knew the following: from the time the temple was rebuilt, there would be seventy "weeks" (with each day of those weeks representing a year) for Jews to return fully to God. That would be 70 x 7, so 490 years. But when does the divine calendar start? Obviously with the rebuilding of the temple. And when was that?

Here Miller turns to another passage. The book of Ezra describes how the Persian empire, which had conquered the Babylonians after Daniel's day, allowed Jews in exile to return home. A key passage in Ezra 7 indicates that the king of Persia, Artaxerxes, sent a letter to the great Jewish scholar Ezra, instructing him to gather wealth from around the empire and take it to Jerusalem in order to restore the temple and thus "glorify the LORD." This decree was traditionally dated to 457 BCE. Four hundred ninety years after that, the efforts of the Jews to attain righteousness would have come to an end.

Do the math: 490 years after 457 is the year 33 CE—the year Jesus died. With the death and resurrection of Jesus, the Jews had their preordained chance for righteousness. But they did not accept Jesus. So how long would it take for the sanctuary of the Jews to be made holy again, after being defiled by the "little horn" of Daniel 8? Exactly 2,300 days (Daniel 8:14)—that is, 2,300 years. And when is 2,300 years after 457 BCE? 1843.

Thus, Miller realized in 1818 that there remained just twenty-five years before the end came. He eventually convinced several pastors, who persuaded other pastors, who informed their congregations, and the movement spread. Miller began being invited to speak publicly, and eventually there were entire conferences of Christian leaders devoted to just this topic—twenty-six of them from 1840 to 1844 alone. Those leaders organized meetings for laypeople—more than 124 of them in 1842 and 1843, some with thousands of Christians in attendance. By some estimates there were around fifty thousand devotees near the end, and possibly a million people who thought that at least *something* significant was going to happen then.[4]

The precise date for the end did vary among different groups of Millerites. At the outset of 1843, Miller began hedging his bet. One gets nervous when disconfirmation is right on the horizon. He began to explain that when he named 1843, he was not using the Gregorian calendar but the ancient Jewish calendar, which began and ended with the vernal equinox. That meant Jesus would return sometime between March 21, 1843, and March 21, 1844. Miller was reluctant to name a specific date: "No one knows the day or the hour!" But eventually he yielded to the pressure of his most fervent followers and broadcast the news. Jesus would return on the last day possible, March 21, 1844. Even before that potentially momentous event, other leaders in the movement came to think the date was wrong, for complicated reasons having to do with different ancient

Jewish calendars. Some argued for September 22, 1844. Yet others insisted on October 22, 1844.

March 21 passed; then so did September 22. As the final option drew near, fevered anticipation grew. But midnight on October 22 came and went, and life went on. This ultimate failure of Miller's prediction brought palpable despondency among the onetime hopeful. As one of the disappointed wrote:

> Our fondest hopes and expectations were blasted, and such a spirit of weeping came over us as I never experienced before. It seemed that the loss of all earthly friends could have been no comparison. We wept and wept until the day dawn.[5]

The effects of this particular instance of end-time thinking were not limited to psychic trauma. The Millerites were subject to widespread ridicule and even to physical hardship. Soon afterward, one of the erstwhile Millerites, Luther Boutelle, explained the real-life consequences of their belief in the imminent end:

> Crops were left unharvested, their owners expecting never to want what they had raised. Men paid up their debts. Many sold their property to help others pay their debts, who could not have done so themselves. Beef cattle were slaughtered and distributed among the poor.[6]

One enthusiast, Ezekiel Hale Jr., a Massachusetts businessman, had given part of his wealth to the movement and divvied the rest among his children, who did not share his religious views. When the end failed to come, he went to court to get his property back.[7]

The Psychology of Frustrated Expectation

One might think a disappointment of this magnitude would have killed the inclination to expect an imminent end of the world. But the human spirit is resilient. Social psychologists have shown that frustrated expectations often lead to renewed fervor in reimagined form. This is the argument of an unusually intriguing book well known to scholars but, unfortunately, not widely familiar otherwise: *When Prophecy Fails* by Leon Festinger, Henry W. Riecken, and Stanley Schachter.[8]

The book is not about the Bible but rather—who woulda thought?—UFO cults. In the mid-1950s, Festinger and his colleagues became interested in the question of what happens to groups such as the Millerites who hold concrete beliefs that can, and then are, proved to be wrong. To find an analogous situation, they had the brilliant idea of studying a UFO cult that expected the world to experience a major calamity on the approaching December 21; they, the members of the group, would be removed from the planet before it hit, picked up by flying saucers, and relocated to some other safe place in the galaxy. Festinger and his colleagues secured a number of observers to infiltrate the group to see how the group would react when it didn't happen. For the group there was no fudging on the date, and when it arrived, members eagerly waited through the night . . . but no flying saucers came.

With this kind of disappointment, you might expect the group to admit its mistake and disband. Festinger and his colleagues, however, thought this was not what would happen. They were right. Just like those who set a date for Jesus's return, the devotees of the coming flying saucers reset the date and became yet more fervent in their belief. What's more, they worked feverishly to attract others to their group. But why?

That was Festinger's question, and he and his colleagues developed the idea of "cognitive dissonance" to account for it. Cognitive dissonance refers to a psychological state that occurs when a group has a set expectation that is specific, concrete, and actionable. That is, the expectation needs to have a serious effect not just on people's mental state but also on their lives—for example, by driving them to quit their jobs or leave their families in anticipation. The expectation also needs to be capable of being concretely disconfirmed, such as: "Jesus will return on October 22 of this year" or "The Martians will come rescue us next Thursday." That disconfirmation then needs to happen. At that point, cognitive dissonance kicks in: reality is dissonant, out of line with what people in the group were convinced would happen.

Instead of admitting they were wrong, however, the group buoys itself by explaining to one another what *really* happened, justifying themselves in face of the disconfirmation by pointing out a slight error in their calculations or claiming the event was intentionally delayed and then resetting the date. But most interesting, the group further resolves the dissonance by becoming more evangelistic, going out to win more converts to their views. Why would a mistake make someone missionary? The theory behind cognitive dissonance is that if more people acknowledge you are right, it eases the psychological trauma of knowing that you are probably wrong. So you set out to win over other devotees.[9]

Thus, the Millerites and their resetting of dates. Each time the expectation is disconfirmed, the group gets larger and more fervent, until the Final Disappointment takes effect.

But even then, the idea does not necessarily go away, nor do the groups themselves. Various American religious groups emerged from the Millerites' Great Disappointment—"at least 33," according to sociologists of religion Rodney Stark and William Sims Bainbridge.[10] Hope springs eternal, and these groups thrive among us today, holding strong eschatological views about the coming end—normally, now, without setting dates. The two break-off groups most familiar to modern readers are the Jehovah's Witnesses and the Seventh-day Adventists.

It is from the latter denomination that another religious movement splintered off, coming to be known as the Branch Davidians, one of the most notorious groups of believers of modern times, famous since the 1993 destruction of their compound outside Waco, Texas, during a clash with the FBI after a fifty-day siege. Eighty people were killed, including the group's leader, David Koresh. The entire disaster occurred, in part, because of Koresh's unusual interpretation of the book of Revelation.

THE DISASTER AT WACO

Koresh and his followers were devotees of the Apocalypse. They did what they did because they were convinced they were the ones prophesied in the book. Koresh himself was the Lamb of God of Revelation 4–5 who was breaking the seals of the divine scroll. One of the seals predicted the Davidians' own martyrdoms.

To understand these views, it is helpful to trace their history, going back to the Millerites over a century earlier.[11] The Millerites often called themselves "Adventists," because they were firmly committed to the view that the second Advent (or "Coming") of Christ was to happen soon. After the Great Disappointment, a group of Adventists began to proclaim that a major event *had* occurred in 1844—not the return of Christ to earth, but an elevation of his status in heaven: he had at last entered into the heavenly sanctuary to perform his role as heavenly priest. Among the leaders of this new group was Ellen G. White, who was understood to be a prophetess. The group took on the name Seventh-day Adventist Church because their teachings emphasized, among other things, the importance of observing the Sabbath—that is, the seventh day of the week, Saturday—as the day of worship, rather than Sunday, which was seen as the first day of the week. Today, the church is one of the most rapid growing of the Protestant denominations, with over twenty million adherents.

In 1934, some seventy years after its founding, a reform movement led to a split in the church. The splinter group was led by a man named Victor Houteff (1885–1955), who called his new group the Davidian Seventh-day Adventists because he especially emphasized the imminent return of the Davidic messiah to reestablish the Davidic kingdom. After Houteff's death, his successor, his wife, Florence, made a specific prediction: the Kingdom was to arrive on April 22, 1959. That led to another disappointment, though this one involved only hundreds of expectants, not many thousands.[12]

The next leader, Benjamin Roden, came to see himself as the one who would organize the coming Davidic kingdom, and so started calling himself the "Branch," an allusion to the future messianic figure who was to come from the ancestral line (or "branch") of King David, according to biblical prophecy (Isaiah 11:1; Zechariah 3:8; 6:12). This provided the new name of the group, the Branch Davidians. Among the curious developments that arose within the group were the theological views of Roden's wife, Lois, who declared that the third member of the Trinity was female and that the soon-to-appear messiah would come as a woman. And who knows? Maybe she's right.

That brings us to David Koresh, who, though male, came to be considered a messiah himself. Koresh was born Vernon Howell in 1959. He had been a troubled youth but found solace and purpose in the Seventh-day Adventist Church, until he was disfellowshipped for his interpretation of Scripture. He joined the Branch Davidians at the age of twenty-two, first as a handyman and then as a prophet. He became close to Lois Roden, who had assumed leadership after her husband (the original Branch) died, and she named him her successor. In 1990, he changed his name to David Koresh, the significance of which is lost on nearly everyone.

Since Koresh saw himself standing in the messianic line of King David, his new first name certainly makes sense. But why Koresh? The name actually reveals a good deal about how Vernon Howell understood himself: it is an English rendition of "Cyrus," the king of Persia in the Old Testament, whom, although a pagan ruler, God remarkably calls "his anointed one," that is, "his messiah." A *gentile* is the messiah? Yes, according to Isaiah 45:

> *Thus says the* LORD *to his anointed [= messiah], to Cyrus [= Koresh]*
>   *whose right hand I have grasped*
> *to submit nations before him,*
>   *and strip kings of their robes. . . .*
> *I will go before you*
>   *And level the mountains,*
> *I will break in pieces the doors of bronze*
>   *And cut through the bars of iron. . . .*
> *(Isaiah 45:1–3)*

Cyrus, then, is God's messiah, whom he will empower to rule the nations. That's the name Howell chose for himself. He was the fulfillment of this prophecy, the non-Jewish messiah predicted in Scripture.

The Book of Revelation and the Disaster at Waco

Most people who know about the tragedy at Waco have some vague idea about Koresh, the Branch Davidians, and the FBI siege that led to the destruction of their compound and a great loss of life. Few people, though, know about the role Koresh's religious views played in the tragic affair.[13]

The Branch Davidians were an obscure group even to scholars

of religion. The first time most of us heard of them was the day of the first assault on their Mount Carmel compound, thirteen miles outside Waco, by the Bureau of Alcohol, Tobacco and Firearms on February 28, 1993. This was "breaking news" back when the phrase actually meant something. Network programming was interrupted to announce that four federal officials were dead and fifteen wounded in a two-hour gun battle with a religious group led by someone with a peculiarly biblical name. New Testament scholar James Tabor, who was listening to the coverage on CNN, was well steeped in biblical prophecy and immediately recognized the name's messianic overtones and began to pay close attention.

As the story unfolded over the next few days, it became clear that the besieged group of Davidians were following what they understood to be divine principles laid out in the book of Revelation. They saw the current situation as a fulfillment of the signs. It also became clear that the FBI, which had been called in to deal with the situation, had no clue what any of that meant. When they repeatedly contacted Koresh inside the compound by phone, he eagerly explained his interpretation of Revelation for hours on end. The agents assumed he was a kook likely to continue whatever nefarious activities he was engaged with inside the compound, or that he might end it all with a mass suicide.

Tabor called a scholar friend, Phillip Arnold, and the pair decided to contact the FBI to explain what Koresh was actually talking about, on the assumption that if you understand someone you are more likely to be able to deal with them. But when Arnold offered their services as experts in Koresh's "Bible talk," the Bureau, to no one's surprise, was not interested. Despite being slighted by the authorities, Tabor and Arnold studied Koresh's biblical interpretations and realized how and why he understood the text of Revelation to be predicting the demise of his community. They also came to believe they could present alternative interpretations of the text that would make sense to Koresh, who, they believed, would be open to other views if presented in language he could understand. Koresh himself indicated to the FBI that he wanted to have discussions with biblical scholars about the matter.

Denied any direct access, Tabor and Arnold began to record expositions of their professional interpretations—geared specifically for Koresh—for a local radio program that the Davidians listened to inside the compound, in hopes that it would provide an opening through which they could mediate a peaceful resolution. Koresh did listen to these broadcasts and, at least according to Tabor and Arnold, seemed willing to discuss the matter. They believed they were close to making a breakthrough, but the FBI was becoming frustrated with what they understandably took to be the stalling tactics of a religious maniac. In the end, after a fifty-day siege, they went in and the disaster resulted. Some eighty Davidians died, including Koresh.

David Koresh and the Coming Apocalypse

So what was Koresh's interpretation of Revelation that convinced him that the Scriptures were looking forward to his own time, predicting that he and his followers might have to become martyrs? As Tabor has explained, Koresh—like his predecessor Benjamin Roden—saw himself as the fulfillment of biblical prophecies. Koresh was particularly obsessed with Revelation 3:7, the letter Christ sent to the church in Philadelphia: "These are the words of the holy one, the true one, who has the key of David, who opens and no one will shut, who shuts and no one opens." Koresh was that one. He did not understand himself to be Jesus Christ, let alone God (as is sometimes reported). He believed that God sent several Christs to earth—including both King Cyrus and Jesus—and that he was the final one, the one who held the "key of David" that unlocks the meaning of all Scripture. Koresh believed that, through his intense studies, God had revealed to him the divine plan for earth, the culmination of which is described in the book of Revelation, beginning with the breaking of the seven seals by the Lamb. He, not Jesus, was the Lamb who appeared to be slaughtered. He, too, was a Christ.

Koresh had proof for his views from the Scriptures themselves. Psalm 40 also refers to a "David" figure who receives a "scroll" from God, but Koresh realized the prediction could not be about Jesus (the key words are in bold):

> *Then I said, "Here I am;*
> **In the scroll of the book it is written of me. . . .**
> *Do not, O LORD, withhold*
> *Your mercy from me. . . .*
> **My iniquities have overtaken me,**
> *Until I cannot see;*
> **They are more than the hairs of my head,**
> *And my heart fails me (Psalm 40:7–8, 11–12)*

The Davidic Christ who has the scroll of God in Psalm 40 is filled with iniquity, with more sins than the hairs on his head. If he is the Lamb who takes the scroll in Revelation 5, then he cannot be Jesus. Jesus was the sinless messiah. Revelation is referring to a sinful messiah. Koresh was the sinful messiah.

Another key passage comes in Psalm 45, which also speaks of a messiah who could not be Jesus:

> *I address my verses to the **king**. . . .*
> **In your majesty ride on victoriously**
> *for the cause of truth and to defend the right;*
> *Your royal scepter is a scepter of equity;*
> *you love righteousness and hate wickedness.*

Therefore God, your God, has anointed you
    with the oil of gladness beyond your companions.
    (Psalm 45:1, 4, 6–7)

Here is a future king who rides to victory as God's "anointed one." But again, it cannot refer to Jesus, this time because of what it says next:

The princess *is decked in her chamber*
    with gold-woven robes;
in many-colored robes she is led to the king;
    behind her the virgins, *her companions, follow.*
With joy and gladness **they are led along**
    as they enter the palace of the king.
In the place of ancestors you, O king, shall have sons;
    you will make them princes in all the earth.
    (Psalm 45:13–16)

This anointed king is married, has sexual relations with other women in his palace, and as a result has a number of sons. But Jesus was single and celibate. The passage therefore refers to a later messiah: Koresh. This passage helped provide the scriptural basis for Koresh's conduct within the compound, as he tried to convinced women followers to sleep with him (the messiah!) and have his babies. Some of them, understandably, left the community. Others, husbands and wives, were more compliant.

Thus, Koresh taught that he, the Lamb of God portrayed in Revelation, was the one who could break the seals—and he had already begun to do so, ushering in the end of time. The community's suffering at Mount Carmel fulfilled the prophecies of catastrophe. Inside the compound, they called the enemy forces aligned against them—especially the FBI—"Babylon." Based on their interpretation of Scripture, they knew that blood would be shed. It had all been described two thousand years earlier in the book of Revelation.

The first assault on the compound on February 28 killed six Davidians. You might expect this would have led Koresh and his followers to rethink their position, but they instead understood the tragedy to be a fulfillment of Revelation 6. When the fifth seal is broken (Revelation 6:9), the prophet sees the souls of those who had been "slaughtered for the word of God," who beg God for vengeance. God assures them that vengeance will come, but not quite yet. The martyrs are told to "rest a little longer, until the number would be complete both of their fellow servants and of their brothers and sisters, who were soon to be killed as they themselves had been killed" (Revelation 6:11). That is, more deaths were to follow. It would be only "a little longer" before another attack in which the surviving Branch Davidians, too, were "soon to be killed."

That verse was key to the strategy Tabor and Arnold hoped to take with Koresh. Their plan was to *concede* his interpretation, agreeing that he was the messianic Lamb foreordained to break the seals, but then point out that there was another way to understand the passage. The words "a *little* longer" did not have to mean "right away." The deaths of the other martyrs—of everyone still in the compound—did not have to be imminent. It could be longer than that. Innocent lives could be saved if he would surrender and let history take its own course.

The FBI agents, of course, had no clue what any of this biblical prophecy business was about. They were focused on the practical realities: there was a madman raving about prophecies, holed up with lots of women and children, with stockpiles of weapons and no hope of winning. They feared that if the siege went on, it might soon lead to a mass suicide—another Jonestown, only this time on American soil. And so the FBI took action, and the prophecy, in a sense, was fulfilled.

Davidians in Sum

Misinterpretations of the book of Revelation rarely lead to catastrophe of this magnitude. But they can and have done so—in fact, throughout the Middle Ages, they sometimes led to much worse.[14] Those of us who watch such events unfold have no difficulty seeing the narcissism of messianic pretenders. But what about the millions of regular old folk—our friends, families, and neighbors—who also genuinely believe they are living the fulfillment of prophecy? Are they delusional, too, when they claim that God's eternal plan is now coming to fulfillment for them in particular, that they are the ones predicted by the ancient prophets of God?

I try not to pass moral judgment on anyone who believes such things. All of us are almost certainly wrong about one thing or another when it comes to ultimate reality. But the belief that the divine plan of the entire human race has now climaxed with *us* (lucky us!) is, if not delusional, then at least a bit narcissistic. Narcissists, like their eponymous ancestor, do not see what is in the water when they gaze into it. Or for that matter what is in the Bible. They see themselves. This is not always disastrous, but it is nearly always sad.

US POLICY ON ISRAEL

The belief that we are living at the very end of time not only affects personal religious views; it also has significant effects on our culture, including our collective decisions. Every eligible voter in our country who thinks the End Is Upon Us has a say, and votes are often guided by their personal religious convictions. That, of course, is how democracy works. We all have our views, beliefs, values, prejudices, and agendas. Even if the Bible does not predict what is going to happen in our near future, many voting Americans believe it does, and this belief can affect policy. I will illustrate the point with an example that has always struck me as surprising, or rather that arouses surprise when I explain it to people. It has to do with the US support for the nation of Israel. I need to say at the outset that I am emphatically *not* taking a stand on the Israeli-Palestinian situation in general or American support of Israel in particular. Still, to understand that support—whatever one thinks about it—it is absolutely essential to understand how deeply it originally was and still is connected to Christian beliefs in a coming Apocalypse.

The short story is this. In traditional Christian thinking, for reasons I will explain, Jesus cannot return until Israel has full control of the Promised Land and all of Jerusalem, including the Temple Mount. In particular, the Jewish temple, destroyed in 70 CE, needs to be rebuilt. Most evangelicals may not know this is the historical grounding for the support for the state of Israel in their tradition, but it is easily demonstrated. This is a clear case where the end times meet modern times in a way that complicates an already virtually hopeless political situation. Who woulda thought the crisis in the Middle East would be about the Antichrist?

Christian Zionism

Christian Zionism has been around as long as modern Zionism itself, going back to Lewis Way and the London Society for Promoting Christianity among the Jews.[15] The presidency of the London Society was taken over in 1848 by Lord Ashley, who was to be become the Earl of Shaftesbury. Ashley was highly connected in British politics and held firm evangelical Christian commitments. He arranged to have a British subconsul appointed to Jerusalem and a Christian church built there, helping to pave the way, as the society saw it, for the restoration of Jews to their traditional homeland, with a Christian presence there when they arrived.[16]

At a conference in 1882, Ashley gave a speech on Jewish restoration that was attended by a young clergyman named William Hechler. The talk inspired Hechler to look into biblical prophecies about the return of Jews to the Holy Land, and he became committed to the cause. Fourteen years later, when the founder of the modern Zionist movement, Theodor Herzl, published *The Jewish State*, arguing for the creation of an independent state for the Jews, Hechler saw the potential beginnings of the End. He arranged for a meeting with Herzl, who also worked in London, and the two became friends. Hechler was one of the three Christian attendees at the First Zionist Congress of 1897.

Zionists like Hechler were certainly interested in converting Jews—and everyone else—to the Christian faith. But even more important was the role a restored Israel could play in the coming of the end-times: "We are now entering, thanks to the Zionist movement, into Israel's Messianic age," Hechler wrote to a friend.[17] This was to become a traditional evangelical view: if Jews would not convert—and it appeared that, by and large, they would not—God's plan would nonetheless prevail. The Jewish people would still return to the land to fulfill prophecy and that would then set the stage for the return of Jesus.

Herzl died in 1904, at just forty-four years of age, but the movement, of course, lived on. One of its active members was Chaim Weizmann, a well-known professor of chemistry in Manchester, who in 1906 began discussions with Arthur Balfour, the recent prime minister (1902–1905). The conversation resumed some ten years later, when Britain was entrenched in the world war and Lord Balfour was the foreign secretary. Israel was, at the time, part of the Ottoman Empire, which had allied with Germany and was bound to dissolve once the country was defeated. Weizmann's conversations with Balfour bore fruit in a way that, in evangelical opinion, set the stage for the fulfilment of biblical prophecy.[18]

Only a small population of Jews lived in Palestine, but the idea of a state of Israel found support among a large number of Christians in Britain and, as a result, in the British government. And so Balfour wrote the famous Balfour Declaration, dated November 2, 1917, in the name of the country's cabinet in a letter addressed to Lionel Walter Rothschild, 2nd Baron Rothschild, a leader in the British Jewish community. This was the first time a major government explicitly endorsed the key objective of the Zionist movement. As the letter states in its opening line: "His Majesty's Government view with favour the establishment in Palestine of a national home for the Jewish people, and will use their best endeavours to facilitate the achievement of this object. . . ." Many Jews saw the declaration as the beginning of the fulfillment of their ancestors' dreams for centuries; many Christians saw it the beginning of the end.

For such reasons Zionism caught hold among evangelicals in America as well, and their support for the state of Israel has been almost unquestionably strong until very recent times.[19] This Christian belief began to assert its influence on American foreign policy most decisively with the appearance of the "Moral Majority" in the late 1970s. According to the founder of the movement, the influential believer-in-the-end-times Jerry Falwell: "You can't belong to Moral Majority without being a Zionist."[20] Given the enormous political clout of this "majority"—all of whom could vote and were urged to do so—it is no surprise that Israeli politicians saw their opportunity, starting with Menachem Begin in the early 1980s. Israeli prime minister Benjamin Netanyahu in particular courted American evangelicals throughout his long tenure. At a Washington evangelical prayer breakfast in 1985, he connected the Christian faith in prophecy with US support for Israel:

> For what after all is Zionism but the fulfilment of ancient
> prophecies? . . . And this dream, smoldering through two

millennia, first burst forth in the Christian Zionism of the nineteenth century—a movement that paralleled and reinforced modern Jewish Zionism. . . . Thus it was the impact of Christian Zionism on Western statesmen that helped modern Jewish Zionism achieve the rebirth of Israel.[21]

Two decades later, in 2003, Falwell would assure his TV audiences, "The Bible Belt is Israel's safety net in the US."[22]

The evangelical support continues, of course. Many evangelicals saw the Trump administration's decision to move the US embassy in Israel from Tel Aviv to Jerusalem as a fulfillment of the plan of God, all part of the end-times scenario that would lead up to the return of Jesus. This much was intimated even in the embassy's dedication ceremony, opened in prayer by megachurch preacher Robert Jeffress, who extolled the "regathering" of God's people to Israel. It is telling that Jeffress has long insisted that Jews (along with Muslims, Hindus, Mormons, and anyone who does not follow his form of Christianity) will be damned for all time. He may be a "friend of the Jews in this life," but in the life to come—not so much.

This has long been the irony of Christian Zionism. Many evangelicals love Israel but believe most of its inhabitants will be sent to the fires of hell. That certainly is the view of the minister chosen to conclude the embassy dedication ceremony in prayer: televangelist and vocal Christian Zionist John Hagee, who has written books with such titles as *The Beginning of the End: The Assassination of Yitzhak Rabin and the Coming Antichrist*, in which he argues that the assassination "fits into events prophesied centuries ago that are recorded in the Bible." That is Hagee's real concern: prophecy. Hagee has claimed that even the Holocaust was part of God's plan to restore the Jewish people to Israel. Apparently not alert to the implications of the idea, he later apologized should anyone have found his comment offensive.

Political support for Israel among evangelicals has waned some-what in recent years, at least among young adults, who have begun to sympathize with the plight of the Palestinians. Even so, evangel-ical commitment to the country remains vibrant—and cannot be separated from evangelical interpretation of Revelation. In a recent poll by Lifeway Research, some 80 percent of evangelicals believe that the establishment of the state of Israel was a fulfillment of bib-lical prophecy that shows that we are now closer to the second com-ing of Christ.[23]

Modern Israel in Ancient Prophecy?

Many people—possibly most—hold some beliefs without know-ing quite why. Because of our upbringing, environment, and news sources, certain ideas just seem like common sense. Those raised in families, communities, and churches that believe the United States needs to provide substantial support for Israel usually know some of the reasons: we need to promote stability in the Middle East, pro-tect American oil interests in the region, and help those who have suffered centuries of oppression. It is important to realize, however, that America's concerns for Middle Eastern stability and oil are rel-atively recent. As we have seen, they are rooted in a certain way of reading the Bible, starting with Genesis, "In the Beginning," and continuing to Revelation, "At the End."

Readers of the Bible have always seen the beginning and the end of human history as intimately connected. Unlike historical scholars who see the Bible as sixty-six books written by different authors at different times with different points of view, these readers see the Bible as a single book with many parts that tightly cohere from start to finish. It is, in effect, a single grand narrative of God's working with the human race. And that narrative has Israel at its center.

In the beginning God created Adam, but he and then his descendants were hopelessly disobedient, so God had to destroy them with a flood—all but Noah and his family. Then humans started anew, but things still went horribly awry, and so God chose one man out of the whole human race, Abraham, and made a pact with him, "an everlasting covenant"—that is, an agreement that would never, ever end: "I will give to you, and to your offspring after you, the land where you are now an alien, all the land of Canaan, for a perpetual holding; and I will be their God" (Genesis 17:18). Abraham became the father of the Jews, and this "eternal covenant" guaranteed the land of Canaan, today comprising Israel and the Palestinian territories, to his descendants forever; they would be his chosen people and he would be their God. Forever means forever. If God favors Israel, followers of God must do so as well.

In this reading of the biblical narrative, even though God is on the side of the Jews as a people, he is not necessarily on the side of Jews as individuals. *That* depends on obedience. When individuals within Israel disobeyed God's laws, he punished the nation; eventually the northern part of the kingdom was destroyed by the Assyrians (721 BCE), to be followed a century and a half later by the southern part, destroyed by the Babylonians (586 BCE). But God was faithful and he restored the southern half, Judah, now called "Judea" (home of the "Jews"), with Jerusalem its capital. Even so, Jews continued to disobey, and when God sent them their messiah to provide salvation, they rejected him. God punished the nation not long after Jesus's death. The Romans conquered Jerusalem, burned the temple, and sent Jews into exile, this time for over eighteen centuries.

But God remained faithful. He had promised the Jewish people the Land, and that promise was fulfilled in recent times. The Balfour Declaration of 1917 set the stage; the establishment of the state of Israel in 1948 was the fulfillment, predicted repeatedly by prophets over the centuries. As the great prophet Isaiah declared:

> On that day the Lord will extend his hand yet a second time to recover the remnant that is left of his people, from Assyria, from Egypt, from Pathros, from Ethiopia, from Elam, from Shinar, from Hamath, and from the coastlands of the sea. He will raise a signal for the nations, and will assemble the outcasts of Israel, and gather the dispersed of Judah from the four corners of the earth. (Isaiah 11:11–12)

When read in its historical context, this passage is predicting a return of Israelites from exile after the Assyrian invasion of 721 BCE. But for most evangelical readers, it is referring to modern history, to the Jews scattered throughout the nations in the centuries after the Roman destruction of Judea. It is a prediction fulfilled in 1948.

So, too, the prophet Ezekiel predicts a return of Jews to the land:

> They shall live in the land that I gave to my servant Jacob, in which your ancestors lived; they and their children and their children's children shall live there forever; and my servant David shall be their prince forever. I will make a covenant of peace with them; it shall be an everlasting covenant with them and I will bless them and multiply them, and will set my sanctuary among them forevermore. (Ezekiel 37:25–26)

The patriarch "Jacob" (also known as "Israel") was the grandson of Abraham; he had twelve sons from whom sprang the "twelve tribes of Israel." These tribes conquered the Promised Land centuries later, but they were driven from that land as punishment for their sins. Ezekiel insisted God would restore them. And importantly, he would "set my sanctuary among them forevermore." Ezekiel is referring to things that would transpire in his own day, soon after the Babylonians conquered Judah, destroyed the temple, and sent many Jews into exile (586 BCE). Ezekiel predicts this exile would end and that the sanctuary (that is, the Jerusalem temple) would be rebuilt. As it was. But evangelical readers can point out that Ezekiel indicates the sanctuary will stand "forevermore." The second temple built after the Jews returned from exile in Babylon was destroyed five hundred years later by the Romans. And so, in the evangelical reading, the prophecy has *not* been fulfilled. That must mean that it will be fulfilled in our own future.

Now it has started: the Jews have indeed returned to Israel, in fulfillment of prophecy, and they will remain there forevermore, even if that requires foreign assistance. Soon the temple will be rebuilt, as Ezekiel clearly indicates. This belief in the rebuilding of the temple is key to understanding evangelical support of Israel.

It is important to stress that evangelicals think God is faithful to Israel even if Jews are not faithful to God. He has fulfilled and will continue to fulfill his promises that Israel will have the Promised Land. But Jews who reject his messiah cannot possibly be saved. That is not God's fault. He is not the one who broke the eternal covenant. Jews did when they rejected their own messiah. Therefore, they will be punished.

To evangelical readers, that is clear from the book of Revelation, which describes "the End" as standing in straight continuity with and in fulfillment of "the Beginning." As we have seen, according to Revelation, the only inhabitants of the earth who will be saved are those who refuse the mark of the beast and instead receive the seal of God. In Revelation 7 the two groups of these divinely sealed saints are discussed. The larger group is "a great multitude that no one could count, from every nation, from all tribes and peoples and languages" (Revelation 7:9). These are explicitly not the people of one nation (such as Israel); they are from around the world, everyone made pure because "they have washed their robes and made them white in the blood of the Lamb" (Revelation 7:14). The other group is smaller, but still sizable: 144,000 Jews who receive the "seal of God" on their head and so become "slaves of God"—twelve thousand "people of Israel" from each of the twelve tribes (Revelation 7:4–8).

Thus, God is faithful to the end. A large, symbolic number of Jews will be saved by converting, to become slaves of God through their faith in Jesus. But the number is not only significantly large; it is also significantly small. Think about the global population of Jews. Even at the time John was writing, there were nearly four million Jews in the world. He would certainly not have known this exact number, but even so: if 144,000 are saved, that would be only 4 percent of just the Roman world. Evangelical Christians, as one would expect, take this, too, to be a fulfillment of Scripture, where God repeatedly says that salvation will come to only a remnant of Israel (Romans 9:27–28).

Why Israel Must Rebuild the Temple

Thus, for evangelical thinkers the entire arc of the biblical narrative from beginning to end shows that prophecies are being fulfilled in our own day. But there's more to it than that. Ezekiel indicated that the temple in Jerusalem had to be rebuilt. That hasn't happened yet. It *has* to happen before Jesus can return. The clearest indication comes not in Ezekiel but in a seemingly obscure passage in the New Testament book of 2 Thessalonians, which I'll discuss in greater detail shortly: Israel not only has to exist as a sovereign state in the Promised Land, it also has to have full control of Jerusalem and, in particular, the Temple Mount. The problem, of course, is that the

Temple Mount is a sacred site for Islam as well, home to the Dome of the Rock for the past thirteen centuries. The dome is located over the site of the original Jerusalem temple. For the prediction of 2 Thessalonians to be fulfilled, the temple needs to be rebuilt there, which means the dome has to go.

It has long been debated whether Paul was the author of 2 Thessalonians; many historical scholars think the book was written by a later Christian in Paul's name.[24] Whoever wrote it, the book tries to explain to readers that the end of the age will not come right away, nor will it happen without warning (contrary to what Paul himself says in *First* Thessalonians, 4:13–5:11). A foreordained sequence of events must happen first. The events involve a mysterious figure, "the lawless one," who will rise to a position of power. This figure is often identified by readers as the "Antichrist" and the "beast" of Revelation (666), even though he is not called either in the passage:

> Let no one deceive you in any way; for that day [the "coming of our Lord Jesus Christ"] will not come unless the rebellion comes first and the lawless one is revealed, the one destined for destruction. He opposes and exalts himself above every so-called god or object of worship, so that he takes his seat in the temple of God, declaring himself to be God. (2 Thessalonians 2:3–4)

The author then indicates that this figure cannot appear yet because a restraining force is keeping him at bay (2:6). When that is removed, "the lawless one will be revealed, whom the Lord Jesus will destroy with the breath of his mouth, annihilating him by the manifestation of his coming" (2:8). That sounds very much like the Final Battle between Christ and the beast as described in Revelation 19:17–20.

What matters most, though, is that before this destruction takes place, the Antichrist figure will take "his seat in the temple of God," declaring himself to be God. That obviously cannot happen until the temple is rebuilt. Jesus therefore cannot return until Israel assumes full control of the Temple Mount. There can be no question, then, about whether or not to support Israel to expand its reach into the Palestinian territories; that was what was promised Abraham "in the beginning." And there can be no question about whether or not to support Israel in the heart of Jerusalem itself. It must destroy the Dome of the Rock and rebuild the temple for the foreordained "end" to come.

Since American Christians who support Israeli control of Jerusalem far outnumber American Jews, it is no wonder that Israeli politicians have long pushed for evangelical support, starting in the 1970s at just the time the evangelical prophecy movement reached a fevered pitch—when Hal Lindsey, Jack Van Impe, and Timothy LaHaye were all preaching that the end was almost here. For these modern-day prophets, one piece left in the puzzle remains: the temple has to be rebuilt and Israel cannot face the opposition alone.

This is not a marginal religious belief held by a tiny slice of American Christendom. It is held by millions, all of them able and encouraged to vote. And this is far from the only way that a belief in an imminent apocalypse influences our government.

THE ENVIRONMENT, CLIMATE, AND THE IMMINENT RETURN OF JESUS

Since the early 1980s, those concerned with protecting the environment and mitigating climate change have worried about the relative lack of support among evangelicals, as repeatedly documented in national polling. The widespread evangelical indifference to such causes is usually understood to relate in some way to biblical beliefs, but rarely do outsiders recognize the real issues.

The Bible is not the only factor, of course. Some researchers have argued, for example, that environmental apathy and climate skepticism thrive because of upbringing and media, and to a certain extent that is obviously right.[25] But many who oppose active involvement in these causes do have arguments and often they come from the Bible.

We saw that, in the case of political support for the state of Israel, specific verses are particularly important. When it comes to environmental issues, what matters more are broad ideas encapsulated in Scripture. Controlled studies have demonstrated that Bible readers who take the texts literally are more inclined to deny (a) that planet earth is facing serious problems, or (b) that humans have anything to do with it, or (c) that it matters much, and/or (d) that there is anything we can do about it. Why would a view of biblical inerrancy lead to such denials? Because God created this world and is guiding its history to a preordained end. His plans for planet earth cannot be altered by human incompetence or even sin. God created the world and he will destroy it. We should probably take care of the place while we're here, but we're not going to inadvertently destroy it ourselves. God has other plans.

The Roots of Evangelical Apathy

Public attention was drawn to potential evangelical apathy to environmental concerns in a rather dramatic way in 1981 after a comment made by Ronald Reagan's Secretary of the Interior, James Watt.[26] Some had not been pleased when Watt was appointed to this position, which made him responsible for managing federal lands and the nation's natural resources. As a private citizen Watt had repeatedly sued the Environmental Protection Agency, the Department of the Interior, and the Sierra Club for environmental overreach, often winning his cases. As environmentalist Robin Veldman notes, with his cabinet appointment, Watt "was being called to oversee an organization whose mission he had previously worked to thwart."[27]

During a briefing with members of the House Interior and Insular Affairs Committee, Watt was asked by Congressman James Weaver, an environmentally concerned Democrat from Oregon, if he agreed that it was important to "save some of our resources . . . for our children." Watt gave his affirmation in rather unexpected terms:

> Absolutely. That is the delicate balance the Secretary of the Interior must have, to be steward for the natural resources for this generation as well as future generations. I do not know how many future generations we can count on before the Lord returns. Whatever it is, we have to manage with a skill to leave the resources for future generations.[28]

Watt's comment about the Lord returning caught many by surprise. It was not typical government-speak. But Watt was a Pentecostal Bible-believing Christian with a Pentecostal Bible-believing eschatology. Many environmentalists found it troubling that his immediate response to a question about preserving resources was based on his religious belief that the world may not have much time left. Those more sympathetic to Watt have pointed out that he didn't say the Lord was coming soon, just that he didn't know. And he does explicitly say it is important to preserve resources for future generations. But for how many generations? And how many resources? If the world is ending in, say, three or four generations, what's the point in skimping now?

It is certainly true that the vast majority of conservative evangelicals who think we are not long for this world are disproportionately uninterested in issues involving the environment and climate change. This was first argued in 1967 in a controversial article by UCLA professor Lynn White, "The Historical Roots of Our

Ecological Crisis."[29] For White, these "historical" roots are biblical traditions, particularly those in the first chapter of the first book of the Bible, where God creates "the heavens and the earth," then the plants, then the animals, and finally humans (Genesis 1). To the humans he gives "dominion" over everything else on earth. According to White, the notion that humans were granted supremacy over all has made Bible-believing Christians unconcerned for the health of the planet. The rest of the world was made for humans, after all, and so could be exploited in any way they choose.

White's view proved to be controversial in part because one could use the Genesis creation story to make just the opposite argument: since God awarded the planet to humans, he expected them to be good stewards of it. Many Christians have understood the passage that way, including increasing numbers of evangelicals today, especially in the younger generations, many of whom are taking climate change more seriously.[30]

How Long Do We Have?

But even if humans are to take care of the planet: For how long? That turns out to be an important question, since studies of evangelical apathy have shifted over the past few decades, away from "protology" (the understanding of how all things began) to "eschatology" (the understanding of how they will end).[31] Opinion polls have provided intriguing data. A 2006 poll of Christians (not just evangelicals) in the US showed that 79 percent believed Jesus will return to earth at some point in the future.[32] A poll in 2010 indicated that nearly half of all Christians in the US believed that Christ will definitely (27 percent) or probably (20 percent) return by 2050.[33] If half the voting public expects the world to last for only forty more years, why would we be overly concerned about the Paris Agreement, which aims to draw down greenhouse gas emissions to zero by 2050? Wouldn't it be a mark of unbelief to be making long-term plans for a planet that Scripture indicates will be re-created by God soon anyway?

Political scientists David Barker and David Bearce have found that those who believe in the second coming are 20 percent less likely to agree that the government should work to fight climate change and 17 percent *more* likely to actively disagree that it should do so (as opposed simply to not caring one way or the other).[34] Anthropologist Sophie Bjork-James has convincingly argued that these positions are based not only on the "temporal" views of evangelical Christians—that the end is "coming soon"—but also on their "spatial" views. Jesus is returning precisely so God can remake the planet with a "new heaven and a new earth." It is the *combination* of time and space that makes the difference. This certainly explains why some evangelical leaders, such as megachurch pastor John MacArthur, think environmentalists by their very nature stand in defiance of God. As he explained to 1,800 avid listeners at a 2008 conference called "The Beginning and End of the Universe":

> This is a disposable planet, a disposable universe. This is only a means for God to put on display, for how else would God reveal his wrath, anger, grace, mercy, compassion, and love? This planet is a theater through which he can put himself on full display and when he is through with this purpose he can lay it to *waste*. This *is* a disposable universe. He can then create a better one in an instant.[35]

The Timing of the End

Many Christians, of course, are somewhat less adamant in thinking that the end will come "soon" and that humans' God-given dominion over the earth gives them license to use and abuse it any way they want. It is nonetheless interesting to note that the belief in Jesus's second coming—even if it is many generations away—still leads to relative apathy on issues related to environmental policy. Barker and Bearce, whom I mentioned above, show that this is because of what is known as "intertemporal choice." (The term "intertemporal" simply means something like "at different points in time.") All of us make decisions about what to do and when based on what also will eventually happen. If taking an action—say, incurring debts to attend medical school or remortgaging the house—costs us a good deal of time, effort, and resources in the short term but will pay off significantly over the long haul, we may be likely to do it. But if we're not confident the action will pay off, we don't bother.

Moreover, if you're convinced that something will be happening imminently, that affects your actions even more. Economist Joel Slemrod showed that, during the Cold War, Americans who feared an imminent nuclear war tended to put less in their savings accounts.[36] Why sock it away for later use if there won't be anything to spend it on? With this in mind, Barker and Bearce entered into their study with the suspicion that for those expecting the return of Jesus, "policies designed to preserve the global community at the expense of incurring some pain now . . . would become less desirable."[37] They suspected this would be true not only for those who think the End is coming right away: "What is more important is that they think it *is going to occur eventually* and that *it could very well happen tomorrow.*"[38] Their study bore out this thesis. On some level, the refusal to tend to dwindling natural resources and rising temperatures has a calculated logic. If God created this world and is himself planning to destroy it, it is not his plan to allow humans to take matters out of his hands with reckless acts of self-destruction. So there really is no need to worry about CO_2 emissions, strip-mining, deforestation, massive extinctions, or poisoning of the air, land, and water. God is in charge and his will be done. In the meantime, take what you want.

I argued earlier that the belief in Jesus's imminent return is largely based on a problematic reading of the book of Revelation. In the next chapter, I'll explore how the book was actually written to be read. For now, I'll just say that the environmental apathy sometimes generated by this misreading is, fortunately, not ubiquitous in the Christian community, or even the dominant one. Millions of Christians believe God has called people to be good stewards of all he has given. The wholesale destruction of natural habitats, the reckless ravaging of resources, the poisoning of the planet—none of that can be sanctioned by the God who looked at his creation and "called it good." Among young evangelicals, such views are taking hold and growing.[39] Those outside their ranks can only be thankful, and hope that their tribe increases.

FIVE

How to Read the Book of Revelation

Ronald Reagan made weekly radio addresses to the nation throughout the years of his presidency. One of the most memorable occurred on August 11, 1984. During a sound check before the talk, thinking the mic was dead, Reagan announced: "My fellow Americans, I'm pleased to tell you today that I've signed legislation that will outlaw Russia forever. We begin bombing in five minutes." It was meant as a joke for the sound technicians, but it was a bad mistake. The comment was picked up and rebroadcast around the world. The Soviets took the joke poorly: Reagan's administration was clearly not sincere in its efforts to improve relations.

Even though many people did not find the comment funny, it was a joke and was known to be a joke. That is only because of its context. If Reagan had spoken the same words not to sound technicians prior to a scheduled radio broadcast but to the nation from behind his desk in the Oval Office, the words would have meant something different. Then indeed it would have been time to look to the skies.

When you change the context, you change the meaning. That is true of written words as well as spoken. If you read in a science fiction novel that a highly toxic virus has accidentally leaked from a top secret governmental lab and infected the entire water supply of New York City, you'd pretty much know where the story's going. But if you read it on the front page of the *New York Times*, you might well get going yourself. The *literary* context of words is therefore just as important as their *historical* context. A science fiction novel is not a newspaper article; a short story is not a haiku; a limerick is not an epic. Every genre of literature involves an unexpressed contract between the author and her readers. Both writer and reader know the rules of this particular game, understanding what is to be expected and how expectations can be met. If the rules are bent or even virtually twisted out of shape, the reader can at least see what the author is doing and grants her the freedom to do so. Even so, there are limits. You will not find serious biographies of FDR that discuss his peace negotiations with the Martians and you will not find nineteenth-century novels comprised of highly compressed metaphors adjusted according to the requirements of rhyme and meter to fit within fourteen lines.

The majority of people who read the book of Revelation never ask about its historical context and literary genre, even though they know (at least implicitly) that these things radically affect a text's meaning. When it comes to this book in particular, that is a terrible mistake. Making the mistake may not be the end of the world, but it may make you think it *is* the end of the world.

WHAT KIND OF STRANGE BOOK IS THIS?

Readers who do not consider the literary context of Revelation typically consider it a one-off, the only book of its kind. It seems so weird, so mystical: How could there be anything like it? Scholars of ancient Judaism and Christianity know otherwise. Revelation is not a sui generis work that requires unique principles of interpretation. A number of ancient writings are very similar to it, such as 1 Enoch, 2 Baruch, 4 Ezra, the Shepherd of Hermas, the Apocalypse of Peter, and the Apocalypse of Paul. These, too, contain bizarre visions given to famous religious figures who learn the heavenly mysteries that can make sense of the puzzling realities of life on earth. Scholars have long understood this genre was in common use among Jews and Christians from 200 BCE to 200 CE. Just as you won't understand how a particular haiku or gothic novel "works" if you don't know something about its genre, you won't understand the book of Revelation without knowing about these other "apocalypses."

HOW AN APOCALYPSE WORKS

It is difficult to provide a one-sentence definition of an entire literary genre, but if I were to take a stab for "apocalypses," it would be something like this: apocalypses are first-person narratives of highly symbolic visionary experiences that reveal heavenly secrets to explain earthly realities.

To show how the genre typically works, it will be useful to explore a representative example. One of the earliest is an important predecessor of Revelation that I have already mentioned: the Old Testament book of Daniel. Taken as a whole, Daniel is quite different from Revelation. For one thing, the first six chapters are not an apocalypse but a series of short narratives about the life and experiences of "Daniel," a young man taken into captivity in Babylon after the destruction of Judah in the sixth century BCE. The second half of the book, though, moves into a series apocalyptic visions whose similarities with Revelation, written some 250 years later, are not accidental. As I have indicated, the book of Daniel exerted a major influence on John of Patmos as he wrote his own work.

But how can the book of Daniel be only 250 years older than Revelation if it is set in Babylon in the sixth century BCE? Already in antiquity, some scholars realized that the book of Daniel was not written by the "Daniel" whose story it tells. We will see reasons for this view in a moment, but for now it is enough to say that nearly all our surviving apocalypses were produced pseudonymously, by authors claiming to be famous religious figures of the past. So, for example, we have apocalypses claiming to be written by the great prophet Elijah, by Abraham, by Enoch, and by none other than Adam himself. There are no scholarly disputes about these works: they were not really written by their alleged authors. But why would someone claim to be a revered religious figure from hundreds of years earlier? Part of the answer is fairly obvious: Who *else* would God choose to show the great mysteries of heaven?

One of the interesting features of the book of Revelation is that unlike nearly all the other apocalypses it does not appear to be pseudonymous. The author calls himself John, and there is almost no reason to think he was someone else.[1] It may be that he did not feel a need to make a pseudepigraphic claim, as the people he was addressing in the churches of Asia Minor already knew him and probably respected his visionary experiences. Most other authors, however, needed a little pseudepigraphic assistance for their bold claims, including the unknown author of the second-century book of Daniel.

I will not be discussing all the visions of Daniel's final six chapters, just the amazing first one in Daniel 7, which is unusually helpful for seeing how the apocalypse genre works. The vision takes only a couple of minutes to read, and I suggest you do so, maybe a couple of times. It is one of the easiest and best ways to blow your mind while staying within the bounds of the law.

THE APOCALYPTIC VISION OF DANIEL 7

Daniel 7 begins by describing "a dream and visions" that Daniel had in the "first year of King Belshazzar of Babylon" (v. 1). From a historical standpoint this is a disheartening beginning, since there never was a Babylonian king named Belshazzar.[2] But that's one of the problems ancient authors had when claiming to be someone living centuries earlier. It is hard to get all those names and dates straight.

The point of the chapter is not the name of the king, however, but the "night vision" itself (v. 2). Daniel sees the four winds of heaven whipping up "the great sea" (i.e., the Mediterranean), and out of it emerge four horrible beasts, one after the other (see also Revelation 13). The first is like a lion with eagle's wings; its wings are plucked off and it is made to stand on the ground like a human (v. 4). The second is like a bear raised up on one side, with three tusks in its mouth along with its teeth; it is told: "Devour many bodies" (v. 5). The third is like a leopard with four bird wings on its back and four heads; it is given "dominion" (v. 6). Finally, Daniel sees the fourth beast, "terrifying and dreadful and exceedingly strong" (as opposed to the others? v. 7). This one is the worst of the lot; it has iron teeth and it devours, breaks into pieces, and stomps whatever is left. The beast has ten horns, but as Daniel looks on, another, small horn comes up, and three of the original horns are plucked out to make room for it. This small horn has eyes and a mouth that speaks arrogant things and makes "war on the holy ones" (v. 21).[3]

As Daniel looks on, he has a vision of God, "the Ancient One" (or "an Ancient of Days"), in his throne room in heaven. God is said to have pure white hair, a throne of flames with a stream of fire flowing from it, and many, many thousands of people around to serve him (see also Revelation 4). While Daniel observes this magnificent sight, he hears the arrogant words the small horn keeps speaking. But then the fourth beast is destroyed and burned with fire (see Revelation 19:17–21); the other beasts are also removed from power but not yet terminated. Finally, Daniel sees "one like a human one"—literally "one like a son of man" (see Revelation 1:12–16)—coming with the clouds of heaven. This one appears before the Ancient of Days, who gives him "dominion and glory and kingship, that all peoples, nations, and languages should serve him. His dominion is an everlasting dominion that shall not pass away, and his kingship is one that shall never be destroyed" (vv. 13–14).

As often happens in these apocalypses, the seer, Daniel, can't make a bit of sense out of what he has just seen. But as also often happens, a divine figure is standing by, an angelic being who can explain everything. The explanation is simple, at least in principle. The four beasts represent "four kings [that] shall arise out of the earth" (v. 16). Who, then, is the "one like a son of man"? He represents "the holy ones of the Most High" who shall "receive the kingdom and possess the kingdom forever" (v. 17).

I will unpack what all that means in a moment. But first, it is important to see how the chapter ends. Daniel is especially interested in the fourth beast, more horrifying and powerful than the others, and in the horns on its head, in particular the little horn that speaks arrogant words. The angel tells him that this beast is a "fourth kingdom" that will ruthlessly devour and trample the whole earth. The horns represent ten kings who will arise to rule the kingdom, and the little horn will be a final king who will usurp the others. And the "arrogant words"? They are most important of all, as they provide a key to interpreting the passage:

> He [the final king] shall speak words against the Most High,
>   shall wear out the holy ones of the Most High,
>   and shall attempt to change the sacred seasons and the law;

and they shall be given into his power for a time, two times, and half a time. (v. 25)

But God will enter into judgment with the beast and all dominion will be taken away from this little horn, and he will be completely destroyed. Then:

The kingship and dominion
and the greatness of the kingdoms under the whole heaven
shall be given to the people of the holy ones of the Most High. (v. 27)

INTERPRETATION

This passage will seem as baffling as the book of Revelation, but it is important to remember that it—like all books from ancient Judaism—is addressing readers of its own time. Like the later readers of Revelation, the original audience of Daniel would have had little difficulty understanding its symbolism. The short explanation is this: the Jewish people at the time of the book's writing (in the 160s CE) were experiencing severe persecution under the rule of the Syrian king Antiochus Epiphanes, who was working to force them to abandon their customs and traditions and adopt Greek culture and religion as a way of making his large kingdom more culturally unified.[4] This opening chapter of Daniel's visions shows that Antiochus (the little horn) will fail, that God will destroy him, and that the Jewish people will become rulers in his place.

You may not have seen that explanation coming. But it has been the standard scholarly understanding of the passage for a very long time and for compelling reasons.[5] For one thing, the chapter almost certainly could not have been composed during the Babylonian Captivity in the sixth century BCE: it is not written in Hebrew, the

language of Judeans at the time, but in Aramaic, a language that became widely used in Israel only starting in the Persian period later.[6]
Even more important, Daniel makes clear references elsewhere in
the book to the rule of the Syrian monarch Antiochus Epiphanes
(175–164 BCE), including a detailed description of his reign in
Daniel 11:21–45. Antiochus is thus almost certainly the little horn
in the vision of Daniel 7. To explain all that requires some historical
background.

In the early sixth century BCE—at the time when the book
of Daniel was *allegedly* written—the Babylonians had established a
massive empire by conquering lands farther west, along the Fertile
Crescent, down through Israel, en route to Egypt. The Babylonians
were themselves conquered by the Persians about fifty years later
(539 BCE), and Persia assumed control of Israel. Two centuries
later, the Persians were conquered by Alexander the Great (356–323
BCE), who was intent not only on spreading his rule but also on
bringing Greek culture to an empire that extended all the way from
Greece to the Indus River. Alexander died young and his empire was
divided up among his generals. Eventually Israel came under control of the Syrian monarchs, who continued Alexander's practices
of "Hellenization"—that is, of urging the populations under their
sway to adopt Greek (which is to say, Hellenistic) culture.

Antiochus IV, known to history as Anthiochus Epiphanes, came
to the throne of Syria in 175 BCE and was particularly intent on
forcing Hellenistic culture on Jews living in Israel. We have accounts
of his vigorous measures in the noncanonical book of 1 Maccabees.
Antiochus made it illegal to follow the laws of Moses, the very laws
that reinforced Jewish identity: Jews were a people set apart, the
chosen ones. But now the practice of circumcision was forbidden.
According to 1 Maccabees, children found to be circumcised were
murdered and hung around their mother's necks. Jews were required
to eat pork or be tortured to death. They were no longer allowed to

own a copy of Scripture, on pain of execution (1 Maccabees 1; see also 2 Maccabees 6–7).

The older empires that had earlier conquered Israel—the Babylonians and the Persians, for example—had no interest in persecuting Jews for keeping their laws and sacred traditions. They wanted the Jews' submission, wealth, and land; they were not interested in their religion or culture. It was different under the Hellenizing Syrians. This, then, is the context for the "little horn" in Daniel 7, said by the angel to be a monarch blaspheming God, persecuting the holy ones, and attempting "to change the sacred seasons and the law" (v. 25). The little horn is Antiochus Epiphanes.

Once the identification of the final horn is clear, the rest of the passage makes perfect sense. Daniel, allegedly living in the sixth century BCE, has a vision of four terrible beasts that come out of the sea, followed by a vision of one like a son of man who, by contrast, comes from heaven. The sea in many texts of antiquity represents the realm of chaos from which the enemies of the gods emerge.[7] So, too, here. The beasts represent a succession of four kingdoms opposed to God and his people. The first represents Babylon, the empire ruling when Daniel is allegedly writing. Next come the Medes, understood by Daniel elsewhere to have destroyed the Babylonians (even though they didn't, but see 5:31 and Jeremiah 51:11, 28). Then were the Persians. Finally came the most horrible fourth beast, the Greeks. The "ten horns" represents a succession of rulers of the Greek empire (as in most apocalyptic texts, the number "ten" is not meant literally; it just means something like "a number of them in sequence"), including the Syrian monarchs who continued the Greek traditions. The last is the little horn, Antiochus Epiphanes, ruling when the *actual* author of Daniel was producing his work, sometime before Antiochus's death in 164 BCE.

That is why the book can be dated so precisely. Both here and elsewhere—see Daniel 11, for example—the allegedly sixth-century author makes very broad "predictions" about "coming" events that actually happened long before his day, but very *specific* "predictions" about what was to happen nearer to his own time. I put "predictions" in quotation marks because obviously if he was writing after the events transpired, he wasn't predicting them. That is an additional and rather significant reason for taking a pseudonym when writing this kind of apocalypse. If you are living in the second century but your reader assumes you are living four hundred years earlier, and you "predict" what is going to happen in the future, you have the rather serious advantage of already knowing that it will indeed happen. Your predictions, then, can be amazingly accurate—except, of course, when you mention a king of Babylon from centuries earlier who wasn't really a king. On the other hand, no one will probably notice the mistake. This was a period when few people could read, there were virtually no public libraries, let alone internet resources, and for most everyone outside the intelligentsia the details of the past were a big blur.[8]

From a rhetorical point of view, if your text predicts things your reader knows did indeed happen, and then starts predicting what will happen *next*, your unwary reader assumes your actual predictions are just as likely to happen as the "predictions" that have already come to pass. When Daniel predicts that Antiochus Epiphanes will be destroyed by God and the rule of the earth will be taken from the Syrians and delivered to the "one like a son of man," that seems just as likely as everything else he has said. We really are living at the end. God will get rid of our oppressors. The one like a son of man will rule gloriously.

But who is this "one like a son of man"? Just as the angel identifies the four beasts as four kingdoms, the one like a son of man is a kingdom comprising the "the holy ones of the Most High" (vv. 18, 22, 27). That is, it is the nation of Israel. God will make Israel the ruler of the nations.

We cannot object to this interpretation by saying that "one like a son of man" must refer to a person (since it is a singular being) rather than to a nation. Remember: the beasts were also individual creatures that represented entire kingdoms. But in another sense, each one represented both the kingdom and its head, the king. The same is true of the "one like a son of man." But who will be that kingdom's ruler? The author doesn't say, which may suggest it is not one of his concerns. For him, what matters is that Israel will come to rule the nations. If he did think about a ruler, one might suppose he was thinking of the future "anointed one" who would rule Israel—that is, the messiah, a king like David. Alternately, some scholars have suggested that since the one like a son of man arrives on clouds from heaven, Daniel has in mind a kind of heavenly ruler, for example, a great angel like Michael.[9] Whoever it is to be, Daniel expects the transfer of power to happen right away. Antiochus will be killed by God and Israel will inherit the kingdom.

One should not object that the passage cannot mean this because it didn't happen: what actually did happen later has no bearing on what the author thought (or at least said) would happen. Ancient apocalypses are filled with expectations that are never realized.

DESCRIBING "APOCALYPSE"

We have explored only one apocalypse, and it is certainly true that you cannot establish how every epic or short story will work on the basis of just one example. But seeing how Daniel's apocalypse works can still help us understand some of the key features of the genre, which will aid us in interpreting the one apocalypse we are most interested in here: the Revelation of John.

Modern scholars who *have* studied all the surviving apocalypses have shown they typically share a number of key features, even if, again, each apocalypse does not necessarily have all of them.[10] Apocalypses tend to be:

- First-person, pseudonymous prose narratives that:
- Consist of visions and dreams, which:
- Are given by God through divine intermediaries, who then reveal their meanings to the human seer. These visions and dreams contain:
- Bizarre images, such as wild beasts and supernatural creatures. The narratives can:
- Come in two forms, either symbolic sketches of the future or peeks into the realms of heaven itself. In both cases the visions:
- Reveal transcendent, heavenly truths that can explain puzzling earthly realities. In particular, they:
- Try to explain why this world involves so much suffering, especially for the chosen ones, if the God who created the world is sovereign. The visions are therefore:
- Typically narrated in a triumphalist mode, showing that in the end God, and all that is good, will win the battle against evil.

Thus, the ultimate goal of these apocalypses is to assure their Jewish and/or Christian readers that God is in control, even if he does not seem to be, given the horrible suffering experienced by his chosen ones. These books show that those who are oppressed and afflicted now will be vindicated later. Their enemies will be destroyed, and they themselves will be exalted.

REVELATION AS AN APOCALYPSE

This, too, is the message of the book of Revelation. Like Daniel and the other apocalypses, it is a first-person narrative of visions given by God through intermediaries to a human seer. The seer in this case is John, a prophet from Asia Minor writing to the Christians of seven churches with whom he is familiar. Unlike most apocalypses, which are written pseudonymously in the names of great religious figures of the past, this one appears to be written by the person who actually claims to be the author. As we will see in chapter 8, Revelation was eventually accepted into the New Testament canon when church leaders became convinced that this John was none other than Jesus's disciple, the son of Zebedee. But there were debates about this for several centuries. Scholars today do not think Revelation was written by that particular John, but then again, as I've indicated earlier, it doesn't claim to be.

John provides a narrative of visions he has had, visions that are "mediated." Recall that in the very opening of the book, John indicates that God gave the vision to Christ, who gave it to an angel, who gave it to John, who is giving it to the members of the seven churches. Why this emphasis on so many intermediaries? The message is too lofty and exalted to come to mere mortals directly from God.

As with Daniel, the visions comprise bizarre images, with beasts and strange beings—the beast of the sea, his false prophet, the Whore of Babylon, and the like. Many of these visions are explained to John by an angel. Some readers over the years have suggested that John used these symbols to hide his meaning from Roman officials, to keep them from understanding he is attacking them. That explanation for the bizarre symbolism certainly adds a scintillating sense of intrigue to the book. But the reality is that most of these symbols would have been quite simple for anyone at the time to discern, whether a devoted Christian or a Roman pagan. Like Daniel before him, the author provides clues (some of them fairly obvious) to unpack the meaning of what he has seen. Just as a reader of Daniel's "prediction" about the little horn would have no trouble recognizing it as the Hellenizing monarch Antiochus Epiphanes, so, too, Revelation's descriptions of the beast of the sea, the False Prophet, and the Whore of Babylon: John's original readers would not have found these hugely puzzling, even though the meanings came to be lost in later generations.

Of the two forms of apocalypse—sketches of what would happen on earth in the "future" and peeks into what is already happening in heaven—Daniel provides primarily a symbolic sketch of the future, a historical narrative of what will next transpire. Daniel does, however, include elements of the other apocalyptic form, the heavenly vision: the prophet sees the awe-inspiring throne of God and the many thousands of worshippers surrounding it. The Revelation of John also utilizes both forms of the genre, but here they are more thoroughly integrated: throughout his vision, John sees both the realms of heaven and the future course of history on earth.

In broad terms, the "transcendent truths" conveyed by Daniel and John are very similar. The world is a hostile place for the people of God, who are experiencing (at least in the author's view) intense persecution. In light of their suffering, it may appear that God is not actually in control. But he is. There is evil on the earth now, but God has planned to destroy it and his plan will soon be carried out. In the near future he will obliterate those who are harming his people and exalt his chosen ones, giving them power and dominion over the other nations, forever and ever.

Thus, both books are written in a triumphalist mode that celebrates the power of God and revels in the glories to come after the slaughter of the readers' enemies. One big difference, however, is that, for Daniel, the future rulers are the people of Israel; for John, they are the followers of Jesus, who will govern the nations from the new city of God. The other big difference is the enemy destined to be slaughtered. For Daniel, it is the Hellenizing ruler of Syria, oppressor of the Jewish people; for John, as we will see, it is the ruler of Rome, persecutor of the Christians.

Like Daniel and the other apocalypses, John was deeply concerned about a situation confronting both him and his readers. In his case, it involved the Roman world of the first century CE. Rome had taken control of what John considered to be the "entire earth." It had economically enslaved the other nations and was dominating all other peoples with its military might. It compelled the worship of false gods, including the emperor himself, and had shed the blood of the Christians. But, John wrote to his readers, this state of affairs was not to last long. The end was coming. God was soon to intervene. He was sending Jesus back in judgment, the "one like a son of man," to unleash the forces of heaven against the tyrants of earth, leading to massive destruction, widespread slaughter of God's enemies, and the overthrow of the Roman state and its heinous emperor. All this was to happen in the near future—as the text states five times in just the closing chapter.

The view that John was writing about his own immediate future rather than ours may seem weird to many readers, but it has been the standard scholarly understanding of Revelation for a very long time. You will remember that the first commentary on the book came from the third-century church father Victorinus, who identified the beast of the sea (the "Antichrist") as Rome. He was right about that: the symbolism throughout Revelation all points in the same direction.

Many scholars since Victorinus have argued for this historical reading through a thorough analysis of every passage in Revelation, from chapter 1 to chapter 22.[11] I will not give a full analysis here, but I will demonstrate the point by looking at four particularly intriguing passages. The first illustrates why futuristic explanations of the images of Revelation as descriptions of what is to happen in our own time simply do not make sense. The other three show how situating Revelation in its own historical and literary context can illuminate its message as an attack on the author's (and God's) own enemies: the first-century Roman empire and its emperor.

THE FATAL FLAW OF FUTURISTIC FANTASIES: LOCUSTS FROM THE PIT (REVELATION 9)

It can be amusing for nonfundamentalist readers who first encounter modern prophecy books to notice how many of them begin by indicating that all of their fundamentalist predecessors had been wrong: they were too precise in picking a date, or they misinterpreted this or that passage, or they were advancing their own agendas instead of listening to what the Bible actually predicts. But *now*, they say, in *this* book we will see what the signs are definitely pointing to. Often the author will insist these are not his own hypotheses but are the teachings of the Bible itself. The implication is clear: if you disagree with the author's claims, you are disagreeing with God.[12]

The invariable thesis of all of these books—that the Bible was not written for its own time but for ours—encounters a rather obvious problem: it would mean that the biblical authors who address specific readers did not expect them to have any clue what they were talking about. That's not how authors, ancient or modern, work. Authors write for readers in their own time and place. When John addressed the first-century Christians in the church of Philadelphia in Asia Minor, he was giving *them* a message. He did not secretly intend the message for twenty-first-century Christians in the church of Philadelphia, Pennsylvania.

Among modern prophecy "experts" who argue to the contrary that Revelation was meant for readers living 1,900 years after its author's death, none has been more outspoken than the aforementioned Hal Lindsey, author of *The Late Great Planet Earth*. In 1970, Lindsey argued that Revelation described what would happen before the end of the 1980s. When his predictions didn't come true, or even close to true, he continued writing books and giving lectures about how *now* the signs were coming to be fulfilled. He's still talking about it on TV. But that must mean that the biblical authors were not, in fact, writing for Christians in the 1970s and '80s, as he originally claimed, but for those in the 1990s, then for those in the 2000s, then in the 2010s, and now in the 2020s. The goalposts continually move. If they didn't, there'd be no reason to keep writing more and more books showing that the prophecies are *finally* now being fulfilled.

In his original book, when Lindsey argues that Revelation was not written to be understood by its first-century readers, he does so with an intriguing sleight of hand. He does indeed stress that we need to put the author in his own time and understand what he understood. But that does not mean that Lindsey wants to understand the book in its own context. Just the contrary. In Lindsey's view, as a first-century Christian, John of Patmos was shown visions of events to transpire 1,900 years later, and he simply could not understand what he was seeing. How could he? How could someone two thousand years ago describe the explosion of a nuclear bomb? He would have to do the best he could using the only images available to him in his first-century context. That's what he did.

Lindsey explains how this works, over and again. His explanations seem to make good sense to his readers . . . millions of them. But the explanations never do quite work when you look at what the biblical author actually says. Most readers don't do that, of course; they just take Lindsey's word for it. They would be better off looking at the passages. Let me give an example, one that Lindsey has repeated over the years. It involves a striking passage from Revelation 9 that describes the plague of torturous locusts unleashed on the earth when the "fifth trumpet" is blown.

Here I quote the passage in full:

> [1] And the fifth angel blew his trumpet, and I saw a star that had fallen from heaven to earth, and he was given the key to the shaft of the bottomless pit; [2] he opened the shaft

of the bottomless pit, and from the shaft rose smoke like the smoke of a great furnace. . . .

³ Then from the smoke came locusts on the earth, and they were given authority like the authority of scorpions of the earth. ⁴ They were told not to damage the grass of the earth or any green growth or any tree, but only those people who do not have the seal of God on their foreheads. ⁵ They were allowed to torture them for five months, but not to kill them, and their torture was like the torture of a scorpion when it stings someone. ⁶ And in those days, people will seek death but will not find it; they will long to die, but death will flee from them. (Revelation 9:1–6)

It is a horrible image of suffering. John goes on to describe these vicious locusts in greater detail, and these details give Lindsey the code he needs to unlock the puzzle of the modern-day reality that the first-century prophet tried to explain. I have highlighted the key words:

⁷ In appearance the locusts were like **horses equipped for battle**. On their heads were what looked like **crowns of gold**; their faces were like **human faces**, ⁸ their hair like **women's hair**, and their teeth like **lions' teeth**; ⁹ they had scales like **iron breastplates**, and the noise of their wings was like the **noise of many chariots** with horses rushing into battle. ¹⁰ They have **tails like scorpions**, with stingers, and in their tails is their power to harm people for five months. (Revelation 9:7–10)

Lindsey uses these details to show what these locusts coming through the air to assault people really are. They are attack helicopters.

The prophet John is seeing a battle scene right out of *Apocalypse Now*, or, for Lindsey, right out of the actual war in Vietnam. These locusts look to John like battle horses because they are mobile creatures rushing into battle. (Note: they are flying through the smoke; is this from napalm?) They seem to have human faces: those are the pilots looking through the windscreens. They have crowns of gold: those are the pilots' helmets. The creatures have something that looks like women's hair. That's a description of the rotors moving so quickly, they appear like wispy strands of hair. They seem to have lion's teeth because under the windscreens are six-barrel cannons that from a distance look like teeth at the bottoms of the faces. And they sound like many chariots rushing into battle because of the overwhelming noise from the rotors, familiar to anyone who has heard the terrifying sound of choppers overhead.

It certainly sounds plausible. And so that's probably it, right?

No. There's a problem with this understanding, and it involves what these locusts are instructed to do. Why, according to Revelation, do they come out of the pit in the first place? What is the catastrophe they are to cause on earth? Lindsey skips that little detail. These creatures are told to torture people for five months . . . but not to kill them. The people they attack do not die. They are not allowed to die. On the contrary, they desperately want to die but cannot. The locusts sting, and the sting is fiercely painful but never mortal. Everyone but the followers of Jesus is forced to endure five months of horrible anguish, with no possibility of death.

These locusts can't be attack helicopters. If they were, why would they not be able to kill anyone? Isn't that the point of an attack helicopter? Has any government ever designed one with, say, a six-barrel cannon meant to inflict unstoppable torment for five months without causing a single death?

The reason Lindsey's interpretation does not work is because he does not take the text seriously enough. Futuristic interpretations almost never do. That is ironic, of course, when they are proclaimed by fundamentalists who think the Bible provides God's own words. But the interpreters choose not to read the words carefully. A large part of the problem is their approach itself, as I've discussed before. These "readers" are not reading: they are assembling a jigsaw puzzle, which leads them to ignore what the text actually says in order to create the picture they themselves have imagined.

Historical scholars do not approach texts this way. To interpret a passage, they see what it actually says before trying to figure out what it means.

A HISTORICAL APPROACH:
THE WHORE OF BABYLON (REVELATION 17)

I will illustrate this historical approach by looking at three key images that may seem confusing but in fact make considerable sense if you are familiar with John of Patmos's historical context. The first is the vision of the great "Whore of Babylon" in chapter 17, seen sitting on a horrendous beast with seven heads and ten horns. We will discuss the beast more fully later; for now, I am interested in the woman sitting on it.

John outdoes himself in descriptive detail in this passage.

> [1] Then one of the seven angels who had the seven bowls came and said to me, "Come, I will show you the judgment of the great whore who is seated on many waters, [2] with whom the kings of the earth have committed fornication, and with the wine of whose fornication the inhabitants of the earth have become drunk."
>
> [3] So he carried me away in the spirit into a wilderness, and I saw a woman sitting on a scarlet beast that was full of blasphemous names, and it had seven heads and ten horns.

⁴ The woman was clothed in purple and scarlet, and adorned with gold and jewels and pearls, holding in her hand a golden cup full of abominations and the impurities of her fornication; ⁵ and on her forehead was written a name, a mystery: "Babylon the Great, mother of whores and of earth's abominations." ⁶ And I saw that the woman was drunk with the blood of the saints and the blood of the witnesses to Jesus. (Revelation 17:1–6)

This is quite a sight, and, as elsewhere, John is completely flabbergasted, with no idea who or what this woman is or what the vision means. Unfortunately, John's horror and amazement may not be evident to those who read the passage in the King James Version. In that translation, after seeing this "whore," John says: "I wondered at her with great admiration" (17:7). This has long been one of my favorite verses in the King James. The prophet sees this grotesque woman and greatly admires her! But, alas, that is simply one of the problems with using a brilliant but four-hundred-year-old English translation. At the time of King James I, the word "admiration" meant "astonishment."

And well *should* John be astonished, not to mention confused. Still, as we are coming to expect, John gets a little help from his friends, or at least a little interpretive assistance from the angel standing by, who unpacks the mystery for him with his explanation:

⁹ This calls for a mind of wisdom: the seven heads are seven mountains on which the woman is seated; also, they are seven kings, ¹⁰ of whom five have now fallen, one is living, and the other has not yet come . . . ¹² And the ten horns that you saw are ten kings who have not yet received a kingdom. . . . These are united in yielding their power and authority to the beast; they make war on the Lamb and the Lamb will conquer them.

> And he said to me, "The waters that you saw, where the whore is seated, are peoples and multitudes and nations and languages. [17] For God has put it into their hearts to carry out his purpose by agreeing to give their kingdom to the beast, until the words of God will be fulfilled.
>
> [18] The woman you saw is the great city that rules over the kings of the earth."

With all that to go on, the symbolism is relatively easy to interpret. The first thing to note is that the whore is called "Babylon." As we have seen, nearly seven centuries earlier, the city of Babylon sent forth its military to conquer the land of Judah, destroy Jerusalem, and burn the temple to the ground. In 70 CE, the armies of Rome also conquered the province of Judea, destroyed Jerusalem, and burned the second temple to the ground. Rome is the new Babylon, the enemy of the people of God.

This "whore" is fabulously wealthy, dressed in expensive purple and scarlet cloth and adorned with gold and precious jewels. Throughout his condemnations of "Babylon" in Revelation, especially in chapter 18, John decries her economic exploitation of the other nations who "fornicate" with her and pay her for her services. Historically, it was not purely for the sake of power that Rome used its military might to overwhelm the lands around the Mediterranean; Rome wanted those lands' resources. The provinces paid tribute in agricultural products, goods, and cash to sustain the wealthiest empire at that point of Western history. As Caesar Augustus boasted near the end of his reign: "I found Rome a city of bricks but left it a city of marble" (Suetonius, *Life of the Divine Augustus*, 29). The entire imperial apparatus was designed to extract resources and revenue from its conquered people, who either cooperated or were forced to pay an even higher price.

John indicates that the Whore of Babylon is drunk with the

blood of the Christian martyrs. It was under the emperor Nero that Rome first became administratively involved with the persecution of Christians. Before that, Christians could be and sometimes were persecuted on a local level when they were seen as troublemakers by some Jews (such as Paul before he converted) and gentiles, often simply because they refused to participate in a city's communal life, as we saw in chapter 2. Nero, though, was the first emperor to attack and martyr Christians directly.

Our principle account of these events comes not from a Christian source but from the Roman historian Tacitus. When the great fire of Rome occurred in 64 CE, destroying large parts of the city, some residents came to suspect that Nero himself was responsible for the blaze, that he had ordered the city torched so he could rebuild it with his own architectural designs. Nero had to shift the blame and, according to Tacitus, did so by rounding up the Christians in the city and subjecting them to horrible forms of public execution, crucifying some, wrapping others in animal skins to be torn apart by ravenous dogs, and having others rolled in pitch and used as human torches to light his gardens (Tacitus, *Annals of Rome*, 15).

John knows about Nero's slaughter and he does not think it was an isolated event. He believes that many, many Christians have been martyred by Roman officials, so that the city is "drunk with the blood" of the saints.

The most decisive indication that the woman is in fact the city of Rome is the angel's interpretation of her very peculiar seat: a wild beast with seven heads. The angel says that these seven heads are the "seven mountains on which the woman is seated" (v. 9).[13] This would have been a dead giveaway to any ancient reader. In antiquity—just as today—Rome was referred to as the "city built on seven hills." But just in case the reader didn't quite get it yet, the angelic interpreter ends by making his point explicit: "The woman you saw is *the great city that rules* over the kings of the earth" (v. 18). And what city ruled the "world" of John's day? Rome, the great whore seated on seven hills, who exploited the nations of the earth and corrupted them, prostituting herself to become massively wealthy and the archenemy of the Christians.

There are other intriguing details connected with John's portrayal of the Whore of Babylon. Among them is John's keen irony: the image he portrays of Rome would have been seen by ancient readers as a caricature. The goddess of the city of Rome was named Roma, often portrayed as an elegant woman in fine clothes and jewels, sitting on a wild animal in conquest. For John, Roma is not a high-class Roman matron. She is a corrupt profligate who has prostituted herself to get where she is. God will dethrone and destroy her.

THE BEAST OF THE SEA (REVELATION 13)

In reading Revelation, it is especially important to realize that, as with all apocalyptic texts, the symbols are multivalent: the author can imbue them with several meanings, but not an infinite number. Moreover, the various meanings are tightly connected. We saw this in Daniel, where both the beasts and the one like a son of man were kings and kingdoms. Both senses would have been understood by readers, just as readers of *King Lear* realize that "Cornwall" actually refers to the *duke* of Cornwall and "France" refers to the *king* of France. The same with the "beast" on which the woman sits in chapter 17. It has seven heads—the seven hills on which Rome sits—but in another sense, the beast actually is Rome.

Earlier, in chapter 13, we also have a vision of the beast. This passage has long been particularly intriguing because we are told that the beast can be known by its number, "the number of a person," 666 (13:18). Who or what is that? Like the beast in the vision in chapter 17, this beast has ten horns and seven heads. Clearly, then, it is the same beast, and anyone who has read the entire book of Revelation will have no trouble realizing the beast's connection with Rome. The beast in chapter 13 has features like a leopard, a bear, and a lion (again, compare this to Daniel's beasts). And it is supported by an even more powerful beast, the "dragon" who gives the beast "his power and his throne and great authority" (13:2). In 20:2 the dragon is explicitly identified as Satan. Rome is thus empowered by the Devil. We are told that the entire earth worships the beast, except the followers of Jesus (13:4, 8). In response, the beast blasphemes God and makes war on the saints (13:4–7). Those who refuse to bow down before the beast are to be executed, and no one can "buy or sell" without accepting the beast's mark on either the forehead or the right hand. That is to say, those who refuse to collaborate with Rome will be cut off from society and left to starve, if not outright executed.

Obviously, there is a good deal of mystery in chapter 13, but two verses in particular tend to confuse readers. The final verse identifies the beast of the sea with a riddle: "This calls for wisdom: let anyone with understanding calculate the number of the beast, for it is the number of a person. Its number is six hundred sixty-six" (13:18). Readers who know (from chapter 17) that this beast is identified with Rome will be alert to the probability that 666 is somehow connected with the city as well. It is odd, though, that some Greek manuscripts of Revelation do not give the number as 666, but as 616. Why would that be?

The other particularly confusing verse of chapter 13 is just as mysterious. In 13:3 we are told that one of the heads of the beast received a "wound unto death"—that is, a wound that killed it—but somehow the wound was healed (13:3). That is, the head died but came back. That may be demonically ironic, since Christ himself died and then returned. But there may be more to the symbolism than that.

Fundamentalist interpreters of Revelation have had a field day with these chapters, providing all sorts of identifications of 666—almost always some nefarious person living long after John's day, in the interpreter's own time, whether Mussolini (the Roman ruler!), Pope John Paul (the enemy from Rome!), Mikhail Gorbachev (that birthmark sure looks like a mortal wound!), Saddam Hussein (the ruler of Babylon!), or . . . pick your person.[14] But supporters of the fundamentalist right are not the only ones who have played this name game; lefties have been good at it, too. When I started teaching at Rutgers in the mid-1980s, some pundits pointed out that Ronald Wilson Reagan had six letters in each name: 666. In more recent times, others on the political left have noted that Donald Trump was elected in 2016, which, as it turns out, is the sum of 666 + 666 + 666 + 6 + 6 + 6. Go figure. And some of my students at the University of North Carolina at Chapel Hill think it is no accident that the phone number of my Department of Religious Studies is 962-5666.

Since the third-century commentary of Victorinus, however, historical readers of Revelation have had little trouble recognizing the identity of 666 (or 616).[15] This much is clear: the author is telling his readers the numerical value of the beast's name.

To understand how it works, we need a bit of background on ancient languages. Neither Hebrew nor Greek used different alphabetical and numerical systems the way we do when we use the Latin alphabet (a, b, c) but Arabic numerals (1, 2, 3). In these ancient languages, the letters of the alphabet served also as numerals. In Greek, the first letter, alpha, was 1, usually written with a tick above it to indicate it was a number, not a letter. Beta was 2, gamma was 3, etc., until you got up to 10, the letter iota. The next letter, kappa, was 20, then 30 . . . up to 100. Then the next letters were 200, 300, and so on. With this system you could express any number with letters of the alphabet.

One unintended result was that every word could be assigned a numerical value; simply add up the numbers represented by each letter. For Hebrew, this method was called gematria, and involved interpreting texts based on the numerical values of the words within it. This ended up being a major interpretive technique in Jewish writings and in some Christian ones, too—though it would not pass muster today with people who engage in historical interpretation. You can't just pick a word in the Gospel of Matthew that adds up to 481 and then a completely different one in Paul's letter to the Romans that also totals 481 and claim they mean the same thing or that one passage is key to interpreting the other. But the author of Revelation is not trying to interpret one text by another: he is telling us the numerical total of the beast's name.

The angel tells John that 666 is the number "of a person." Recall that the image of the beast of the sea is multivalent: in some sense it is the city of Rome, in some sense the empire of Rome, and in some sense the emperor of Rome. In this case it is a man, which is to say, the emperor. John is especially incensed that the beast is persecuting and martyring Christians. As we have seen, the first Roman emperor to do so was Nero, who ruled from 54 to 68 CE. And this is where the gematria kicks in: if you spell "Caesar Nero" in Hebrew letters, the name adds up to 666.

But why would the author be referring to the name as spelled in Hebrew rather than Greek? Numerological puzzles are inherently intriguing, and perhaps John is simply heightening the mystery. That would be one reason he introduces the discussion by saying: "This calls for wisdom." It's not gonna be simple.

There's an additional curiosity. Why do some early manuscripts of Revelation give the number as 616? As it turns out, there are two ways to spell "Caesar Nero" in Hebrew, one with and one without an *n* at the end of his name (Neron or Nero). In Hebrew, an *n* is the letter *nun*. When used as a numeral, *nun* represents 50. There it is:

spelled with the *nun*, Nero's name adds up to 666; without the *nun* it is 616. John is definitely talking about Nero.

But how do we make sense of the statement that the head of the beast (the ruler) received a deathblow (a "mortal wound") from which he recovered? This is where it gets even more interesting. Faced with enormous political opposition, Nero committed suicide in 68 CE. Rumors began to circulate that he had not died but had fled to Parthia, the enemy empire to the east. Nero allegedly had made a pact with the Parthian leaders and was soon to return at the head of their armies to reassume power over the Roman world. We have historical records of impostors appearing after his death, claiming to be Nero, including one during the reign of Domitian, just at the time John was writing his book.[16] And stories of "Nero redivivus" ("Nero alive again") can be found in a number of sources. One second-century Christian writing called the Sibylline Oracles gives an explicit discussion of Nero returning as a kind of Antichrist figure to plague the followers of Jesus.[17]

The "head" of the beast is said to be one of the rulers of the great city; it received a deathblow but then somehow recovered. This is a prediction of Nero redivivus, Nero come "back from the dead" to wreak havoc at the end of the age.

MORE HISTORICAL RICHES:
THE OTHER BEAST OF REVELATION 17

It should be clear by now that the beast of Revelation 13 is not a future ruler of a global government ("the European Union"!), an Antichrist yet to come. John is writing for his own day. The beast is first-century Rome, its empire, and its emperor all rolled into one: haughty against God, controller and exploiter of the entire world, worshipped by all nations, and persecutor of Christians.

Most readers pay less attention to the second beast (13:11–18), which is subservient to and a promoter of the first (16:13; 19:20; 20:10). This other beast comes not from the sea but from the earth—presumably meaning that it is a human creation. Its main task is to make sure everyone on earth worships the first beast; it convinces them to do so through fantastic miracles ("great signs") that convince people to make an "image" of the beast of the sea (17:12–15). Anyone who does not worship this image is to be killed. This second beast is the one that requires everyone on earth to be "marked on the right hand or the forehead" with the "name of the beast or the number of its name" in order to engage in any economic activity (17:16–17).

Who or what is this second beast that urges and requires the worship of the beast of the sea—that is, Rome and its emperor? Historically there cannot be much doubt about it: in the Roman world, the worship of the emperor as a divine being was promoted by the Imperial Cult. This second beast is not an individual but an institution. To understand the image more fully requires, again, a bit of historical context.

In the ancient world it was not unheard-of for great and powerful rulers to be worshipped as divine.[18] The pharaohs of Egypt were considered gods; the founder of Rome, Romulus, came to be considered a god after his death; and when Julius Caesar was assassinated, his nephew and heir, Octavius (later Caesar Augustus), declared he had been made a god. Octavius was reluctant to be worshipped as divine when he became the first emperor, as was his successor, Tiberius. But they both did allow temples to be built for them in response to requests by some of the leading cities in various Roman provinces. Later in the mid-first century, the living emperor was widely considered divine and worshipped. Caligula, Tiberius's successor, actually encouraged it.

This did not mean that the emperor was worshipped as the only god or even as one of the great gods of Mount Olympus. The polytheistic religions of the empire all recognized many gods with various powers and abilities. The emperor was generally known to be a human born to human parents, but he was also recognized as far more powerful than mere mortals. He had godlike powers and could therefore be considered and worshipped as divine.[19]

Imperial "cults" eventually sprang up throughout the provinces. Wherever a temple was built to the emperor, priests would be appointed to perform sacrifices and other sacred duties. Scholars have long understood that the central Roman government did not push these cults onto the subjected peoples of the provinces as a kind of propaganda tool. The cults were started by local rulers and other elites, who were required to ask permission to do so. There were social and political advantages to making the request. A city's shrine to the emperor-god would add cachet to its municipality as one specially favored by Rome.

As a result, worshipping the emperor was understood as a political act of subservience. Since everyone in the empire apart from Jews was "pagan"—that is, a worshipper of many gods—and since none of the empire's religions insisted that it alone was to be followed, it was commonplace for people to join new religions and worship new gods without abandoning their old ones. That meant there was absolutely no religious or moral problem with worshipping the emperor. And if someone refused? It presumably meant the holdout did not support Rome. That is, it would be an act of treason.

Jews were exempt from worshipping the emperor because they had ancient traditions that required them to maintain their monotheistic practices: they alone were not allowed by their religion to worship other gods. They were not, therefore, required to participate in the imperial cult, so long as they prayed for the emperor and, while there was still a Jewish temple, perform sacrifices on his behalf.

By the time of John, however, most Christians did not identify as Jews and Roman authorities did not recognize them as such. It is easy to see why. Most Christians came from gentile stock, they did not worship in synagogues on Saturday but in their own communities on Sunday, and they did not follow customs widely recognized as distinctively Jewish: the males were not circumcised, and neither males nor females kept kosher food laws or observed Jewish festivals. To outsiders, Christians were not Jews, which meant they were not exempt from worshipping the emperor.

By the early second century—not long after the book of Revelation was written—we hear of Christians being persecuted for not participating in the imperial cult. One piece of evidence comes to us from 110 CE in a letter written by Pliny the Younger, the Roman governor of the province of Bithynia-Pontus in Asia Minor, to his emperor, Trajan. In the letter, Pliny asks for advice about the pestiferous Christians he has encountered. He indicates that when Christians were brought up on charges before him, he required them to perform a sacrifice in the presence of an image of the emperor. If they refused, he had them executed. Pliny asks Trajan if that is an acceptable practice; by return mail, the emperor assures him it is (Pliny, *Letters* 10.96, 97).

The second beast ("from the earth") in Revelation is said to promote and enforce the worship of the image of the beast ("from the sea"). Those who refuse are to be killed. This second beast, then, does not represent a political entity, but a religious one. It is the imperial cult, meant to enforce the political power of Rome through religious worship; it is called a "false prophet" because it advances a religious perspective that is opposed to the truth of God. Like Rome and the emperor, it, too, is bound for destruction.

IN SUM

The book of Revelation is filled with exaggerated claims. That often happens in situations of conflict: the "enemy" is portrayed as massive and unstoppable, an inherent threat to decency and truth. For John, Rome rules with an iron fist; everyone in the empire has to bow before the image of the emperor or be slaughtered without mercy. Only the followers of Jesus refuse. As a result, they are martyred, myriads and myriads of them. But they will be avenged when God, the world's true power, intervenes and disposes of his enemies: the beast, his false prophet, the Devil who empowers them, and all who side with them. "Babylon the Great" will be destroyed and God will bring in a glorious New Jerusalem for his faithful, who will replace the Romans as the great power to whom all peoples are subject and subservient.

This is a message written for John's day. Followers of Jesus are not only assured that these things will happen, they are repeatedly told they will happen "soon." Futurist interpreters who claim these events are yet to transpire are misreading the book, not heeding its literary genre and not paying attention to its historical context. However, even though Revelation was not written for people living two thousand years after John's time, that does not mean it is irrelevant to readers today. It is hugely relevant. Not because it predicts what will happen in our own future, but because it conveys ideas that must be taken seriously by readers of all times—ideas about who God is, how he interacts with his world, what he expects of people, what he exacts from those who do not give him what he demands, and how he rewards those who do.

In the following chapters we will see that when we interpret the book of Revelation in light of these concerns, it presents a very different set of problems, very grave ones. The difficulty with Revelation is not that it predicts a future that never happened but that it presents a view of God that is deeply unsettling. Even readers from Christian antiquity often found it disturbing. Is it not disturbing that, in the end, the unstoppable justice of God triumphs over his mercy? That in his wrath God sends catastrophes upon the planet, indiscriminately bringing misery and destruction, and then casts most of the humans who have ever lived into a lake of fire?

Various readers will come to different conclusions. But whatever answers each of us prefers, it is important at least to ask the questions. Does Revelation encapsulate the message of love and mercy found elsewhere in the New Testament? Does the Apocalypse of John embrace the Gospel of Jesus?

SIX

The Lamb Becomes a Lion: Violence in the Book of Revelation

F ar more people revere the Bible than read it. This has always struck me as both interesting and inexplicable. I've known thousands of people who insist that the Bible is the very Word of God who have never bothered to read it, or at least not read much of it, let alone read it carefully from beginning to end. But if God wrote a book, wouldn't you want to see what he had to say?

This is especially true of the Christian Old Testament, by far the largest part of the Bible. Many churches have brief, carefully chosen readings from the Old Testament as a prelude to a Gospel reading, but scarcely ever are the Old Testament passages the topic of a sermon or a lesson in Sunday school. Many Christians admit they are just not that interested in the Old Testament because its teachings have been surpassed and even superseded by the coming of Jesus and because, well, they find it boring. I wonder what its author would say about that.

The one thing many Christians do know about the Old Testament, or at least say about it, is that it portrays a wrathful God of judgment, and that this portrait changes when we get to the New Testament, where we find a God of love and mercy who has kindly offered salvation to people who are lost. As a rule, these believers do acknowledge that both are the same God. But how, then, can the difference be explained? Did God mature over time? Did he get old and kindly? Did he change strategies? Or was it his plan all along to scare the hell out of people in the Old Testament before offering them heaven in the New?

My sense is that most people don't really think about the problem. But if I had a nickel for every time I've heard someone say that the God of the Old Testament is a God of wrath, but the God of the New Testament is a God of love, I could buy a summer home on Santorini. I always wonder if these people have ever read the book of Revelation.

JOSHUA AND JESUS

One of the ways people point out the difference between the God of the Old Testament and the God of the New is by contrasting the stories of Joshua and, say, the Battle of Jericho with the stories of Jesus and, say, the Sermon on the Mount. There is an irony here most people have never considered: these two figures share a name. Jesus is the Greek version of the Hebrew Joshua.

The Hebrew Joshua was a warrior who led Israelite troops in the slaughter of entire cities as part of the divine plan. Centuries earlier, according to the book of Genesis, God vowed to give the Promised Land to the descendants of Abraham, the father of the Jews. When it came time for the promise to be fulfilled, there was a rather obvious problem: there were already people living in the land. These current inhabitants had homes, families, farms, jobs, towns, and cities. They were civilized people presumably doing what they could to eke out a living. But God had promised their land to someone else. How was that someone else—the people of Israel—to acquire the land, property, and possessions of others? They had to take them by force. The Old Testament Joshua/Jesus leads the charge—or rather the slaughter. There is no need to dwell at length on all the carnage. Just consider the account in Joshua 6 of the taking of Jericho.

We used to sing a song about it in Sunday school, a lovely ditty that ends with "Joshua and the Battle of Jericho, and the walls come a-tumblin' down!" As kids we thought it was marvelous. God orders Joshua/Jesus to march the troops around the besieged city once a day for six days. Then on the seventh day they are to march around it seven times, blow their trumpets, and shout—and the walls will fall. They do. What we were not told in Sunday school is what happens next. The divinely inspired Joshua/Jesus tells the soldiers to enter the defenseless city and slaughter every man, woman, and child—including the infants—along with every animal. They do so. It is a mass murder of every living thing.[1]

How does that stack up against the Joshua/Jesus of the New Testament? The one who said: "Love your enemy," "Turn the other cheek," "Pray for those who persecute you"; the one who taught not to take up the sword lest you die by the sword; not to seek retaliation; not to desire what others have, but to give anyone who asks for your coat, your shirt as well?[2] Do the Old Testament Joshua/Jesus and the New Testament Joshua/Jesus represent the same God?

From the early days of Christianity there have been Christians who have thought not. Already in the second century, a prominent theologian named Marcion took this view to a logical extreme: the God of Jesus was *literally* not the God of the Old Testament. For Marcion, the God of the Israelite prophet Elisha who called on two she-bears to maul forty-two boys to death because they had been calling him names ("Baldy! Baldy!" 2 Kings 2:23–24) was not the same God who told his followers, "Let the little children come unto me" (Matthew 19:14). The leaders of the church of Rome declared Marcion a heretic and kicked him out of the church, the first time we hear of an official excommunication. Marcion, however, did not give up on his message: he planted churches throughout the Roman empire, and many of them thrived. One could argue that Marcion still has lots of Christian followers today, even though they have never heard of him and do not realize that thinking the God of the Old Testament is different from the God of the New is an ancient Christian heresy.

There are also lots of Christians today—not to mention Jews— who object to the idea that the God of the Old Testament is principally a God of wrath. For one thing, he is also very much a God of love. The key commandment given to every Israelite is: "Hear, O Israel: The LORD is our God, the LORD alone. You shall love the LORD your God with all your heart, and with all your soul, and with all your might" (Deuteronomy 6:5). This is the origin of the "Shema" (a Hebrew word that means "Hear"), which is to be recited by Jews three times each day. God urges love, and not only love directed to him. He also commands: "You shall love your neighbor as yourself" (Leviticus 19:18; Mark 12:31). Jesus did not invent these words; he was quoting Jewish Scripture. The Old Testament God commanded his people to love. And the New Testament God is a God of wrath. Anyone who thinks otherwise has never taken seriously the Bible's final book, the very climax of the Christian Scriptures. Here God ordains and oversees the bloody massacre of the majority of the inhabitants of earth.

I agree with those who consider the New Testament the most important collection of books in the history of civilization, and I have devoted most of my life to studying it. Even so, I do not ignore what it actually says and pretend that it says something else. The Bible can be a brutal book, and the Apocalypse of John is the most brutal of all. To demonstrate the point, I need to delve deeper into the scriptural idea of the wrath of God in both the Old Testament and the New. I will not give a full account, just some of the lowlights—not to delight in the gore, but to show why Revelation presents the dark side of Christianity.

STORIES OF GOD'S WRATH

I start with an Old Testament account far less known than the Battle of Jericho but equally gruesome. The narrative is set at the end of Israel's forty-year sojourn in the Wilderness, just before Joshua's conquest of the Promised Land. God has saved the people of Israel from their slavery in Egypt (Exodus 1–15); he then gives them his Law through Moses on Mount Sinai (Exodus 20–40; Leviticus 1–27). From there, the goal is to enter the Promised Land, but because of the Israelites' disobedience, God prevents them from doing so. An entire generation has to pass away before they are allowed to begin the conquest. When the forty years are over, Moses is still alive and directs the opening stages of the operation in the area east of the Jordan River comprising the lands of Edom and Moab.

It is Moses, therefore, who begins the slaughter of the non-Israelites. One of his early military conflicts is particularly horrific and illustrates well the targets of God's wrath in the conquest narratives. The episode involves two peoples, the Moabites and the Midianites.

In Numbers 25, some Israelite men take up with Moabite women and have sexual relations with them. For Yahweh, the God of Israel, this is very bad: he is jealous for his people and insists they abstain from outside influence, otherwise they may be led away from worshipping him alone. And that's what happens. The Israelite men join their Moabite womenfolk (prostitutes? wives? illicit lovers?) in religious ceremonies and start worshipping the pagan god Baal of Peor (Numbers 25:1–3). God is incensed and punishes this malfeasance by sending a plague against Israel—all the people, not

just the offenders. Before God relents, twenty-four thousand Israelites are killed (Numbers 25:9), not for their own transgressions but
because of the sins of others. While the plague is still raging, Moses
instructs the people to avert "the fierce anger of the LORD" (25:4);
this will require human sacrifices. The "chiefs of the people"—that
is, the leaders of the various Israelite tribes, who again were not
among the guilty—are ordered to be impaled under the hot sun,
apparently because they could not keep their people in line. More
understandably, the men who have joined in the worship of Baal are
also executed. When the executions are finished, God relents. But
that is not the worst part of the story.

Interwoven with the account is another grisly episode, involving the Midianites. While the plague is still raging, an Israelite man
brings "a Midianite woman into his family" (Numbers 25:6). It is
not clear if that means he marries her or just brings her home for
a romp. In any event, he takes her into the privacy of his tent. But
people have seen her arrive and know what's happening. One particularly zealous Israelite, Phinehas, decides to put an end to the
matter. He enters the tent and drives a spear through the two lovers
while they are still engaged in coitus, killing them both. God is
extremely pleased with this outcome and issues a special blessing
on Phinehas, giving him "my covenant of peace" because he "made
atonement for the Israelites" (Numbers 25:13). It was an atonement
made by the blood of the murdered lovers.

That, though, is not the end of God's punishment on the Midianites. Six chapters later, God commands Moses to take care of
them once and for all: "The LORD spoke to Moses, saying 'Avenge
the Israelites on the Midianites'" (Numbers 31:1). Moses does so
by sending out twelve thousand troops to attack the people of Midian. They are massively successful: they kill "every male" (Numbers 31:7). But they spare the "women of Midian and their little
ones," taking them captive (Numbers 31:9), along with all their

livestock and possessions, before burning all their towns and encampments to the ground.

Moses, though, is not satisfied with this mass murder and destruction: it is not massive enough. What were the soldiers thinking? He orders that all the surviving male children, including infants, be slaughtered, along with every woman or girl who has ever had sex. But the Israelite men are to "keep alive for yourselves" all the "young girls who have not known a man by sleeping with him" (Numbers 31:18). We are later told the hitherto virgin girls now enslaved to Israelite men number thirty-two thousand.

The entire Old Testament is not about such brutality against God's enemies, but a good bit of it is. And it is striking that in this particular account, God destroys both those outside of Israel and those within. The outsiders are portrayed as dangerous because they can lead the Israelites astray to the worship of other gods; God cannot allow that. It is better to remove these people completely. It doesn't matter if the targets of slaughter are decent people who love their spouses and children, who give graciously to those in need, and who do their best to live a good life. The Old Testament authors don't care or even think about that. Israel has to be holy, a people apart, distinct from all others. Anyone who might badly influence the people of God must be destroyed.

In other parts of the Old Testament, God vows to take out nations that have used their power maliciously, not against the Israelites but other people. The prophet Amos, one of our earliest known authors (eighth century BCE), claims God will destroy Damascus and send the Syrians into exile for national misbehavior. He will also destroy the Philistine cities of Gaza, Ashdod, and Ashkelon; burn down the city of Tyre; and attack the Edomites, the Ammonites, and the Moabites (Amos 1:3–2:6).

Most of the Old Testament, though, focuses on God's punishment of his own people. One of the most hair-raising reports of what God does (or will do) to his chosen people comes in some of the final words of Moses. Near the end of the book of Deuteronomy, just before the children of Israel enter the Promised Land, Moses delivers a final speech (Deuteronomy 28). In it, he describes the blessings God will shower upon the Israelites if they obey the laws he has given, and the divine curses he will inflict if they do not. Fourteen verses are devoted to describing the blessings, but fifty-three to the curses. The emphasis is clear: there can be good rewards or *massive* punishments.

The blessings are relatively straightforward: if the people of Israel obey, they will thrive. They will be set above all the other nations of earth, they will be blessed wherever they go, their crops will be abundant, their livestock will increase, they will be prosperous, and they will have large families (28:1–14). What could be better? But if they disobey, things will be very bad indeed, and Moses provides a good bit of gory detail in his threats. If the people are disobedient, all the blessings will be reversed: they will be cursed everywhere they go, the crops will fail, and the livestock will die, as will the children (28:15–19). But more than that, the people will experience "disaster, panic, and frustration in everything" they do. There will be "pestilence . . . consumption, fever, and inflammation"; they will experience "heat and drought," with "blight and mildew" (28:21–22). They will lose their wars; other nations will be horrified at what has happened to them (28:25); their corpses will be devoured by scavengers. They will be afflicted with "boils, . . . ulcers, scurvy, and itch" that cannot be healed (28:27); they will lose their minds (28:28); their children will be sold into slavery (28:32); and . . . well, the afflictions are described for another thirty-six verses.

Scholars call the narrative books in the Old Testament that immediately follow Deuteronomy (Joshua, Judges, 1 and 2 Samuel, and 1 and 2 Kings) the "Deuteronomistic History." These were written by a single author who took Deuteronomy's idea of "blessings and curses" very seriously, and described the entire history of Israel in light of its obedience and disobedience to God.[3] Failure dominates. After many warnings, God reacts to the disobedience of those living in the northern part of the land, the nation called "Israel," by having the Assyrians destroy it, never to exist again (721 BCE). Those in the southern part, the nation of "Judah," go on for another 150 years, but they, too, succumb to disobedience and are wiped out by the Babylonians (586 BCE). The southern nation will eventually be restored, but there will be unspeakable suffering first.

In Deuteronomy, God promises wrath for those who refuse to keep his law, and in the subsequent Deuteronomistic History, he delivers on his promise, with full vengeance.

The Wrath of God in the Prophets

This theme of God's wrath against those who fail to worship him properly appears not just in the narrative books of the Old Testament but regularly throughout. It is the relentless drumbeat of all the prophets: Isaiah, Jeremiah, Ezekiel, Hosea, Joel, Amos, and . . . take your pick. God's people need to obey him or he will enter into judgment with them. If they do suffer disaster, it is because God is punishing them. They need to return to obedience if they want to live.[4]

These prophets are decidedly not fortune-tellers predicting what will happen in the distant future—say, in 1988 or 2027. Nor do they have any interest in predicting a messiah to come hundreds of years later to deliver his people from their sins. They are speaking to people of their own time, the chosen ones, Israel (in the north) and Judah (in the south). The prophets' only future concerns are for the *immediate* future. These prophets are not "foretellers" describing events to transpire long after their day. They are "forth-tellers," speaking God's word to people faced with crisis, telling what they need to do to survive.

In the context of these forth-tellings, the prophets repeatedly emphasize the realities of divine wrath. God will punish those who disobey him and will do so in violent ways. His wrath is meant to lead people to repentance; if they refuse, they will suffer horribly and perish. There is no need for me to demonstrate this book by book; simply read Isaiah, Jeremiah, or any of the others and see. But I will illustrate the point with examples from two of our earliest prophets, Amos and Hosea.

The Wrath of God in Amos

Amos is a gem of a book and it is a real shame it is not read more. The message it contains is terrifying, but it is delivered with powerful rhetorical skill. Amos does not restrain himself from attacking the people of Israel for their unethical behavior: they enslave fellow Israelites for not paying their debts, they abuse the needy, and they "trample the head of the poor into the dust" (2:6–7). God deplores these kinds of economic exploitation. The people are also guilty of sexual immorality: a man and his son, for example, are both having sex with the same girl (2:7). And many people oppose those who are committed to religious service (2:12).

What is God's response? These are the people he chose, yet they refuse to obey him. So God tells them: "Only you have I known of all the families of the earth; therefore I will punish you for all your iniquities" (3:2). How will he punish them? National destruction.

> *Therefore thus says the Lord GOD:*
> *An adversary shall surround the land,*
> *And strip you of your defense*
> *And your strongholds shall be plundered. (3:11)*

Amos chooses not to end there; he continues attacking the bad behavior of the Israelites, including the luxurious lifestyles of rich women in Samaria, who "oppress the poor, who crush the needy, who say to their husbands, 'Bring something to drink'" (4:1). God is especially aggravated because he has tried to compel the people to return to his ways, but they refused. He tried starving them—"I gave you cleanness of teeth in all your cities, and lack of bread in all your places"—but it didn't work (4:6). He caused drought, "yet you did not return to me" (4:7–8). He brought blight, mildew, and locusts to destroy the crops, "yet you did not return to me" (4:9). He "killed your young men with the sword" and "yet you did not return to me" (4:10). (Note: God himself killed the men.) He destroyed some of their cities, "yet you did not return to me" (4:11). And so, having tried everything else, he has only one option.

> *Therefore thus I will do to you, O Israel*
> *Because I will do this to you,*
> *Prepare to meet your God O Israel! (4:12)*

In this context, "meeting your God" is not a happy prospect. God will meet them with the full force of his divine power. He will wipe them out.

The Wrath of God in Hosea

Amos's eighth-century contemporary Hosea has a similar message, but uses a different powerful image to convey it. Here the problem is not so much Israel's ethical transgressions but its cultic ones. Israel has refused to worship the Lord and him alone. The people have turned to other gods, thinking these other divinities could provide what they need—like a lover on the lookout for something better. God, in Hosea's imagery, is not merely a judge of his people; he is a jilted lover and Israel is a "whore" who enjoys wanton sex with others. Her true husband, God, will therefore give her what she deserves. God speaks to the children of Israel:

Plead with your mother, plead . . .
That she put away her whoring from her face
  And her adultery from between her breasts
Or I will strip her naked
  And expose her as in the day she was born
And make her like a wilderness
  And turn her into a parched land,
  And kill her with thirst
Upon her children also I will have no pity,
  Because they are children of whoredom. . . . (2:2–4)

The condemnation and threats of punishment go on for thirteen chapters, leading to even more graphic images about what God will do to the unfaithful people of Israel:

So I will become like a lion to them,
  like a leopard I will lurk beside the way.
I will fall upon them like a bear robbed of her cubs,
  and will tear open the covering of their heart;
there I will devour them like a lion,
  as a wild animal would mangle them.
I will destroy you, O Israel; who can help you? . . .
They shall fall by the sword,
  their little ones shall be dashed in pieces,
  and their pregnant women ripped open. (13:7–8; 16)

You may think God is justified in his anger. But having infants dashed to pieces and pregnant mothers ripped open?

In Sum: The Wrath of God in the Old Testament

As I have said, I know a number of people, including scholars of Judaism and the Hebrew Bible, who insist it is wrong to think of the God of the Old Testament as a God of wrath. On the whole, they would say, the Scriptures emphasize God's love, grace, goodness, and kindness. I would agree to an extent. But for most of the Bible, God's love comes to very few: he rewards only those among his elect who steadfastly obey his specific commands. Any outsider who threatens the purity of God's people or acts in ways that he cannot abide is subject to his wrath. So, too, even his chosen ones. And he exacts this wrath in horrifying ways, inflicting terrible suffering and death on innocent boys, girls, and infants because of the sins of others.

Back, then, to my original question: Is this the God of the New Testament?

It depends on which parts of the New Testament you choose to read. Many Christians would say that nowhere in the New Testament can you find divine violence like the horrifying destruction of the entire population of Jericho in Joshua 6, or the brutal executions and enslavement of the Midianites in Numbers 25 and 31. That really is as bad as it can get. How could it get any worse? But it does get worse: just read the book of Revelation, described by biblical scholar John Dominic Crossan as "the most relentlessly violent book in all the canonical literature of the great religions of the world."[5]

VIOLENCE IN THE BOOK OF REVELATION

When people read the Bible, they tend to see what they want to see. One of the points of scholarship is to help people see what is really there. Because the book of Revelation came to be included in the Bible—albeit after a long period of debate among church leaders (as we will see in chapter 8)—it is often read today with sympathetic eyes by those who do not expect to see anything seriously problematic in Scripture. That is true of many Christian laypeople, but also of a large number of Christian scholars who are totally convinced there is nothing really wrong with God destroying most of the humans on the planet by having them thrown into a lake of fire.

I myself thought that for a long time, reasoning that God is just and justice requires judgment, so those who offend God are the ones at fault. After all, God has provided a way for people to be forgiven of their sins by having his own son die for them. Anyone who willfully rejects this incredible gift of grace brings judgment on themselves. If they prefer judgment to salvation, they are simply getting what they deserve. No one can blame God for that.

Even more, I thought that those who have accepted God's gracious gift of salvation had been oppressed, persecuted, and martyred. They deserve justice. Those who mistreated the innocent people of God must pay the price.

At times my thoughts went even further: God is above our understanding of ethics and right and wrong. Whatever he does is right by definition. It would certainly not be right for my next-door neighbor to inject scorpion venom into someone's veins and allow them to suffer in anguish for five months, refusing to put them out of their misery when they begged to die. And no one could justify a tyrant who chose to torture his people and then throw them into a vat of burning sulfur. But God is not my next-door neighbor or an earthly tyrant, and so he cannot be judged by human standards. If God does such things in the book of Revelation, who are we, mere mortals, to object? We simply cannot judge the Almighty.

I do not see it that way any longer. I am not saying I am more moral or just than the true God. I am saying that, in my view, the God of Revelation cannot be the true God. I certainly would not be inclined to think the true God was like the God of Revelation if the book were *not* in the Bible. And the fact that later church fathers eventually thought it should be included in Scripture surely can't compel me to say that its views are necessarily right. If Revelation told me that night is day, evil is good, and hate is love, I wouldn't believe it. So, too, if it tells me that the supreme ruler of the universe is all-loving and also plans to torture the majority of humans and then throw them into a lake of burning sulfur. The God of Revelation is not all-loving, not even close. Neither is the Christ of Revelation. They favor only Jesus's devoted followers. All others are tormented and then horribly destroyed, including many Christians, those whom John considers lukewarm in their faith or misguided in following practices he disagrees with. All are tossed into the lake of fire.[6]

It is somewhat ironic that so many readers of Revelation think, as I did, that the God portrayed there is above all human sense of right and wrong. Most of these same readers also believe that our own sense of right and wrong has been given to us by God. This, as you probably know, is a commonly invoked "proof" that God exists. According to this argument, if there were no superior moral being who created us, we could not explain why we have such an innate knowledge of what is good and bad behavior. Our morality, it is argued, must be rooted in the character of God, given to us as creatures made in his image, whether we choose to follow our God-given sense of morality or not.

But if our own sense of right and wrong reveals the character of God, what if God's moral code requires him to torture and destroy those he disapproves of, those who refuse to become his slaves? ("Torture" is not too strong a word here: Remember those locusts.)[7] If God is like that, and we are told to be "godly" people—told to imitate God in our lives—then surely it follows that we should imitate him in how we treat others. If God hates those who refuse to be his slaves and hurts and then destroys them, shouldn't we do so as well?

Are we to act "godly" or not? And what does it mean to be Christlike if Christ's wrath leads to the destruction of nearly the entire human race? Are we really to be "imitators of Christ"? Should we, too, force our enemies to suffer excruciating pain and death?

I know I am putting these reflections in unusually harsh terms, but unlike the wrath of the God of Revelation, my words will not kill anyone. I ask these questions because it is important for us to consider the implications of our views.

Let me stress the question: If the book of Revelation had been left out of the canon of Scripture, would Christians be so invested in saying there is nothing wrong in accepting the vengeful, jealous God of violent wrath portrayed here? And would Christian scholars be inclined to say that God is actually not portrayed that way here? Would any careful reader seriously claim this is not a violent book? And would readers really find this to be an image of God they want to embrace? Even speaking on purely historical grounds: Is this an image of God the historical Jesus himself would have embraced?

Scholars who defend a reading of Revelation as nonviolent do so in a variety of ways. Some stress that the book never urges humans to assume the role of God and inflict violence on others. This is an extremely common view, but it is simply not true. In chapter 18, when an angel pronounces the "fall of Babylon," a voice comes from heaven telling the followers of Jesus: "Come out of her, my people, so that you do not take part in her sins." That is, the saints are told to leave the wretched place that is to be destroyed (18:4). But the angel goes on to order them about what to do to Babylon. This may not be clear to English readers. But in Greek the commands of verses 5–6 are given to the same "people" mentioned in verse 4, not to a divine power (such as an angel or Christ): "[You people] render to her as she herself has rendered, and repay her double for her deeds; mix a double draught for her in the cup she mixed. As she glorified herself and lived luxuriously, so give her a like measure of torment and grief" (18:6–7). These are the orders delivered to the followers of Jesus: Rome has made you suffer, so return the favor double. Torment and grieve the supporters of Rome twice as much as they tormented and grieved you.

This is not nonretaliation; it is retribution.

Most of the book, of course, is not about human violence but about the terrible violence brought by God and his divine agents. How can that be denied? All the catastrophes—the wars, famine, economic collapse, natural disasters, tortures—are sent precisely from heaven. They aren't ordained by the forces of evil or Satan, or inflicted by wicked people. The seals that are broken—ushering in all this destruction—are broken by *Christ*, the Lamb. John explicitly states that the book is all about the "wrath of God" and the "wrath of the Lamb" (6:16–17; 11:18; 14:10; 16:19; 19:15).[8]

The most common argument scholars make to claim the book is nonviolent is that its controlling image of Christ is as an innocent victim, "the Lamb that had been slain."[9] This, for these scholars, is the key: Christ is portrayed as the meek, mild, and submissive Lamb that had been sacrificed, showing that the author supports nonviolent resistance to the forces of evil in imitation of the suffering Christ, whose blood was shed for the sake of others.

It is a beautiful thought, and it would make sense if it were what Revelation says. But, on the contrary, the book emphatically and repeatedly portrays the slaughtered Lamb in an opposite light. He is out for blood. This is not a meek Lamb who conquers because of or through his willingness to be sacrificed, but a Lamb that comes back from the dead with a vengeance. Nowhere in the book does he passively submit to suffering. That happened before. Now, *after* his suffering, he comes for revenge, tormenting and destroying those who oppose him and his followers.

That this is the overarching image of Christ can be shown from the very beginning of the narrative, where the Lamb is first introduced.

THE WRATH OF THE LAMB WHO WAS SLAIN

As we have seen, at the outset of his visions, John is taken up to heaven into the throne room of God (chapter 4). There he sees God with the scroll sealed with seven seals and learns that the only one with the authority to break the seals is the "Lion from the tribe of Judah." He looks for the mighty Lion, but instead sees a "lamb as if slaughtered" (5:6). This is the creature who takes the scroll from the hand of God. It cannot be emphasized enough: it is the Lamb, not the Lion, who breaks the seals. Does that mean that it is the innocence of Christ—his decision to die for others, his willingness to submit to evil forces in the world—that brings victory for his followers? That the sacrificial lamb conquers precisely because he is a lamb?

In my judgment this is a complete misreading of the entire book of Revelation. The book is not about a lion that becomes a lamb; it is about a lamb that becomes a lion. An Almighty Lion who is not king of the forest but of the world, the "King of Kings and Lord of Lords" (17:14). It is as King over all other kings that Christ now engages with his enemies. They may have shed his innocent blood the first time, but now he wreaks vengeance—not just on those who opposed him in life, but even on those who had nothing to do with his death. And he is not the only one out for blood; his followers pray that he will avenge their own deaths: "How long before you judge and avenge our blood on the inhabitants of the earth" (6:9–10).[10] Note: They, too, want vengeance on everyone on the planet—all "the inhabitants of the earth." And Christ does what they ask. In the end, everyone except Christ's devoted followers is slaughtered.

Despite what is sometimes said, it is a mistake to think that Christ *first* appears in Revelation as the Lamb, as if this were the guiding image of the narrative. On the contrary, Christ first appears as the cosmic judge of the earth, the "one like a Son of Man" (1:13), whose coming in Scripture leads to the destruction of the enemies of God and their rule (Daniel 7:13–14). In John's opening vision of Christ (1:12–16), he is dressed in a white robe and gold sash, just as the mighty angels who will later pour out the bowls of God's wrath (15:6). But he is far mightier than these earth destroyers. His hair is white, not to show that he is old and decrepit, but to reveal that he is the One who has ruled from eternity past (see Daniel 7:9), the "alpha and the omega" (22:13). Most important, he has a two-edged sword coming out of his mouth. I noted earlier that this may represent him as the one who speaks the Word of God, but for John this Word is not a peaceful, soothing communication to calm the souls of those on earth. It is the word "judgment." Later Christ tells the Christians they should repent or "I will make war against them with the sword of my mouth" (2:16).

This opening description of Christ can usefully be compared with the final one near the end, at the battle of Armageddon (19:11–21). These two descriptions bracket the narrative, providing the interpretive guide to Christ's role in all that comes between. It is not at all a narration of the Lamb's passive resistance to the forces of evil. At the end, the beast appears on earth with his armies to fight Christ and his heavenly forces; Christ comes forth from heaven on a white horse and wages a war of righteous judgment. He is called "the Word of God" and we are told that he is clothed with "a robe dipped in blood" (19:13). He will not be shedding his own blood again; he will now make his enemies pay for his earlier sacrifice. Once more he is said to have a sharp sword coming from his mouth. Now there is no doubt what this sword is for: it is to avenge blood with blood. The sword will "strike down the nations" so that Christ can rule the world with a "rod of iron" (19:15). He treads "the wine press of the fury of the wrath of God Almighty" (19:15) by killing all the enemy troops; the scavenging birds of heaven feast on the battlefield, eating "the flesh of kings, the flesh of captains, the flesh of the mighty, the flesh of horses and their riders—flesh of all, both free and slave, both small and great" (19:17–18). In a grisly conclusion we learn that "the birds were gorged with their flesh" (19:21).

This is not the proponent of nonviolent resistance who inspired Mahatma Gandhi and Martin Luther King Jr. This is the lamb who has become a lion, set to destroy everyone who is not a slave of God. And this destruction is not quick and painless.[11] Even though the narrative is meant to be understood cyclically, not as a linear description of what will happen in chronological sequence, it is worth noting that the horrors increase through the progression. Some of the first set of disasters affect a fourth of the earth, the next set a third of it, and the third set seemingly all of it. Disaster after disaster, all released by the Lamb.

THE HORROR, THE HORROR

These chapters are not even the most violent parts of the book. Three passages I've already mentioned compete for that dubious honor, and all reveal a Christ who is out for blood. The first passage comes as an interlude between the seven trumpets and the seven bowls of God's wrath (14:14–20). Here we have another vision of "one like the Son of Man," who is seated on a cloud, wearing a golden crown and carrying a sharp sickle (14:14). An angel emerges from the heavenly temple and calls to this (grim) reaper, "Use your sickle and reap, for the hour to reap has come, because the harvest of the earth is fully ripe." In other words, it is time for judgment to begin. Christ wields his sickle, "and the earth was reaped" (14:16).

Had the author stopped there, the reader would assume that those opposed to God had been suddenly killed. But then the account becomes painfully graphic. Another angel emerges from the temple also bearing a sickle, and yet another issues a fearful command: "Use your sharp sickle and gather the clusters of the vine of the earth, for its grapes are ripe" (14:18). Now we understand this is a grape harvest, of sorts. The vines are cut down, their grapes removed, and the grapes thrown into "the wine press of the wrath of God," where they are trodden (14:19). It is not red wine that flows, however, but human blood. And it is a vintage crop: "the blood flowed from the wine press, as high as a horse's bridle, for a distance of about two hundred miles" (14:20). This is what happens to people who do not worship God properly. With an effective mixed image, the angel explains their fate: it is not that they will be trodden into human wine but that they will "drink the wine of God's wrath" (14:9–10).

The second passage involves not just drinking but also eating. Before the final battle, an angel tells the seer John: "Blessed are those invited to the marriage supper of the Lamb" (19:9). Christ, the Lamb, is to be united with his bride, the church of his followers, and there will be a celebration. That sounds festive. But who are the banqueters? And what is on the menu?

Those who eat the marriage supper of the Lamb are the scavenger birds; their meal is the flesh of Christ's enemies. As we have seen, after Christ puts forth his "sharp sword" in order to "strike down the nations" in the Final Battle (19:15), an angel calls out to "all the birds that fly in midheaven," inviting them to enjoy "the great supper of God" (19:17). They come to the feast, to devour the cadavers of Christ's enemies slain in battle. The battle is over in a flash. "The beast and the kings of the earth" (so not just Rome but also all its supporters) have gathered their armies, and as soon as they appear, they are overwhelmed. The beast and his false prophet are cast into the lake of burning sulfur, where they will suffer but never die, while all their troops are slaughtered by Christ himself, "by the sword of the rider on the horse, the sword that came from his mouth" (19:21). Let the feast begin.

The third passage shows that Christ directs his violence not only against pagans who do not accept his message and the Jews who worship in the "Synagogue of Satan" but also against his own followers, even active leaders and teachers in his church. We should never forget the injunctions and warnings of the seven letters in chapters 2 and 3. Christ regularly threatens to remove his favor and protection from his churches and their members (for example, 2:5, 15; 3:3). From the rest of the book, it is easy to infer their fate.[12]

John does not always leave this up to the imagination. One of the most horrifying images of the book comes in the aforementioned letter to the church of Thyatira (2:18–29). Recall that John slanders a prophetess in the church whom he calls Jezebel, a teacher whose views John vigorously rejects.[13] She believes it is acceptable for Christians to eat food offered to idols and may even encourage it (2:20). John thinks this view is idolatrous and licentious. He may be using sexual imagery as Hosea did to refer to "getting into bed" with other gods. Whatever the intent behind his imagery, he thinks the prophetess Jezebel is wrong. And not just wrong but damnable.

There is no knowing what the historical "Jezebel" actually said or taught. One can easily give her view a generous read: Suppose Christians in the community of Thyatira had pagan family members, friends, and neighbors who sometimes invited them to their homes for a meal. At the meal, they ate what had been prepared, which sometimes included meat purchased at the local temple. Rather than offend the non-Christians who offered them a gracious invitation, these church members accepted and enjoyed their time together. Perhaps they used the meal as a chance to talk to their dinner companions about their faith and try to convince them to learn more about Christ. "Jezebel," in this reading, thinks this is a completely reasonable approach to being in the world and possibly a helpful strategy for spreading the good news.

John, however, does not give the situation a generous read. He thinks participating in meals with pagans with meat purchased in a temple is an offense that would lead straight to the lake of fire. And he is forthright about what Christ himself thinks of this social and possibly evangelistic move. In his letter, Christ says: "I am throwing her on a bed and those who commit adultery with her I am throwing into great distress." Earlier I pointed out that this is not called a sickbed and Christ does not make her ill. Men come and have sex with her. Does she welcome them as a willing partner? Or do they rape her? In either event, they themselves are punished, too, though we are not told specifically how. One can imagine medical possibilities.

But that's not the worst of it. Christ concludes by assuring his readers that he will punish her with an extreme act of violence, taking his vengeance on her innocent offspring. He is going to kill them. That is what John imagines Christ will do to those who allow Christians to participate in a meal with pagans: "I will strike her children dead" (2:23).

SYMBOLIC VIOLENCE?

I have difficulty seeing how a text can be much more violent than this. Most of the book, of course, is not about what will happen to Christians whom John considers wayward but to those outside the church. These inhabitants of earth will suffer incomprehensible catastrophes before being thrown alive into a lake of burning sulfur.

Why would it have to be this way, even if God is just and decides to avenge his persecuted or even martyred followers and to wipe out the masses of the ungodly? Couldn't he simply give them a simultaneous and fatal coronary? Or just disintegrate them with a cosmic ray gun? Not for John. The wrath of God and the Lamb needs to be satisfied. The Christian martyrs plead for vengeance, and God gives it to them. Everyone except the most devoted followers of Jesus will suffer torment and then be subjected to a hideous death.

I anticipate many people reading this will be thinking that the book of Revelation is *symbolic* and that I'm making a mistake in supposing any of this is *literally* going to happen. Jesus is not actually going to kill babies, torture almost everyone on earth, and then execute them in the most horrifying way he can imagine. The book is all a metaphor about how God will restore justice, destroy evil, and make the world good again, a paradise for those who are faithful.

On one hand, I agree. I do not think John imagines the events he narrates will literally happen as he describes them. He is using symbolism in order to convey a message. And that message does provide hope for those who are—or who at least feel—persecuted and oppressed for their faith. In the end, God will triumph and evil will be destroyed. That part is good. But why does the author tell this story in such incredibly violent and gory terms?

It is important to realize that even though the author's account is symbolic, his symbols embody his understanding of God, the world, and humanity. The beast represents Rome, and there is good reason to believe John really does think Rome is soon to be destroyed by God. It is not clear if John thinks God will use Christian soldiers who'll engage in battle, or an angelic host, or even the returning Son of Man. The final option would not be at all odd for someone living in John's time who was familiar with the biblical and extra-biblical Jewish tradition. Many Jews, including Jesus himself, expected something similar, an apocalyptic intervention that would annihilate all those opposed to God, so his people would rule in the future kingdom.[14] But, as I will show in chapter 8, Jesus thought about this in a very different way from John. He did not celebrate the violence and did not think this intervention was about vengeance, domination, or the mind-boggling material glories to be enjoyed by saints. John does. And he is very much looking forward to the time when people like him will rule the nations (22:5).

Even so, if his narrative is meant to be *symbolic* of God's coming victory, why should I be bothered by the symbols he uses to describe it? It is because the symbols themselves are important. Symbolic images reveal an author's deepest values, commitments, perspectives, and beliefs. And John's are deeply disturbing. As New Testament scholar Pieter de Villiers has put it:

> This is language that soaks the imagination of readers in
> violence. . . . It is language that draws its listeners into
> an atmosphere of bitter and agonistic opposition against
> others and that categorize people in terms of either good
> or evil with dangerous consequences.[15]

He goes on to argue that such "harsh, violent language can create violent behavior." It can and has.

It would have been simple for John to write a *nonviolent* account of the glorious future to come for the followers of Jesus. He did not need blood running up to the horses' bridles for two hundred miles. He could have told a completely different story if he had wanted, perhaps an account of highly successful missionary campaigns by the apostles of Christ, who convert the nations to the truth of God and the message of Jesus by their divinely inspired rhetoric and great miracles of healing, with all the lands of the earth appointing rulers who were most the spiritual men and women among them to guide them into the glorious future God had prepared. Why not? Why do you need them all tortured and killed?

That John tells the story the way he does reveals his understanding of God as a God of wrath. Love hardly features at all in this account. John does say that Christ "loves" his followers and "freed them from their sins by his blood" (1:5), and in the letters he dictates Christ does indicate that he loves some of his followers (3:9, 19). But these are the only three places Christ is said to love anyone in the entire book. And John says not a word, not a single word, about God himself loving anyone or anything. His God is a God of wrath, determined to wreak vengeance through heaven-sent catastrophes and torments.

To be sure, the followers of Jesus are well taken care of in the end: they inherit an incredibly glorious city. But John never indicates that God rewards them because he loves them. It is because they alone are unerringly obedient "slaves" who are committed to worshipping him day and night.[16] And so to say that this is all "just a story" completely misses the point. The story conveys a message, an understanding of right and wrong and of what really matters before the Almighty. The book celebrates judgment, condemnation, bloody vengeance, and divine wrath—not love, mercy, forgiveness, and reconciliation. In the end, the Lamb who was once bloodied avenges his blood a thousandfold. For John, Christ came the first time in meekness but is coming back in anger. History will be guided by the vengeance and wrath of God and his Lamb.

Is this what Jesus thought?

SEVEN

The Ideology of Dominance: Wealth and Power in Revelation

DH. Lawrence is famous for his racy novels: *Sons and Lovers, Women in Love, Lady Chatterley's Lover, The Rainbow.* But sex was not his only passion. There was also religion. Traditional Christianity was no mysterium tremendum for him, no dangerous but irresistible attraction. It was a psychic horror. Few people know that Lawrence's final book was *Apocalypse*, an analysis of the book of Revelation, written not out of love but out of loathing. Lawrence hated the book and ended his career by explaining why.[1]

Lawrence had been raised in a conservative environment, required to attend church and forced to hear the Bible read over and over again. He escaped as soon as he could, but came away both highly knowledgeable and deeply resentful of the Christian Scriptures. He could cite them at will, but did not do so to promote Christian values. On the contrary, his penetrating mind and uncanny ability to see through pious pretention made him a formidable opponent of the faith.[2]

Biblical scholars today who know about Lawrence's final book typically glance at it to get the general picture so they can write off his extreme views with a passing remark. When I first read the book, I had the opposite reaction. I found it brilliant. Not as a scholarly analysis of the historical background and setting of Revelation; Lawrence was not a specialist in the field and his assertions about the origin and the sources of the book will convince almost no one today.[3] But his assessment is brilliant at a much deeper level. With characteristically penetrating insight, Lawrence realized that the entire visionary narrative of the Apocalypse is driven not by a flowery message of the goodness of God or the Christian virtue of sacrificial love for others. It celebrates their opposite: raw and undisguised Christian envy. God, in the narrative, uses brutal force to give his people what they desire: the massive wealth and unstoppable power held by the empire of Rome. In fact, the Christians will acquire far more wealth and power. In the end, they will gleefully see their enemies destroyed before their very eyes so they themselves can become incomparably rich and rule the entire world.

Lawrence stresses that, unlike John of Patmos, some leaders of the early Christian tradition (including Jesus and Paul) understood wealth and power to be problems in and of themselves and urged their fellow believers to eschew them in their quest to live humble, spiritual lives. John had a contrary view. For him there was no problem with wealth and power per se. The problem was that the wrong people had them.[4]

Lawrence argues that wealth- and power-envy relate to two kinds of human nature. Jesus and Paul were strong personalities, confident and self-sufficient. As a result, they could pull away from the things of the world, the material possessions and power so desired by others. But, Lawrence says, "John of Patmos felt himself weak, in his very soul," and like other weak and needy personalities, he hated those who had worldly power. As a result,

> the Christian religion . . . became dual. The religion of the strong taught renunciation and love. And the religion of the weak taught *down with the strong and the power powerful, and let the poor be glorified.* Since there are always more weak people than strong, in the world, the second sort of Christianity has triumphed and will triumph. . . . The rule of the weak is *Down with the strong!*[5]

After a fuller analysis, Lawrence summarizes his view:

> These early Christians fairly lusted after the end of the world. . . . [T]hey insisted that the whole universe must be wiped out, sun, stars, and all—and a *new* Jerusalem should appear, with the same old saints and martyrs in glory, and everything else should have disappeared except the lake of burning brimstone in which devils, demons, beasts, and bad men should frizzle and suffer for ever and ever and ever, Amen!
>
> Oh, it is the Christianity of the middling masses this Christianity of the Apocalypse. By the time of Jesus, all the lowest classes . . . had realized that *never* would they get a chance to be kings, *never* would they go in chariots, never would they drink wine from gold vessels. Very well then—they would have their revenge by *destroying* it all . . . all the gold and silver and pearls and precious stones and fine linen and purples, and silk, and scarlet. . . . All these that are destroyed, destroyed, destroyed in Babylon the great—how one hears the envy, the endless envy screeching through this song of triumph.[6]

Lawrence concludes with his ultimate assessment: This "is the dark side of Christianity."[7]

After spending many years studying the book of Revelation, I have trouble disagreeing with him. I do not subscribe to Lawrence's analysis of the literary sources of Revelation, but it is hard to reject his sense of the values the book promotes. For decades I had read the account as a story of hope: written to Christians who were ruthlessly oppressed and persecuted, and meant to show them that in the end justice would be done, good would triumph, God would overcome the miseries of this world, and his followers would be rewarded for their faithfulness.

I still do see the book that way. But how will they be rewarded? God will destroy every other man, woman, and child on earth, everyone who has not accepted the author's particular way of following Jesus—no matter who or where, whether good or wicked—so the true followers of Jesus can have all the wealth and power in the world. That is what John yearns for.

We have already seen that the book is massively violent. In this chapter I want to stress that the violence of the book is not an end in itself but a means to an end. The ultimate goal is revenge. But more than that, it is limitless possessions and power. In the end, the right people will get what the wrong people have now. As New Testament scholar Christopher Frilingos has so succinctly expressed, the book is all about who will dominate the world: "A frankly imperialist narrative, Revelation predicts the end of the Roman Empire and the beginning of a Christian one."[8] Revelation does not adopt a new Christian attitude toward wealth and domination. It instead affirms the attitude promoted by Roman culture, the same view held by most people who choose *not* to follow the teachings of Jesus: wealth and domination can be ultimate goods.[9]

Again I ask: Is that what Jesus had in mind?

WEALTH IN THE TEACHINGS OF JESUS

Our earliest Gospels have a good deal to say about Jesus's attitude toward wealth, in passages perennially discomfiting to Christians with significant material resources, or even Christians with simply more than they need. One of the best-known passages comes in Matthew's Sermon on the Mount, where Jesus explicitly tells his followers not to accumulate wealth:

> [19] Do not store up for yourselves treasures on earth, where moth and rust consume and where thieves break in and steal; [20] but store up for yourselves treasures in heaven, where neither moth nor rust consumes and where thieves do not break in and steal. [21] For where your treasure is, there your heart will be also. (Matthew 6:19–21)

Wealthy followers of Jesus have almost always read this passage as urging a both/and proposition—those who are wealthy in material things should also seek spiritual treasures. But that is not what Jesus says. He is presenting an either/or proposition, insisting that it is one or the other. Your heart will *either* be here, with your material possessions, or up above with God. Which do you choose? It is understandable that readers may not want Jesus really to mean this, but it is what the passage says.

Many Christians—wealthy or otherwise—have also interpreted Jesus's reference to "treasures in heaven" as actual material abundance in the world to come: faithful Christians will be granted fantastic resources in the great beyond. A friend of mine recently overheard a group of Christians at the next table in an upscale restaurant talking about how they, as followers of Jesus, would be given multiple mansions and golf courses in heaven. (Seriously? Golf courses?) But one of them did concede: "Of course, my golf course won't be as nice as Billy Graham's."[10]

These people appear to have overlooked a rather important point. Jesus said that treasures in heaven would come to those who abandoned their wealth on earth. (Maybe they should have chosen a cheaper restaurant.) But more than that, Jesus was not giving his followers shrewd advice about how to become fabulously wealthy for all time: just postpone your passion for material possessions now and you'll be incomprehensibly more affluent later. That's the opposite of what he taught. Jesus contrasted earthly *materialism* and the constant drive to acquire more with the greater *spiritual* goods that can come only by abandoning earthly desires and tending to the soul. Material goods are not what matter. You should not suffer hardship now *so that* you can enjoy munificence later. The money and the things it provides are not what matter, pure and simple. Putting any attention on what doesn't matter will necessarily distract you from what does.

For Jesus, the "things of God" are far more precious than your most prized possessions. In fact, Jesus maintained that the things of God are far more important than the basic necessities of existence. In the same sermon, Jesus tells his followers not to worry about "what to eat or what to drink, or even what clothes to wear" (Matthew 6:25). Instead they are to focus on God, and he will take care of their needs. It obviously is not practicable to neglect food and clothes, but it is a mistake to think Jesus must be practicable. He states his views clearly. Birds don't have to work to eke out an existence; God himself gives them their nourishment. The lilies of the field don't worry about what they'll wear, and yet God dresses them better than kings (Matthew 6:28–29). If God clothes the grass that lives a short while and then is burned, won't he do so for those who follow him? There certainly have been Christians over the centuries who have taken Jesus at his word, but not many. I've never met one.

Jesus himself took these ideas seriously, or at least he does in the Gospels. Most readers of the New Testament understand that Jesus left his work and home to become an itinerate preacher and that he convinced twelve other men to do the same. But rarely do people think about what that might have meant for them. How did they live? The answer is pretty clear: they were impoverished beggars who relied on others for their sustenance, interpreting the kindness of strangers as, literally, a godsend.[11] It is hard to imagine they weren't hungry and cold a good bit of the time. Jesus wants his followers to live like *that*? Well, he certainly says he does.

Most people, of course, don't want to hear it. So they say he doesn't mean it.

SURELY JESUS DIDN'T MEAN IT. DID HE?

Nowhere is that more obvious than in the widespread interpretations of a key passage of the Gospels first found in Mark 10:17–31. A rich man approaches Jesus and asks him how to "inherit eternal life." Jesus immediately tells him to keep God's commandments. The man says he already does so: he doesn't murder, commit adultery, steal, and so on. But he knows he is still lacking something. Then comes one of the most poignant lines of the Gospels: "Jesus, looking at him, loved him" (Mark 10:21). It is poignant because it means that Jesus loved the man enough to tell him the full story: "You are lacking one thing. Go, sell everything you have and give to the poor, and you will have treasure in heaven." If the man does that (and only after he does), he can become Jesus's follower ("*then* come, follow me"). The man is devastated; he simply can't do it. He is wealthy and can't bring himself to give all his possessions away. He goes away crestfallen.

It is not enough to obey all of God's commandments: you have to abandon everything to attain the "wealth" of heaven. Jesus explains to his disciples that he really means this: it is almost impossible for a wealthy person "to enter the kingdom of God" (Mark 10:24). The disciples find this hard to believe. Like so many Christians after them, they think that surely wealth is a sign of divine favor. God bestows material blessings on those he holds dear, right? Wrong. Not for Jesus. To the disciples' astonishment, Jesus claims it is "easier for a camel to pass through the eye of a needle than for a rich person to enter into the kingdom of God" (Mark 10:25). But how can that be? If rich people aren't favored by God, who is? Who can possibly enter the kingdom? Jesus informs his disciples that salvation is impossible for humans to achieve, but God can make it possible.

Here again is a passage widely misunderstood by readers who, like the disciples, can't believe what Jesus is saying. It should be clear, however, that when Jesus says "it is possible" with God, he is decidedly *not* saying that sometimes God *will* save rich people who are unwilling to give away their possessions. If that were what he meant, he could have told the rich man not to worry: God would save him anyway. But that's not what he says. He is saying that God makes it possible for some people to decide to give up their wealth. It's rare, so rare that it might seem impossible. But God can make it happen. These people are saved not despite the fact they are rich but because they have abandoned their wealth.

Almost all interpreters, though, have tried to get around the problems of Jesus's words by softening them a bit, or, more often, a lot. Among the common interpretations you hear is that Jesus is referring to a camel passing through a low gate in the wall of Jerusalem that was called the "eye of the needle." The camel would have to stoop to get through, but it wasn't literally impossible. But there was no such gate in Jesus's time. Others say that Jesus didn't actually say the word "camel" but "ship cable" (spelled similarly). That may make better sense in some ways, but, realistically speaking, threading a needle with a thick rope isn't possible, either. Jesus's point is that it can't be done.[12]

That has disturbed Gospel interpreters for as long as there have been interpreters. Already in the second century we have a sermon by the church father Clement of Alexandria called "What Rich Man Can Be Saved?"[13] Clement's interpretation of the passage must have warmed the cockles of every wealthy person's heart in his congregation. It certainly would warm many wealthy hearts today. Clement insisted that Jesus could not and did not mean that rich people should give everything away. That would make no sense: if the wealthy gave everything away, they would have nothing left to give to the poor. Jesus must have meant that rich people should not be *attached* to their wealth. Their hearts should be with God, not with their possessions—even though they might have wealth and should definitely keep it. This is an early interpretive attempt to have it both ways—to keep your goods but be more interested in God. And it is not difficult to see why a pastor of a congregation with wealthy members might want to interpret the passage this way; it is the wealthy who provide funds for the church.

Since Jesus is no longer around to explain himself, it is easy to insist he didn't really mean what he said. And it is easy to imagine his twelve disciples wished he didn't mean it, either. They probably would not have minded a nice bed at night or something decent to eat without begging. In this very account, Peter seeks for assurance that they have done the right thing by giving up "everything" in order to follow Jesus (Mark 10:28). Many modern readers overlook the significance of the term "everything." He does mean everything: possessions, homes, jobs, friends, families. The families are surely the most heart-wrenching. In the first-century world, the husband was the head of the household and almost always the sole breadwinner. Women could not work outside the home to make money. If the man left his family, the wife became a de facto widow and the children orphans. Especially in a world where most people's own relatives could barely get by on their own, an abandoned family could normally survive only by begging or by doing things that are not pleasant to imagine. Jesus demands *that*?

When he responds to Peter, Jesus does not dwell on the fate of the families who have been left behind. He praises the disciples for taking on abject poverty for the sake of the kingdom. But his response is also often misinterpreted: "Truly I tell you, there is no one who has left house or brothers or sisters or mother or father or children or fields on account of me and the gospel, who will not receive a hundredfold in the present time—houses and brothers and sisters and mothers and children and fields—with persecutions, and in the age to come eternal life" (Mark 10:29–30). Often this is taken to mean that those who follow Jesus by leaving everything behind will actually become richer than they were before, both now and in heaven. But again, a close look at Jesus's words shows that he is *not* saying that. How does one acquire "hundreds" of "mothers"? Obviously not in the literal sense. And so Jesus is not talking about literal houses and fields to replace the ones that have been abandoned, either. Jesus must mean that those who leave their own homes and families to follow him will be welcomed into many other homes and so will have hundreds of other people treat them as kin and allow them to share their resources. The point is not to get rich here on earth; it is to abandon material possessions. Do so and God will take care of you. And what of the wife and children you've left to fend for themselves? Oddly, Jesus doesn't say anything about them. Possibly he thinks God will miraculously take care of them, too.

A passage that confirms this understanding that future heavenly wealth for the faithful is purely spiritual comes in the famous account of the Jewish leaders who ask Jesus whether it is right to pay taxes to the Roman Empire (Mark 12:13–17). This may sound like a relatively innocent question, but in fact Jesus's opponents are laying a trap for him. If Jesus says, "No, don't pay taxes to those filthy Romans who have taken over our Promised Land," then his enemies can turn him over to the authorities for opposing the state. But if he says, "Yes, do what the ruling authorities ask and faithfully pay what they demand," they can accuse him of being a collaborator and an enemy of the Jewish people. As happens elsewhere, though, Jesus's opponents do not know whom they are up against. Jesus never, ever gets caught in these traps. On this occasion he asks for a Roman denarius and when it is produced he asks whose image is on it. He already knows the answer, of course: imperial coins were issued with a likeness of the emperor to emphasize his control over all things, even daily purchases. Jesus's opponents tell him the coin bears the image and inscription of Caesar, and that allows him to demolish their trap: "Then give to Caesar the things that belong to Caesar and give to God the things that belong to God" (Mark 10:17). For Jesus, the things of this world belong to the mighty and powerful who rule it. God has nothing to do with such trivialities. He does not care about material goods. He wants your soul.

So give him your soul. Devote yourself completely to God. Then you will become truly rich, not in material possessions but in what really matters: the knowledge and love of God. That is why, elsewhere, Jesus says that if someone wants to take your coat, give it to him; in fact, give him your cloak as well (Matthew 5:40). Why not? In fact, give everything away. Being rich in God requires being poor in possessions. Wealth is not merely a matter of indifference, it is an impediment.[14] Those who want it—now or later—will never enter the kingdom of God. That's the teaching of Jesus.

The book of Revelation has a very different view of the matter.

WEALTH IN THE BOOK OF REVELATION

It is worth noting that John's visions begin and end with acclamations of heavenly opulence: glorification of wealth brackets the entire vision narrative as a controlling theme. The account begins with John's vision of the magnificent throne room of God, which is far more spectacular than anything ever seen on earth. That is to be expected, of course: God is the Almighty Creator of all things (4:3–6). Still, it is striking that John finds that God himself can be described only in terms of precious jewels, like jasper and carnelian. His throne is surrounded by a rainbow like an emerald. In front of the throne is a sea of glass like crystal. On earth Jesus may have embraced destitution as an itinerant beggar, but the opulence of his Father's throne room beggars description. Imagine what the whole palace must look like.

So, too, the first humans John sees in the heavenly realm, the twenty-four elders. They also are sitting on thrones and are dressed in white garments, with golden crowns on their heads. They are God's co-rulers, far subservient to him, but also surrounded by fantastic splendor. Devoted to God alone, in exchange, they live like kings. That will be true later for God's other worshipful slaves.

This opening vision, all jewels and gold, is quite terse, as indeed one might expect. A vision of God necessarily defies description; little could be added apart from yet more jewels and other superlatives, which would still only describe what it is all "like." There are no words that can encapsulate the magnificent reality itself. At the book's end, however, John goes into considerable detail about the future dwelling place of the saints, the new Jerusalem, which so far exceeds anything on earth that it, too, is nearly impossible to imagine, far beyond what Caesar Augustus could have dreamed for Rome, his "city of marble" (Suetonius, *Divine Augustus*, 29). The new Jerusalem is made completely of gold, with a wall of jasper, gates of pearl, and a foundation of jewels. It is not at all what we today would consider (merely) a large city; it is 1,500 miles cube, half the size of the United States. The ground alone is covered by two million square miles of solid gold. It defies the imagination and is supposed to. The followers of Jesus will live in opulence beyond anyone's dreams. By comparison, ancient Rome would look like a termite nest.

The bulk of Revelation does not focus on the fantastic wealth awaiting the followers of Jesus, of course. But the narrative does highlight the significance of this ending scene by way of a none-too-subtle comparison. The persecuted slaves of God will dwell forever in unimaginable material splendor. And the enemies of God? For them it's the lake of fire.

Just as visions of *divine* wealth bracket John's vision of heavenly realities (chapters 4 and 21), images of *demonic* wealth bracket his discussions of God's major earthly enemy, the beast of the sea (chapters 13, 18–19). Probably the most notable feature of this beast is that he provides a literary counter to Christ, an evil doppelgänger, an "Anti" Christ. He is a horrible "beast" (13:1–2) instead of an ideal "one like a son of man" (1:13); he comes up from the "sea" (13:1) instead of from heaven (19:11); he is empowered by Satan (13:2) instead of by God; he is an earthly ruler who received a mortal wound that has been healed (13:3) instead of a sacrificed lamb who has died and risen to heaven (1:18); and so on. There is also a focus on wealth in this early description of the beast. He is a ruler with ten diadems. More than that, he controls the world's economy, to the obvious detriment of his enemies; only those with the mark of the beast "can buy or sell" anything (13:17). The beast hoards all the money, all the economic power; Jesus's followers have none at all.

The description of the Whore of Babylon emphasizes these same points: she is wantonly luxurious, flaunting wealth in the face of God's people, dressed in incredibly rich fabrics (scarlet and purple), and adorned with gold, jewels, and pearls (17:4). John debases her grotesque affluence. Yet that description of Babylon will come to be duplicated in the new Jerusalem, which is also portrayed almost

entirely in terms gold, jewels, and pearls (22:15–21). In the end, the
followers of Jesus will get what Rome has now, only more so. For
John, fantastic wealth is not a material obsession that draws a person
away from God. It is the ultimate end of the saints' existence.

John's focus on wealth becomes even more clear when he celebrates the fall of "Babylon" in chapter 18. The great sins of the
city are derided at her downfall. And what are those sins "heaped
high as heaven" (v. 5)? "She glorified herself and lived luxuriously"
(v. 7). The Whore of Babylon exploited the entire world for her own
prosperity. When "the kings of the earth" who "committed fornication and lived in luxury with her" see her demise, they "weep and
wail" (v. 9), and "the merchants of the earth weep and mourn for
her," not because they loved her but because they profited from her
(18:15). Now, alas, there is no one to buy "their cargo," their "gold,
silver, jewels and pearls, fine linen, purple, silk, and scarlet, articles
of ivory, costly wood, bronze," along with exotic spices, foodstuffs,
livestock, and, worst of all, "human bodies and souls" (18:17). And
what about the denizens of heaven? They could not be happier.
With exalted schadenfreude, they cry out: "Hallelujah! Salvation
and glory and power to our God, for his judgments are true and
just; he has judged the great whore who corrupted the earth with
her fornication, and he has avenged on her the blood of his slaves"
(19:1–2). All the merchants' pomp and luxury, all their niceties,
every bit of their wealth, has been wiped off the planet.

Or at least transferred. Two chapters later, the followers of Jesus
will be given material possessions that people would die for, and in
fact have. The saints of Jesus have died for their faith, and this is
their reward.

Despite the claims of televangelists and preachers of the "Prosperity Gospel," this surely is not what Jesus had in mind. Jesus insisted that his followers not care what they eat, drink, or wear. They
were to live spiritual lives removed from material concerns. No one

can focus on material goods and God at the same time: "No one can serve two masters; for a slave will either hate the one and love the other, or be devoted to the one and despise the other. You cannot serve God and wealth" (Matthew 6:24). And no one should pretend they can live in abundance but not really care about their possessions. Material things need to be abandoned. So when Jesus talks about treasures in heaven, he isn't referring to golden mansions and pure white, no-need-to-wash raiments. Jesus does not advise giving up abundance now precisely to acquire more of it later.

John of Patmos agreed that material things are not what matter in this life, but from his description of the new Jerusalem, he certainly thinks they matter in the life to come. God's slaves will be rewarded for their faithfulness, and while there will indeed be spiritual rewards—they will be able to worship God forever—they can also look forward to fantastic material wealth in a city made of gold with gates of pearl. It is a pleasant thought, indeed. But it is not a thought Jesus had.

JESUS'S VIEWS OF DOMINATION

Wealth is not the only worldly passion John of Patmos imagines awaiting the slaves of God: there is also power. In his vision, Christ will rule the nations "with a rod of iron" through his saints; together, they "will rule forever and ever," with all the nations of earth subservient to them (22:5; 21:24–26). In what's becoming a familiar theme, John of Patmos has no problem with the harsh realities of "power" and "dominance" in the Roman Empire per se. He does not think they necessarily run contrary to the ways of God. For John, the problem is that the wrong people are ruling with iron rods. Again, what about Jesus?

Jesus's own teachings about power and dominance are, on the contrary, countercultural and counterintuitive, perhaps the most striking aspect of his proclamation. The way to greatness is through humility; the way to power is through service; the way to mastery is through slavery. Anyone who thinks that Jesus understood humility, service, and sacrifice as the ironic means to domination in the life to come has completely missed the point. Service is not the means but the goal.

This kind of teaching may seem contrary to all sense today, even—or possibly especially—among the vast majority of Jesus's followers. But it is clearly attested throughout the Gospels, where even Jesus's disciples don't believe he can mean it. Here I will focus my attention on our earliest Gospel, Mark, which repeatedly emphasizes that Jesus is the messiah who must suffer. His disciples cannot get the idea into their heads. For them, the messiah was to be the great and powerful ruler who overthrew the enemies of the people of God and set up rule on earth. If Jesus is the messiah, he will assert his power and they will stride with him to victory. Mark repeatedly shows this traditional view of the messiah is precisely wrong.[15]

As the narrative progresses, Jesus's disciples come to realize he is the "messiah" only after they have spent a good deal of time hearing him teach and observing his miracles. In the first half of the book they are impressed by his power and his teachings but appear clueless about his identity. Early on they ask, "Who then is this?" (4:41); later they "did not understand" (6:51–52); later still, in exasperation, Jesus asks, "Do you not yet understand?" (8:21). It is only at this point, after eight chapters of incomprehension, that Peter, his closest disciple, begins to get a glimmer of an inkling. Jesus has asked the twelve who others say he is, and they tell him that some think he might be a prophet come back from the dead: John the Baptist, or Elijah, or one of the others. He then asks who *they* think he is, and Peter confesses, "You are the messiah" (8:29). Jesus tacitly confirms this confession by instructing them not to tell anyone. But right away, in the very next verses, he reveals that he is not the messiah they are imagining—the great warrior who will assert power over the enemy. He must go to Jerusalem and be rejected, suffer, and be executed before being raised again (8:31).

Peter immediately rebukes him for saying so. This is not what will happen to him: he's the *messiah* (8:32). Jesus then rebukes Peter in turn, calls him "Satan," and tells him he is thinking like a human, not like God. God's ways are not human ways. God values service, not domination. And so Jesus begins to teach the crowds: following him will lead to great self-denial and suffering, not glory. His followers must take up their own crosses and be willing to give their lives for others: "For whoever wants to save their life must lose it and whoever loses their life for my sake and the sake of the gospel will save it" (8:34–36). Jesus never says that those who are willing to submit to the ruling authorities now, even to the point of death, will later come back to force them into submission. They will indeed be rewarded with true life, just as he would be when he was raised from the dead. But this true life is not a life of dominance. Jesus is not urging deferred pleasure; he is explaining a paradox. It is no wonder the disciples could not understand him.

This account occurs almost precisely in the middle of Mark's narrative, and it sets the stage for the second half of the Gospel. Mark drives the point home by narrating very similar encounters in both of the next two chapters. In 9:31, Jesus again tells the disciples that he has to be executed but will be raised from the dead. Again Mark indicates that they "did not understand" and shows it: right away the disciples begin to argue among themselves about which of them "was the greatest"—as if the point was to be "great." Jesus can hardly believe it. He tries to explain again: "If anyone wants to be first he has to be the last of all and the servant of all" (9:33–35). He does not say that those willing to serve now will become ruthless tyrants later. His message is far more radical than that: serving itself is the mark of greatness.

The point is made yet more forcefully in the third incident. Jesus once more indicates that he must experience a humiliating fate: he will be handed over to the gentile rulers, "and they will mock him and spit on him, and flog him, and kill him" (10:34). Immediately after he predicts this humiliation, two of his closest disciples, James and John, approach him to ask to be his co-rulers in the coming kingdom: "And they said to him, 'Allow us to sit, one at your right hand and the other on your left, when you come into your glory'" (10:37). The two brothers do realize they may have to suffer first (they will "drink his cup" and be "baptized with his baptism"), but their goal is the glorious reward that will await. Suffering will be the gateway to power and dominion. In response, Jesus calls all the disciples together and tells them, "You know that those who are thought to rule over the nations exercise lordly power over them and their great ones assert their authority. But it is not to be like this among you. Whoever among you wants to become great must be a servant, and whoever wants to be first among you will be the slave of all" (10:43–44).

The disciples simply do not understand. Deferred gratification makes sense: Suffer now to rule later. But how can service *itself* be the point? For Jesus, that is nonetheless the message: being the greatest of all means being a slave to all. Even if the disciples do come to rule in the kingdom—as Jesus elsewhere indicates they will (Matthew 19:28)—it will not be through asserting their will and forcing others to do what they, the disciples, want. If they rule, it will be a rule of service to others, because it is service, not power, that matters before God.

The Gospels are unified in portraying Jesus himself as the model of this kind of service. I do not need to provide a full discussion of this here—that would require an entire book. But no episode portrays the point more graphically than a famous scene in the Gospel of John, the last of our canonical Gospels. At his final meal with his disciples, Jesus rises from the table and takes on the role of a slave by washing their feet in turn (John 13:1–11). Peter wants nothing to do with this: Jesus is the master and he, his disciple, will not join in the charade. But Jesus tells him it is no charade. Peter must allow him to do what he came to do—to serve others—or he will have no part of him. For John's Gospel, following Jesus means following his example. He is not a master but a slave, and his followers are to be enslaved to the well-being of others as well. They are not to dominate but to serve.

Just as many Christians throughout the ages have not accepted Jesus's teachings about material possessions, so, too, with his teachings about lives devoted to service. Many readers suppose he could not have meant it, or at least didn't mean it for everyone. He may have meant that his followers should be good people and help others out on occasion, but he can't have meant that they should focus entirely on serving others for as long as they live. And he certainly did not envision an *eternity* of service to others. What kind of eternity is that? If Jesus comes from God, and God is Almighty, then surely the followers of Jesus are to be mighty, right?

HOW JESUS'S TEACHINGS MADE A DIFFERENCE: THE CHRISTIAN IDEOLOGY OF SERVICE

Even though many followers of Jesus over the centuries have rejected his teachings about power and dominance, not all have. Arguably the most significant impact Christianity made on the social and political world of antiquity involved its insistence that those with means should provide for those in need. This idea that the powerful should help the weak, that those who have should support those who have not, upended the understanding of human relations in the Roman world.[16]

If you had to choose one word to describe ancient Roman ideology, it would almost certainly be "dominance." The doctrine of dominance was not unique to the Romans, of course; it had been the unquestioned organizing principle of most societies since they came into existence. It was true politically, socially, and interpersonally. Scarcely anyone in antiquity challenged the idea that a more powerful city or empire should conquer one that was weaker, and there was almost no ethical problem with slaughtering the defeated population and enslaving any survivors.[17] Rome ran a slave economy: most slaves were prisoners of war and their descendants; it was not a racially based institution. Among the many treatises devoted to moral discourse by thinkers in antiquity from a range of philosophical schools—including the writings of, say, Seneca, Plutarch, and Marcus Aurelius—there is almost no moral objection to the ruthless activities of conquering armies or to slavery.

The ideology of dominance involved not just war but social practices. Great leaders were expected to dominate their subjects. Those who were powerful physically, mentally, or economically were expected to dominate the weak, the uneducated, and the poor. Recent studies have shown that something like 40 percent of the urban population in the Roman Empire was hovering around the poverty line, defined in this case as having enough resources to provide sufficient food, clothing, and shelter to survive. Another 30 percent was destitute. There was no ethical problem with that—no ethical need to help the impoverished.[18] As a bevy of studies has shown, in the Roman world, when the wealthy elite gave money away it was not to assist those in need. It was either a way for the rich to help out those in their own socioeconomic class—for example, family members fallen on hard times—or to fund municipal projects such as the construction of buildings or the financing of public entertainments that would bring honor to themselves. These contributions could indeed sometimes help those who were not well-off, who might be able to use the public buildings and enjoy some of the gladiator shows. But that is not *why* the wealthy funded these projects. It was all about advancing their public recognition; that is, for personal gain. Nearly the only time wealthy leaders bestowed funds on the poor was to buy their vote. These may seem like broad generalizations, but they are substantiated in our surviving sources time and time again.[19]

Dominance also happened within the home. Adults, of course, dominated children, which is why it was so surprising for Jesus to say that a person had to become a child to enter the kingdom. And naturally, men were expected to dominate women domestically, financially, and sexually. Nor was there any problem with a master making his slaves do what he wanted, including sexually. Indeed, there was no shame in a male master having sex with a male slave, no moral problem with it being "unnatural." Quite the contrary: domination was natural.

The Christians who propagated Jesus's teachings argued for a different ideology. I am not saying they all followed this ideology or even that most of them did. But Christian leaders in the early church began to preach that it was important to serve others. Those with means were to provide for those without. Widows and orphans were to be helped and the destitute were to be cared for. Helping those in need now would bring "treasures in heaven."

But it was not long before Christians began to imagine that this meant material treasures, that giving money to the poor was a kind of long-term investment in the bank of heaven. That was decidedly not what Jesus said, but it was a misunderstanding that in some respects ended up doing the world a considerable amount of good.

Christians transformed the idea of paying for municipal buildings and public entertainments into the idea of giving charity to the poor. This was not a Christian invention, of course; it arose centuries before within Judaism.[20] Jesus stood in a long line of Jewish prophets who insisted that the people of God help those in need. His followers picked up the charge—not in the radical way he preached, but enough to make a significant difference. Prior to

Christianity, there were no such things as hospitals, orphanages, or organized charities to help the poor. These are Christian institutions that emerged in the Roman world.

This was a shift in the dominant paradigm, but not all Christians came on board. Many, many Christians continued to follow their human impulse for economic, physical, and social power. Eventually the Roman empire became Christian, and the impulse to dominate became ever more possible for Christians to fulfill. Among other things, many (most?) of the most highly placed Christian leaders urged their own understandings of religious belief and practice, leading to the almost complete domination of Jews, pagans, and Christian heretics through imperial policy backed with legislation supporting the established church.[21]

The Christianity that passed through Late Antiquity, the Middle Ages, the Reformation, and down till today was and is highly complex and incredibly diversified. But at every point in history one can ask: Were there Christians who actually took Jesus seriously when he said that the way to be great was to live a life of service and to be willing to give one's life for others? Absolutely yes. There were and are. There are far more, however, who have thought he didn't really mean for his followers to be so extreme about it, or who have believed that the point of service now is to attain domination later—that love of others in the present is the path to complete control over them in the future. Others go further still: once their period of service is over, they will happily watch those they served be slaughtered before their eyes.

DOMINATION IN THE BOOK OF REVELATION

Where does John of Patmos fit on this spectrum? There is really not much doubt. In his narrative, when the catastrophes have run their course, Jesus's followers are granted world dominion. To understand more fully what that might mean, we have to consider what remains of the population of earth at that point. That task, as we have seen, is complicated by the hopeless stream of inconsistencies in the final two chapters of Revelation.

John's enthusiasm for widespread destruction, in the end, got the better of him. Already in chapter 6 of Revelation, the entire cosmos falls apart. But in chapter 7, the world and the people in it live on. The obvious explanation is that John is not literally describing the end of the sun, moon, stars, and sky. But that creates a problem. If John constantly engages in rhetorical excess, how can we imagine what he actually envisages?

This problem becomes especially acute at the end of the account, when God grants the martyrs their wish to have their blood avenged on "the inhabitants of earth," not just those responsible for their deaths. At the last judgment, *everyone* whose name does not appear in the "book of life"—that is, everyone who is not a follower of Jesus—is sent to the second death in "the lake of fire" (20:11–15). There does not seem to be much room for discussion. Doesn't "everyone" mean *everyone*? John makes this point even more emphatic: after all the people not found in the book of life are thrown into the fiery lake, then Death and Hades themselves are. There will be no more death, no more realm of the dead, no more people to sin and die. Only those who follow the Lamb are left, and immediately the prophet sees the new heaven and new earth appear, the "holy city, the new Jerusalem, coming down out of heaven from God" (21:1–2).

So that is that. Except it's not. As we have seen, after John describes the glorious new city of gold, we learn that "the nations will walk by its light" (21:24). But why are there nations? We also learn that "the kings of the earth will bring their glory into" the new Jerusalem (21:24). What kings? No one "who practices abomination or falsehood" will enter the city (21:27). Who is practicing abomination (idolatry) or falsehood (sin) if there is no one left? The answer seems obvious: for the saints to dominate, there need to be others left.

However one resolves the inconsistencies and however much metaphor one wants to assign to the text, there can be no mistake about its controlling motif. John's passion for complete domination completely dominates.

And not only at the book's end. The idea that God and his Christ hold absolute power permeates the book from the very beginning. In the opening lines, Christ is described as "the ruler of the kings of the earth" (1:5), who by dying received the "glory and dominion forever and ever" (1:6). With his own first words, God proclaims his universal dominance: "I am the Alpha and the Omega, says the Lord God, who is and who was and who is to come, the Almighty" (1:8). The English word "Almighty" is a bit weak for the Greek term used here: *Pantokrator*, a rare word, or at least it was before the book of Revelation. The word almost never appears in Greek before the New Testament and only once in all the other twenty-six books of the New Testament combined (2 Corinthians 6:18). But John uses it nine times. It means something like "the one who exercises his power over all things." That is, of course, what "Almighty" means, but that more common word gets used so often that its force has been tamed. The *Pantokrator* is more powerful than anything in existence.

Conquest is another major feature of Revelation. The verb "conquer" is used seventeen times in the book, more than in all the rest of the New Testament. It is important to realize, though, that this "conquering"—which God's slaves are urged to do—does not mean only "destroying." It also means "dominating" those who are not destroyed. We see this early on in the book, in the letter to the church of Thyatira, where Christ promises his followers: "To everyone who conquers and continues to do my works to the end, I will give authority over the nations; to shepherd them with an iron rod as when clay pots are shattered" (2:26). This is a harsh image, taken from Psalm 2:7. These "shepherds"—the followers of Jesus—will not have a wooden crook to keep their flocks in line, but a "rod of iron" capable of shattering pots and (presumably) cracking skulls (22:3).

Thus, the book of Revelation is all about levels of domination. God the Father is *Pantokrator* (*All*-mighty). Christ who implements God's will is the conqueror of earth, the Lord of Lords and King of Kings. His followers have been purchased by him and are his slaves but are also kings of earth who rule over all other nations, those left outside the city who can only benefit from the light it casts out. And the minor rulers of the other nations bring whatever "glory" they have to the golden city to benefit their lords. This is world domination, world without end.

IN THE END: SERVICE OR DOMINATION?

Is this obsession with domination consistent with the teachings of Jesus? As I have already noted, there is not a single word in all of Revelation about God loving others and no instruction to the followers of Christ to do so, either. Instead, they are called to be "conquerors." Once they overwhelm the rest of the earth with divine military might, they shall become its rulers, kings who control "the nations with a rod of iron." Whether John meant this literally is beside the point. This is how he sees God, Christ, his followers, and the rest of the human race: as powerful rulers and abject subjects.

Is this what Jesus meant when he told his followers to abandon all desire for greatness? To live lives of service? To become slaves? In the book of Revelation, Christ's followers are slaves, but only to God. They hate everyone outside their rank and want their blood to spill (6:10), just as Christ himself despises those who are not true believers—even members of his own churches (2:6, 15, 2–23). The slaves of God are not instructed to love, serve, or help anyone—even when they have the power to do so. They live in the new Jerusalem, a city where their every need is met and life is so good they no longer ever shed a tear, for all eternity. Do they use the city's wealth to help those outside? No. Those outside don't matter, except to the extent that they bring their wealth into the city. But no one who engages in abomination or falsehood can do so, because no sinners could possibly set foot in the city of gold where Christ resides. Was that Jesus's view? Did he shun sinners? In Revelation, Jesus and his followers do not come to serve and to give their lives for others. They come to destroy the lives of others and to be served. It is difficult indeed to see how Jesus would countenance such a view.

John of Patmos is certainly a committed Christian. He is a passionate follower of the Lamb who wreaks vengeance on earth, a slave of God to the very end. But is he the kind of Christian that Jesus would recognize? In the final chapter I reflect further on that question.

EIGHT

The Apocalypse of John and the Gospel of Jesus

The book of Revelation was one of the least copied and read books of the New Testament and had difficulty making its way into the canon. In the first four Christian centuries, it was accepted mainly by the churches of the western part of the empire, where some leaders such as Irenaeus, Hippolytus, and Victorinus cited it as an authoritative text. Other writers found its message dangerous and claimed it was forged in the name of the apostle John. In the eastern empire, the book was for the most part not well received, for two reasons. For one thing, many church leaders found its crass materialism offensive. As Christian leaders began to stress the importance of a spiritual union with God rather than carnal, physical rewards for obedience, they considered Revelation hopelessly indebted to a view of leisure and pleasure embraced by the wider culture. The Christian faith was supposed to be different. The book, then, did not represent a revelation of the true God and his Christ.

In addition, eastern Christian leaders questioned whether the book was apostolic. The only books that could be truly authoritative were produced by one of Jesus's apostles or those close to them.[1] The author of Revelation certainly claims to be John, but there were numerous "Johns" in the early Christian community. The only "apostolic" John was Jesus's disciple, John the son of Zebedee. By the end of the second century, a virtual consensus emerged that he had written the Gospel of John and at least one of the letters that eventually became canonized (1 John; only later did 2 and 3 John came in on its coattails). These books all shared similar points of view and were closely connected in their themes and writing styles. What about Revelation?

The Apocalypse was often seen as quite different from the other writings, even in terms of style and grammar. This case was made most compellingly around 260 CE by a prominent bishop of Alexandria named Dionysius, in a long letter quoted by the fourth-century church historian Eusebius (*Church History* 7.25). Dionysius begins his assessment of Revelation by pointing out that some earlier church leaders had spurned the writing, in part because no one could make sense of it:

> Some of our predecessors rejected the book and pulled it entirely to pieces, criticizing it chapter by chapter, pronouncing it unintelligible and illogical and the title false. They say . . . it is not a revelation at all, since it is heavily veiled by its thick curtain of incomprehensibility.[2]

Since the apostles communicated their message clearly for the benefit of their readers, Dionysius's predecessors argued the so-called revelation could not have been produced by John or any other member of the apostolic band. Some came to think it had been forged in John's name by an infamous Christian heretic named Ce-rinthus.[3] His reason for doing so? To provide an allegedly apostolic sanction for his sensual lifestyle:

> This, they say, was the doctrine [Cerinthus] taught—that Christ's kingdom would be on earth; and the things he lusted after himself, being the slave of his body and sensual through and through, filled the heaven of his dreams— unlimited indulgence in gluttony and lechery at banquets, drinking-bouts, and wedding feasts.

Dionysius himself is not inclined to reject the book outright, since other Christians hold it in high regard. And he (humbly? coyly? disingenuously?) suggests that he is possibly simply too thick to un-derstand it. He goes on to say that since the author calls himself John, he sees no reason to deny that was his name: "But I am not prepared to admit that he was the apostle, the son of Zebedee and brother of James, who wrote the gospel entitled According to John and the gen-eral epistle (i.e., 1 John)." His main reason for assigning it to some different John was its "linguistic style and . . . general tone."

Toward the end of his letter, Dionysius provides a philological comparison of Revelation with the other Johannine writings, using arguments that scholars even today could, and often do, agree with:

> By the phraseology also we can measure the difference between the Gospel and Epistle and the Revelation. The first two are written not only without any blunders in the use of Greek, but with remarkable skill as regards diction, logical thought, and orderly expression. It is impossible to find in them one barbarous word or solecism, or any kind of vulgarism.

For Dionysius, this clarity and quality of style stand in stark contrast with what we find in the book of Revelation. Unlike the apostle John, the man really just can't write. So it must be a different author.

The views expressed by Dionysius struck a chord with many church leaders in the east—not surprisingly, since they were reading the books of the New Testament in Greek. (The west mainly used Latin.) It was well over a century before the book came to be accepted more widely as a part of Scripture. This acceptance was driven by several factors. For one thing, Revelation proved useful for orthodox thinkers during the great theological controversies of the fourth century. The most significant debate involved the nature of Christ: Was he a divine being who was subordinate to God the Father, a second-level divinity who came into existence at some point in eternity past? Or was he completely equal with God the Father in power and fully eternal? The latter position eventually won out, and the book of Revelation proved useful to that end. As I have noted, God identifies himself as "the Alpha and the Omega" twice in the book (1:8 and 21:6). But Christ does as well: "I am the Alpha and the Omega, the first and the last, the beginning and the end" (22:13). If both God and Christ claim to be the beginning and end of all things, they are, then, equal and both fully eternal, at least in the argument of the orthodox theologians.

Another factor leading to the acceptance of the book involved the "spiritualized" reading of Revelation popularized by the great authoritative figure Augustine. As we have seen, in this reading, the book is not about upcoming calamities, which will end with the sensual glories of a literal thousand-year reign of Christ and his saints. The millennium is happening now. Jesus's followers have been made alive in the spirit and been granted power over the forces of evil; the Devil cannot touch those with the spirit of Christ. If that's what the book means—if it was not, in fact, a celebration of a coming age of exquisite banquets and exotic pleasures—then for many ancient readers, there was no real obstacle to taking it as apostolic. Once that hurdle was cleared, church leaders became more forgiving of its writing style and came to think that it probably was written by the apostle John after all. As with all the books of the Bible, there was no actual *vote* at a worldwide church council to include Revelation in Scripture; it came to be accepted more or less as a matter of informal consensus.[4]

Doubts lingered, however, and as I have indicated, the book was not widely read over the centuries. Well over a millennium later, at the time of the Protestant Reformation, when Martin Luther produced his classic German translation of the Bible, he placed Revelation in an appendix along with three other books (Hebrews, Jude, and James) because he did not think that they "preached Christ." That is, he did not think Revelation presented the ideas of Christ's salvation adequately (or at all); it was therefore, he believed, not authoritative on the level of the other books of the New Testament.

THE COMING DESTRUCTION: JOHN AND JESUS

Whatever Martin Luther thought, it is clear that John of Patmos believed he was "preaching Christ." He was a fiercely devoted Christian with unusually firm ideas about what it meant to follow Jesus. But we need to return to a question raised in earlier chapters. Is the Christ that John proclaims the Jesus of the Gospels?

Readers today should bear in mind the objections raised to John's Apocalypse by its opponents in the early church, who found its views inconsistent with the Christian message, largely because of its materialist bent. Most modern Christians might be less concerned about the sensual character of the book per se, since few believe bodily pleasure should be wholly avoided in the pursuit of an ascetic style of life, especially for all eternity. But the materialism of the book is still troubling, especially in comparison with the New Testament teachings of Jesus. So, too, is its emphasis on sheer violence and passion for dominance.

I do not want to paint an overly rosy picture of Jesus in the New Testament accounts of his life. Throughout the Gospels, Jesus, too, declares that a judgment of God is soon to come, a judgment that will involve widespread destruction. Or at least he makes this apocalyptic proclamation in three of them. It is striking that this is not Jesus's message in the final Gospel, the Gospel of John. This creates the rather enormous irony, not lost on modern scholars, that the Apocalypse of John and the Gospel of John embrace completely different understandings of the "end-times." The Apocalypse is all about the judgment that will hit this planet when God destroys his enemies and brings his followers into a heavenly city here on earth for life everlasting. The Gospel maintains that those who believe in Jesus *already* have eternal life and that at death they will be rewarded with the glories of heaven (for example, John 5:24, 6:47, 14:1–7)— *not* in an earthly city of God. These views appear to be at odds, and they help confirm that the two books are by two different authors.

In the earlier Gospels, however, Jesus does regularly proclaim that the Kingdom of God is soon to arrive here on earth and that if people want to enter into it, they need to repent; otherwise they will be destroyed. We find this message already in the oldest recorded saying of Jesus. His first words in our earliest Gospel, Mark, are: "The time has been fulfilled; the Kingdom of God is near. Repent and believe the good news" (Mark 1:15). This is an apocalyptic image: God's kingdom is almost here and people need to prepare. That it is reported as "good news," not "bad news." It is a message of hope, of salvation. All those who return to God, who "repent" of their misdeeds and their misguided lives and begin to live in ways God approves, will receive a glorious reward. Jesus does not call on people to believe in him for salvation or to avoid all contact with

Rome. And he offers this advice freely. Unlike in the book of Revelation, he does not threaten to attack them with the sword if they refuse.

Jesus does indeed portray God as a judge in Matthew, Mark, and Luke, and God will certainly condemn those who do not turn to him. But it is important to stress: in these Gospels salvation comes to those who accept Jesus's call to live differently. Those who live as God directs—in service to others—will be saved in the coming conflagration. Salvation is not based on any particular religious beliefs, nationality, or cultural heritage. It is based on the commandment to love.

In an earlier chapter, I discussed the rich man who approaches Jesus and asks how to have eternal life. Jesus tells him simply, "Keep the commandments" (Mark 19:17). He then enumerates them: Don't murder, don't commit adultery, don't steal, etc. When the man pursues the question about whether he has done enough, Jesus instructs him to sell all his possessions and give his money to the poor. His entire response addresses the man's behavior. Jesus does not say, "Believe in me for salvation, become my slave, and definitely, absolutely, do not eat meat offered to pagan idols or I will kill your children."

One of the most informative and powerful of Jesus's teachings about the coming judgment is found in the parable of the sheep and the goats (Matthew 25:31–46), which encapsulates the contrast between the views of Jesus and John of Patmos. Jesus describes the future king at the end of time sitting on his throne with "all the nations" of earth before him. These are assembled into two groups, the "sheep" on his right and the "goats" on his left. The king first speaks to the sheep and calls them blessed, welcoming them into the kingdom God has long prepared for them. And he tells them why they have been saved: "Because I was hungry and you gave me something to eat, thirsty and you gave me something to drink, a foreigner and you welcomed me, naked and you clothed me, sick and you visited me. . . ." The sheep are overjoyed, but, at the same time, surprised: they have never seen the king or done any of these good things for him. But he tells them that since this is how they acted toward the most lowly of his brothers and sisters, they did so to him.

He then turns to the goats and tells them they are cursed and must enter into the fire that is prepared for the Devil and his angels. Again he explains why: unlike the sheep, they ignored him when he was hungry, thirsty, a foreigner, naked, and in prison. They, too, are surprised: they have never seen him in need. But again he explains: he means they did not take care of "the least of these," his brothers and sisters in need. The offenders are therefore sent to the flames to be destroyed.

In making sense of this parable, it is important to stress the most obvious point: the sheep and goats, who come from all the nations of earth, are judged according to how they lived their lives in relation to others who were in need. These are not lifelong followers of Jesus who have faithfully obeyed him for years. They've never seen him—hungry, thirsty, in prison, or otherwise. For Jesus himself, salvation does not hinge on what nation a person comes from (e.g., Israel), or what customs they follow (e.g., Jewish), or what god(s) they believe in. It does not depend on a personal commitment to Christ and him alone or a refusal to have anything to do with Rome and its rulers. Salvation depends on whether or not a person has helped those in need.

This message is repeated throughout Jesus's teachings. We learn of the "Good Samaritan" who is praised for helping a man left half-dead by the side of the road; the Samaritan is not a follower of Jesus, and certainly not a Jew (Luke 10:25–37). He is (in the story) a sworn enemy of the Jews. But he helps someone who is in need, and so he is praised for having fulfilled the Great Commandment, "You shall love your neighbor as yourself," in contrast to the religious leaders who refuse to offer any help.

It is a poor widow who gives her "two mites" who is praised by Jesus, not because of her sizable donation, but because she gave everything she had (Mark 12:41–44). Jesus did not track her out of the temple and urge her to become his follower. She had done what was needed.

It is rich Zacchaeus who has earned salvation in Jesus's eyes, because he gave half of all his goods to help the poor and, if he defrauded anyone, gave fourfold restitution (Luke 19:9). The passage says nothing about him becoming one of Jesus's followers or about his annual Roman tax bill.

I am not saying that Jesus did not seek followers in the Gospels. He preached his message precisely so people would accept his views and follow him. But in our earliest Gospel traditions, following Jesus meant following his example. It did not mean believing certain things about him, or accepting certain "truths" about his identity as a way of salvation, or taking a certain stand on imperial rule. Jesus told his followers to give of themselves for the sake of others, rather than focus on their own wants and needs. Those who never met him or had never heard of him could do that: thus the sheep and the Samaritan. Those who had met him were told to follow his own example by "denying themselves" (Mark 8:34), for "whoever would save his life" would have to "lose it" (Mark 8:35).

Yes, Jesus thought destruction was coming for sinners. He repeatedly discusses it. Strikingly, though, he never says anything about divinely sent misery, torture, or protracted deaths. The end will come suddenly, when no one expects it, and it will be decisive. Destruction would come to all who placed themselves above others, who refused to help others, who insisted on promoting their own pleasures and position even if it meant hurting others. People like that would be annihilated, but they would not be tortured. More-over, Jesus never talks about eternal torment; he talks about destruc-tion. And he certainly never regales his listeners with tales of blood and gore that will satisfy their longing for vengeance.[5]

Jesus was not out for vengeance in the early Gospels. He never uses his miraculous powers to hurt, maim, or kill anyone. He be-lieves in giving himself for others, going out of his way for others, giving his life for others. How different from the book of Revela-tion, where Christ is out for blood, ready to torture people into submission and then destroy them with the sword before raising them from the dead and having them thrown into burning sulfur.

As I have stressed: John of Patmos absolutely considered himself a follower of Christ. So did many others and so do many others. But it is important to recall one of the most trenchant passages of the entire New Testament, where Jesus indicates that many who have considered themselves his followers—who believe they have done his will, proclaimed his message, and been filled with his power—will be condemned at the end.

> Not everyone who says to me, "Lord, Lord," will enter into the kingdom of heaven, but the one who does the will of my Father in heaven. Many will say to me on that day, "Lord Lord, did I not prophesy in your name, and in your name cast out demons and in your name do many great deeds?" And then he will declare to them: "I never knew you. Depart from me, you who do evil." (Matthew 7:22–23)

Notice who these people are. They are those who call Jesus Lord. They not only believe in him, they devote themselves to doing mi-raculous deeds in his name. But they are condemned to judgment. Why? Because they did not do the will of God; they practiced evil.

That does not mean they were perversely wicked people. It means they did not do what Jesus told them to do. He told them to do the "will of my Father in heaven," and throughout his ministry he repeatedly told them what that was: helping those in need, giving to the poor, helping the sick, visiting the lonely, loving others as much as they loved themselves. Or even more: giving up their lives for others. Those who think following Jesus means doing "great deeds" in his name, but who do not act in loving ways toward others, are lost, even if they do insistently call Jesus their Lord.

This is the gospel of Jesus.

IMITATING JESUS—BUT WHICH ONE?

In one of the most influential scholarly assessments of Jesus ever written, *The Quest of the Historical Jesus*, theologian Albert Schweitzer argued that each generation of scholars has painted Jesus in its own image.[6] That is to say, the historical and cultural contexts of biblical scholars affect how they understand Jesus; they invariably portray him as a person of their own time who proclaimed their own perspectives. Schweitzer showed, for example, that Enlightenment scholars who rejected the supernatural wrote accounts of a non-miraculous Jesus whose alleged "miracles" were simply misunderstood by the pre-Enlightenment authors of the Gospels. That makes sense: if a scholar influenced by philosophical rationalism does not believe miracles are possible, then obviously he would be disinclined to believe Jesus performed miracles.

Schweitzer's view has been borne out with a vengeance over the past forty years. More than ever, it has become de rigueur to portray Jesus according to one's own ideological perspectives. And so we have scholars (not to mention preachers) who celebrate the Capitalist Jesus, the Marxist Jesus, the Feminist Jesus, the Countercultural Jesus, and the Political Revolutionary Jesus. The Nazis had an Aryan

Jesus. Among us still today there is a White Nationalist Jesus. Name your ideological preference and write your book.

This phenomenon has real-life consequences. Not only do people interested in Jesus paint him in their own image, they also model their lives on the image of Jesus they have painted. Those who see Jesus as a pacifist tend to oppose war and work for peace. Those who see Jesus as an advocate for the poor and needy often engage in volunteer work and generously share their own resources. Those who take to heart Jesus's teaching "Do not judge lest you be judged" are often open to the opinions and perspectives of others—not to mention their race, gender identity, nationality, religion, and everything else about them that makes them human. Those who see Jesus as one who loves and saves all people equally often work to bring justice and equality to the world. Scriptural portraits of Jesus in these modes can and do make the Christian message a beneficial reality.

But what about a portrait of Jesus that shows him as vengeful? Filled with wrath against those who do not believe in him? Infinitely powerful and determined to use his almighty force to dominate those he disapproves of, to harm them, torture them, and massacre them? The Jesus who once suffered but is now out to destroy his persecutors? The Jesus who is concerned with incredible displays of material wealth, whose followers will be rewarded with power and domination and allowed to rule the other peoples of earth with "a rod of iron"?

This is not the Jesus of the Gospels, but it *is* the wrathful Lamb of the Apocalypse. It is also the portrait of Christ many people prefer today. It is a portrait that enables and encourages Jesus's followers to embrace violence, vengeance, domination, and exploitation, to do whatever it takes to assert their will on others. Some of these people have been our neighbors. Some of them have been our leaders. Some of them very much want to be our leaders.

What would the Jesus of the Gospels make of them?

For those of us who choose to follow Jesus—whatever religious tradition we call our own—our understanding of Jesus will almost certainly affect how we model our lives. Is he the loving, peaceful Jesus found in the Gospels, ever attentive to the needs of others? Or is he the wrathful, vengeful Jesus of the Apocalypse, who seeks to hurt and destroy everyone outside his band? Each of us has to decide.

Notes

ONE: The End Is Near

1   It is rather difficult to differentiate cleanly between the religious views of "fundamentalists" and other "evangelicals," in large part because conservative Protestantism is a continuum. This is how I'm using the terms: "evangelical," in the broad sense, refers to Protestant Christians who are committed to the idea of personal salvation through a deeply spiritual experience, often described as being "born again." Only those who have this kind of personal relationship with Christ will be saved at death and awarded with heaven. Because of this belief, evangelicals are committed to propagating their faith by seeking to convert others (i.e., they believe in "evangelism"—literally, spreading the "good news"). Evangelicals have a high view of Scripture as the authoritative revelation of God that is true in what it affirms—though, for some evangelicals, not necessarily in every detail.

    Fundamentalism is a kind of far-right evangelicalism that stresses the inerrancy of the Bible. Scripture makes no mistakes of any kind, not just about theology but also about science, history, and everything else. Fundamentalists place a heavy emphasis on the literal truth of such traditional Christian doctrines as the virgin birth, the physical resurrection of Jesus, the atoning work of Christ's sacrifice on the cross, and his imminent second coming. These are among the Christian "fundamentals"—hence the name of the group, originally a moniker that leaders of the movement embraced. Fundamentalists tend to be distrustful of "human knowledge," scientific or otherwise, that goes beyond what the Bible says.

For an important and unusually interesting study that argues most American evangelicals and fundamentalists today do not define themselves in such theological terms, or indeed even think much about them, see Kristin Kobes Du Mez, *Jesus and John Wayne: How White Evangelicals Corrupted a Faith and Fractured a Nation* (New York: Liveright, 2000). Du Mez argues that most American evangelicals understand their movement in terms of nationalism and rugged masculine values, rather than biblical authority, evangelism, and a "born-again" experience.

2 Edgar Whisenant, *88 Reasons Why the Rapture Is in 1988* (Nashville: World Bible Society, 1988).

3 Here is one of the simpler ones. In the Old Testament book of Daniel, the great king of Babylon, Nebuchadnezzar, has a dream during the second year of his reign (602 BCE). Nebuchadnezzar was eventually responsible for the destruction of Judea and the temple in Jerusalem. In Scripture the Babylonian conquest is interpreted as God's punishment of his people for their disobedience. In the dream, Nebuchadnezzar has a symbolic vision of the course of future history, with the overthrow of one kingdom after another until all are destroyed by a hidden divine force. The dream comes to be interpreted by the protagonist of the story, the Jewish prophet Daniel, who, unlike most of his compatriots, was faithful to God and therefore given unusual wisdom and an uncanny knack of interpreting dreams. Daniel explains to the king that the dream was about "what will happen at the end of days" (Daniel 2:28).

Whisenant argues that we who live thousands of years later can understand the dream only when we link it with another biblical text. He finds the key in Leviticus 26:28. Here God indicates that he will punish Israel "seven times" for its sins. That must mean "seven years," and since in the Jewish calendar a year is 360 days, and since often in the Bible a "day" means a "year"

(2 Peter 3:8), then: 7 x 360 shows that Israel will be punished for its sins for 2,520 years. The initial phase of the suffering began with the Babylonian exile experienced by Daniel, and it lasted for seventy years. And so, by subtracting the seventy years of captivity from the year of the dream itself (602 BCE minus 70) we come to 532 BCE. If the suffering then will last 2,520 years, it will end, remarkably, in 1988 (–532 + 2,520).

4 Whisenant, *88 Reasons*, 8.

5 Hal Lindsey with C. C. Carlson, *The Late Great Planet Earth* (Grand Rapids, MI: Zondervan, 1970).

6 See Paul Boyer, *When Time Shall Be No More: Prophecy Belief in Modern American Culture* (Cambridge, MA: Harvard University Press, 1992), 126.

7 For a particularly useful brief and accessible history of the misinterpretation of the book of Revelation, see Gerhard A. Krodel, *Revelation*, Augsburg Commentary on the New Testament (Minneapolis: Augsburg, 1989), 13–32.

8 One other major battle fundamentalists have won involves what it even means to be a Christian. Large numbers of theologians and less conservative lay Christians find it highly aggravating that fundamentalists have convinced the public that anyone who thinks the Bible has contradictions, historical mistakes, and various other problems can't be a Christian. What a strange view. Just to start with: If being a Christian means believing the Bible is literally true and without mistake, does that mean that the followers of Jesus living in the centuries before there was a Bible were not Christians? You will notice—if you pay attention to such things—that none of the traditional Christian creeds such as the Apostles' Creed, and the Nicene Creed says a single word about having to believe the Bible. The creeds do indicate what Christians jointly believe, but the Bible isn't mentioned. That's because the heart of Christian faith has always been belief in *Christ* as the way of salvation with the God who made the world. It is Christianity, not Biblianity.

9   Amy Johnson Frykholm, *Rapture Culture: Left Behind in Evangelical America* (New York: Oxford University Press, 2004). Frykholm also helpfully points out that this view of things can have very serious implications not only for personal religious belief but also for American social and political policies. That will be the subject of chapter 4.

10 See my comments in note 14.

11 Historian of modern religion Ernest R. Sandeen mentions one particularly egregious example: "Michael Baxter, a hardy British publicist, managed to predict incorrect dates from 1861 through 1908, presumably being saved only by death from an infinite series." Sometimes his predictions could be rather precise: "He once predicted that the second coming would be on March 12, 1903, between 2:30 and 3:00 p.m." Ernest R. Sandeen, *The Roots of Fundamentalism: British and American Millenarianism, 1800–1930* (Chicago: University of Chicago Press, 1970), 59, n1.

12 Edgar Whisenant, *The Final Shout: Rapture 1989 Report* (Nashville: World Bible Society, 1989).

13 Norman Cohn, *The Pursuit of the Millennium: Revolutionary Millenarians and Mystical Anarchists of the Middle Ages*, 2nd ed. (New York: Oxford University, 1970), 35.

14 Another intriguing example—out of many—is the aforementioned evangelist Jack Van Impe, who preached that the end was coming any day now from at least the early 1970s—when I heard him speak to a large convention—until his death in 2020. In his 1979 book, *Signs of the Times* (Royal Oak, MI: Jack Van Impe Ministries, 1979), Van Impe assures his readers that the rapture will be "very, very soon" (p. 9). His reason for thinking so: the Signs are "already in progress" (p. 19). He then lists these compelling signs that are different now from ever before in history. The list includes wars, famines, pestilences, earthquakes, illicit sex, drunkenness, and widespread iniquity. Seriously: that's what makes the world different in 1979 than ever before. Based in part on these shocking phenomena, Van Impe

comes up with a precise calculation for the rapture: it could be no further than three years away. But he acknowledges that his calculations "might be off by five years" (p. 66). When the rapture obviously hadn't happened three and then eight years later, he wrote another book explaining that *now* the signs were near. His list of signs was practically the same as before (Jack Van Impe, *11:59 . . . And Counting!* [Nashville: Thomas Nelson, 1987]). Then he wrote another book a decade later. So it goes, world without end.

15 For a sensitive and revealing documentary on Camping, recorded both while he was making his predictions in "the last days" and then in the aftermath of his final disappointment, see Zeke Piestrup, dir., *Apocalypse Later: Harold Camping vs. the End of the World*, 2013.

TWO: The Most Mystifying Book of the Bible

1 Quotations taken from Werner George Kümmel, *The New Testament: A History of the Investigation of Its Problems*, trans. S. McLean Gilmour and Howard Clark Kee (Nashville: Abingdon Press, 1972), 21–26.

2 He also questioned the authority of the books of Hebrews, James, and Jude. Luther pointed out that church fathers had had some doubts about all these books. He himself was not convinced the books "preached Christ" adequately. See Kümmel, *The New Testament*, 21–26.

3 If you're interested in a more detailed explanation passage by passage, see Bruce Metzger, *Breaking the Code: Understanding the Book of Revelation* (Nashville: Abingdon Press, 1993). The best scholarly commentary on the book, in my judgment, is Craig Koester, *Revelation*, The Anchor Yale Bible (New Haven, CT: Yale University Press, 2014). You can find a popular summation of Koester's commentary in his accessible book *Revelation and the End of All Things*, 2nd ed. (Grand Rapids, MI: Eerdmans, 2018).

4   In his popular book *Revelation and the End of All Things*, Koester gives a good early example: "A very literal translation of Rev. 1:4 would read that John sends greetings 'from He the is and He the was and He the coming one.'" Koester goes on to argue that John cannot be seen as a bad writer. Instead, since there are other places where his grammar is correct and his writing lucid, he simply chose to write strange Greek. I don't find that at all persuasive: I could say the same thing about the sophomore term papers I get every semester. Sometimes they get it right.

5   For anyone who wants to dig deeper into the issue, see Joseph Verheyden, "Strange and Unexpected: Some Comments on the Language and Imagery of the Apocalypse of John," in *New Perspectives on the Book of Revelation*, ed. Adela Yarbro Collins (Leuven, Belgium: Peeters, 2017), 161–206. The final option I give here is the one advanced by Koester, *Revelation*, p. 141, but laid out more extensively in his Great Courses course "Apocalypse: Controversies and Meaning in Western History," lecture 4, "Origins of the Book of Revelation."

6   Scholars today do not think that John the disciple wrote the Gospel, either, though that was the common view of Christian leaders starting at the end of the second century.

7   As Robert Royalty has pointed out, it is unusual (in both antiquity and today) to write an "open letter" criticizing a number of different communities, available for all to read in a kind of public airing of dirty laundry. Was the public nature of the letters meant to provide additional incentive for the churches to correct their ways?

8   See Adele Yarbro Collins, *Crisis and Catharsis: The Power of the Apocalypse* (Philadelphia: Westminster Press, 1984). This is a major study that gives evidence for the dating of Revelation to the time of Domitian, around 95 CE, and discusses at length the question of John's historical context.

9   See Yarbro Collins, *Crisis and Catharsis*, 84–110.

10 In antiquity authors who "dictated" letters were considered to

have been their "authors," even though someone else physically put pen to papyrus (see, for example, Romans 16:22, where "Tertius" calls himself the "writer" of Paul's letter to the Romans). It is surprising to many that Jesus is not only never said to have written anything but also that there is only one passage of the Gospels that indicates he could *read* (Luke 4:16–20).

11 I do not think that the fact that both Paul and John deal with the same issue shows that John is necessarily writing to "Pauline" Christians; the problem of whether to partake of meat offered to idols surely was a problem in many early Christian communities.

12 In 1 Corinthians 8, Paul agrees that pagan gods don't exist, but he does point out that eating the meat might lead astray other Christians who lack that understanding. Somewhat oddly, two chapters later, in 1 Corinthians 10, Paul argues that Christians should definitely not eat the meat because it involves Christians in demon worship. It is hard to reconcile these two views, but in either case he is considerably more relaxed than John.

13 John frequently alludes to Old Testament texts in describing his visions, especially to Ezekiel and Daniel; that is no surprise, since for him the Old Testament was authoritative Scripture. It is interesting, however, that he never quotes the Old Testament directly. In many instances he is almost "riffing" on these earlier texts, as scholars have long noted. Seeing how he has amplified and modified his source materials can help show what he is trying to emphasize. John's allusions to earlier writings can be seen through numerous verbal and conceptual parallels—as when, for example, he, like Daniel, speaks of a beast with seven heads and ten horns coming out of the sea. See pp. 132.

14 This strikes me as more likely than other interpretations, including the theory that they represent the twenty-four books of the Hebrew Bible (which number thirty-nine in English translations). The elders are people who have been rewarded with crowns; it seems implausible to me that they are anthropomorphized books.

15 God himself, of course, could have broken the seals, but that not only would have more or less destroyed the plotline, it also would not have made any sense: Why would he seal a document meant for someone else if he was going to break the seals? Just leave it unsealed.

16 It is striking that Revelation uses a different Greek word for lamb (ARNION) than the Gospel of John (AMNOS). It is not clear if or how the difference is significant.

17 For a good English translation of Victorinus's commentary, see William C. Weinrich, ed., *Latin Commentaries on Revelation* (Downers Grove, IL: Intervarsity Press Academic, 2011), 1–22; an introduction to his views is found on pages xx–xxiv. For an influential, modern endorsement of this view, see Yarbro Collins, *Crisis and Catharsis.*

18 We know of only a few Christian martyrs from the first century; even the persecution of Nero would almost certainly not have involved hundreds, let alone thousands. See Candida Moss, *The Myth of Christian Persecution: How Early Christians Invented a Story of Martyrdom* (San Francisco: HarperOne, 2013). On John of Patmos's *perception* of opposition, see Yarbro Collins, *Crisis and Catharsis.*

19 A third interlude introduces another beast, the "dragon"—an image of Satan—who appears in order to persecute a pregnant woman, who represents the nation of Israel, and so, the people of God (ch. 12). The woman gives birth to the child (Christ) who is to rule the nations. The dragon tries to swallow (that is, destroy) Christ but is unsuccessful. It then proceeds to persecute the children of the woman, who now represent the church. The vision is gloriously rich and complex, but all part of John's emphasis that the forces of evil in the world are empowered by Satan.

20 I am intentionally using the word "whore," as the author wants to castigate this figure as lascivious and dangerous; she is not a sex worker in the modern sense.

21 Many people have wondered if John used peculiar imagery in such passages in order to keep his message secret so only Christians would understand. The theory is that he did not want Romans to realize he was attacking them (leading to further persecution). It is an interesting theory, but biblical scholars have long considered it implausible, both because no one would expect non-Christians to have any interest in the book in the first place and because the symbols John uses would have been easily recognizable to anyone in his day. Any educated person at the time would have had no difficulty understanding what the "great city" that "ruled the nations" and was seated on "seven hills" would have been.

22 For a fuller discussion of this point, see my book *Heaven and Hell: A History of the Afterlife* (New York: Simon & Schuster, 2020), 213–32.

THREE: A History of False Predictions

1 See my discussion in Bart D. Ehrman, *The Apostolic Fathers*, The Loeb Classical Library (Cambridge, MA: Harvard University Press, 2003), 85–89. My quotations of Papias come from that edition.

2 It is included among the books of the New Testament in the important fourth-century manuscript Codex Sinaiticus.

3 Many of us will remember well another prediction that the world would end six thousand years after creation, this time in Y2K. This theory was based on the number crunching of the seventeenth-century Irish bishop James Ussher. (See the intriguing account of Stephen Jay Gould, *Questioning the Millennium: A Rationalist's Guide to a Precisely Arbitrary Countdown* [New York: Harmony, 1997], ch. 1.) By compiling numbers from a variety of sources, such as the lifespans of the earliest humans in Genesis, Ussher determined that God said, "Let there be light" on October 23, 4004 BCE, at noon. Ussher did not round his date of creation off to 4000 BCE because he, like everyone else

who knew about such things, believed Jesus was born in 4 BCE. (When the modern calendar was invented in the Middle Ages, it miscalculated the date of the death of Herod the Great, king of Israel when Jesus was born according to both Matthew and Luke. Herod died four years earlier than thought, in what became 4 BC. It is an intriguing error, since it would mean that Jesus was born four years Before Christ. See further Gould, *Questioning the Millennium*.) But that means that if Ussher was correct about the date of creation, and creation was to last six thousand years, it should have ended on October 23, 1996. Still, January 1, 2000, sounds more credible, so that was the date chosen.

4   See the intriguing study of R. Landes, "Let the Millennium Be Fulfilled: Apocalyptic Expectations and the Pattern of Western Chronography, 100–800 CE," in W. Verbeke, D. Verhelst, and A. Welkenhuysen, eds., *The Use and Abuse of Eschatology in the Middle Ages* (Leuven, Belgium: Leuven Katholieke Universiteit, 1988), 137–211.

5   See Landes, "Let the Millennium Be Fulfilled."

6   See William C. Weinrich, ed., *Latin Commentaries on Revelation* (Downers Grove, IL: Intervarsity Press Academic, 2011).

7   Philip Schaff, ed., *Nicene and Post-Nicene Fathers*, First Series (Peabody, MA: Hendrickson, 1994; originally published 1877), vols. 1–8. For a description of the extent of Augustine's writings and his view of Revelation, see Timothy Beal, *The Book of Revelation: A Biography* (Princeton, NJ: Princeton University Press, 2018), 49–69.

8   Translation of Marcus Dods, *The City of God* (New York: Random House, 1950).

9   This view is sometimes called "amillennialism," to distinguish it from "premillennialism" and "postmillennialism," which I will discuss later; see pp. 65–71.

10 See Beal, *The Book of Revelation*, 49–69.

11 For short introductions, see Norman Cohn, *The Pursuit of the Millennium: Revolutionary Millenarians and Mystical Anarchists of the*

Middle Ages, 2nd ed. (New York: Oxford University Press, 1970), 108–12, and Bernard McGinn, *Visions of the End: Apocalyptic Traditions of the Middle Ages* (New York: Columbia University Press, 1979), 126–42. For a translation of Joachim's writings, see McGinn, *Apocalyptic Spirituality* (Mahwah, NJ: Paulist Press, 1979), 97–148.

12 See Cohn, *Pursuit of the Millennium*, 108–12, and McGinn, *Apocalyptic Spirituality*, 149–82.

13 Ernest R. Sandeen, *The Roots of Fundamentalism, British and American Millenarianism, 1800–1930* (Chicago: University of Chicago Press, 1970), 5–7.

14 Edward King, *Remarks on the Signs of the Times* (London: George Nicol, 1798); from L. E. Froom, *The Prophetic Faith of Our Fathers*, vol. 2 (Tacoma Park, WA: Review and Herald,1948), 767. (See Sandeen, *The Roots of Fundamentalism*, 7.)

15 These were not the only contributing factors, of course. Also important were conservative Christian reactions to modernism in general, especially to the sciences (and not just Darwin), as well as to historical-critical studies of the Bible emanating from Germany.

16 See the helpful biography of Stanley Price and Munro Price, *The Road to Apocalypse: The Extraordinary Journey of Lewis Way* (London: Notting Hill Editions, 2011).

17 Price and Price, *The Road to Apocalypse*, 5.

18 The house still exists and is now registered with the National Trust.

19 Price and Price, *The Road to Apocalypse*, 8.

20 Price and Price, *The Road to Apocalypse*, 16–19. For a full study of the rise and ongoing effects of Christian Zionism, see Donald M. Lewis, *The Origins of Christian Zionism: Lord Shaftsbury and Evangelical Support for a Jewish Homeland* (Cambridge, UK: Cambridge University Press, 2014).

21 Sandeen, *The Roots of Fundamentalism*, 44.

22 According to Donald Kraus, the executive editor for Bibles at Oxford University Press in New York, in a private communication. It continues to sell extremely well today.

23 See, for example, Sandeen, *The Roots of Fundamentalism*, 222–24.

24 The Scofield Bible was anticipated in 1908 by the "Thompson Reference Bible," originally produced by Frank Charles Thompson. It, too, was highly conservative and also used the King James Version, but it was not nearly as commercially successful or influential as the Scofield.

25 The Scofield Bible published a second edition in 1917 and underwent a third revision in 1967, just four years before I was given my own engraved copy. For the matter-of-fact presentation of the seven dispensations as embedded in the Bible itself, see C. I. Scofield, ed., *The New Scofield Reference Bible* (New York: Oxford University Press, 1969), note on Revelation 20:4, 1373–74.

26 Most dispensationalists today focus on three of the dispensations, Law (with Promise seen as part of this), Church, and Millennium. For dispensationalist views before Darby, see Craig Blaising and Darrell Bock, *Progressive Dispensationalism* (Grand Rapids, MI: Baker, 1993), 118–19.

27 See my discussion of 1 Thessalonians 4:13–18 on pp. 9–12.

28 Among the most useful discussions of how these views developed over the years and so became the dominant perspective of conservative evangelicals are Paul Boyer, *When Time Shall Be No More: Prophecy Belief in Modern American Culture* (Cambridge, MA: Harvard University Press, 1992); Jonathan Kirsch, *A History of the End of the World: How the Most Controversial Book in the Bible Changed the Course of Western Civilization* (San Francisco: HarperOne, 2006); George Marsden, *Fundamentalism and American Culture*, 2nd ed. (New York: Oxford University Press, 2006); Sandeen, *The Roots of Fundamentalism*; Matthew Avery Sutton, *American Apocalypse: A History of Modern Evangelicalism* (Cambridge, MA: Belknap Press, 2004); and Timothy P. Weber, *Living in the Shadow of the Second Coming: American Premillennialism, 1875–1982*, enlarged ed. (Grand Rapids, MI: Zondervan, 1983).

29 For a discussion of the fuller range of issues connected with fundamentalist thought and history, see especially Sandeen, *The*

Roots of Fundamentalism, and Marsden, *Fundamentalism and American Culture.*

FOUR: Real-Life Consequences of the Imminent Apocalypse

1 Helpful overviews can be found in Ernest R. Sandeen, *The Roots of Fundamentalism: British and American Millenarianism, 1800–1930* (Chicago: University of Chicago Press, 1970), 50–54; Kenneth G. C. Newport, *Apocalypse and Millennium: Studies in Biblical Eisegesis* (Cambridge, UK: Cambridge University Press, 2000), 150–72; and, more fully, Stephen D. O'Leary, *Arguing the Apocalypse: A Theory of Millennial Rhetoric* (New York: Oxford University Press, 1994), 93–133.

2 Miller, *Apology and Defense,* 11–12, quoted in Newport, *Apocalypse and Millennium,* 160, n31.

3 For modern ways of understanding Daniel's visions, see the discussion of Daniel 7 on pp. 111–19.

4 Timothy P. Weber, *Living in the Shadow of the Second Coming: American Premillennialism, 1875–1982,* enlarged ed. (Grand Rapids, MI: Zondervan, 1983), 15.

5 Quoted in O'Leary, *Arguing the Apocalypse,* 108.

6 Quoted in Ronald L. Numbers and Jonathan M. Butler, eds., *The Disappointed: Millerism and Millenarianism in the Nineteenth Century* (Knoxville: University of Tennessee Press, 1993), 209.

7 Ronald D. Graybill, "The Abolitionist-Millerite Connection," in Numbers and Butler, *The Disappointed,* 143.

8 Leon Festinger, Henry W. Riecken, and Stanley Schachter, *When Prophecy Fails: A Social and Psychological Study of a Modern Group That Predicted the Destruction of the World* (Minneapolis: University of Minnesota Press, 1956).

9 As might be expected, the theory of cognitive dissonance has been widely used and discussed in the seventy years since *When Prophecy Fails* first appeared. For a helpful collection of essays,

see Jon R. Stone, *Expecting Armageddon: Essential Readings in Failed Prophecies* (New York: Routledge, 2000). For an interesting application of the theory to ancient Christianity, see John Gager, *Kingdom and Community* (Englewood Cliffs, NJ: Prentice-Hall, 1975).

10 Rodney Stark and William Sinns Bainbridge: *The Future of Religion: Secularization, Revival, and Cult Formation* (Berkeley: University of California Press, 1985), 487.

11 See Newport, *Apocalypse and Millennium*, 197–229.

12 Early Christianity scholar James Tabor alerted me to a video of members of the group that was recorded on the day of their disappointment. It is worth watching: https://youtu.be/ehZ0d1 jfTxM.

13 Particularly helpful is the synopsis in James D. Tabor, "The Waco Tragedy: An Autobiographical Account of One Attempt to Avert Disaster," in *From the Ashes: Making Sense of Waco*, ed. James R. Lewis (London: Rowman and Littlefield, 1994), 13–22; for the full account, see Tabor and Eugene V. Gallagher, *Why Waco: Cults and the Battle for Religious Freedom in America* (Berkeley: University of California Press, 1995). I have drawn my information from these two discussions. For a popular account, see Malcom Gladwell, "Sacred and Profane: How Not to Negotiate with Believers," *New Yorker*, March 24, 2014.

14 See especially Norman Cohn, *The Pursuit of the Millennium: Revolutionary Millenarians and Mystical Anarchists of the Middle Ages*, 2nd ed. (New York: Oxford University Press, 1970), and in particular the hair-raising account of the takeover of Münster, Germany, by militant Anabaptists in the 1530s, who believed they were initiating the new Jerusalem in fulfillment of the prophecies of Revelation, leading to massive starvation and slaughter (pp. 223–80).

15 Its roots, in fact, are much deeper, going back to seventeenth-century Calvinism and its understanding of the Jews as the chosen people; see especially Donald M. Lewis, *The Origins of*

Christian Zionism: Lord Shaftsbury and Evangelical Support for a Jewish Homeland (Cambridge, UK: Cambridge University Press, 2014), 8, 68. On Lewis Way, see pp. 62–65.

16 For an extensive account, see Lewis, *The Origins of Christian Zionism.*

17 Quoted in Stanley Price and Munro Price, *The Road to Apocalypse: The Extraordinary Journey of Lewis Way* (London: Notting Hill Editions, 2011), 106.

18 For an insightful discussion of Balfour and the Balfour Declaration, see Lewis, *The Origins of Christian Zionism,* especially pages 1–10.

19 As Stanley and Munro Price have pointed out, "Christian Zionism has been a core belief of millions of Americans since the late nineteenth century." Price and Price, *The Road to Apocalypse,* xiv.

20 As Quoted in Price and Price, *The Road to Apocalypse,* 114, 1.

21 Cited in P. R. Wilkinson, *For Zion's Sake: Christian Zionism and the Role of John Nelson Darby* (Colorado Springs, CO: Paternoster, 2007), 221.

22 Price and Price, *The Road to Apocalypse,* 114.

23 Joel C. Rosenberg, "Evangelical Attitudes Toward Israel Research Study: Evangelical Attitudes Toward Israel and the Peace Process," Chosen People Ministries, https://lifewayresearch.com/wp -content/uploads/2017/12/Evangelical-Attitudes-Toward-Israel -Research-Study-Report.pdf.

24 See Bart Ehrman, *Forged: Writing in the Name of God: Why the Bible's Authors Are Not Who We Think They Are* (San Francisco: HarperOne, 2011), 19–21, 105–8.

25 See especially the recent study of Robin Globus Veldman, *The Gospel of Climate Skepticism: Why Evangelical Christians Oppose Action on Climate Change* (Oakland: University of California Press, 2019). Veldman provides a helpful corrective to the idea that doctrinal beliefs are entirely responsible for evangelical apathy; in my judgment, however, she goes too far in the other direction, underplaying the theological underpinnings of the apathy.

In Veldman's accounting, conservative evangelicals regularly informed her they were not concerned about the environment because "God would take care of it" or because "Jesus is coming back soon anyway." See the interviews she cites on pages 63, 64, 69, 72, 102, 113—among others. We should also not forget that there are millions and millions of atheists and agnostics as well who contribute to environmental and climate apathy.

26 Veldman provides a useful discussion of the matter: *The Gospel of Climate Skepticism*, 28–35, 37–39.

27 Veldman, *The Gospel of Climate Skepticism*, 30.

28 As quoted in Veldman, *The Gospel of Climate Skepticism*, 38, with bibliography.

29 Lynn White, "The Historical Roots of Our Ecologic Crisis," *Science* 155, no. 3767 (March 10, 1967): 1203–7.

30 Sophie Bjork-James, "Lifeboat Theology: White Evangelicalism, Apocalyptic Chronotopes, and Environmental Politics," *Ethnos* (November 2020): 1–21, esp. 14–17.

31 See especially James L. Guth et al., "Faith and the Environment: Religious Beliefs and Attitudes on Environmental Policy," *American Journal of Political Science* 39, no. 2 (May 1995): 364–82.

32 "Many Americans Uneasy with Mix of Religion and Politics," Pew Research Center, August 24, 2006, https://www.pewfo rum.org/2006/08/24/many-americans-uneasy-with-mix-of-reli gion-and-politics/.

33 "Public Sees a Future Full of Promise and Peril: Section 3: War, Terrorism, and Global Trends," Pew Research Center, June 22, 2010, https://www.pewresearch.org/politics/2010/06/22/section -3-war-terrorism-and-global-trends/.

34 David C. Barker and David H. Bearce, "End-Times Theology, the Shadow of the Future, and Public Resistance to Addressing Global Climate Change," *Political Research Quarterly* 66, no. 2 (May 1, 2012): 272.

35 Bjork-James, "Lifeboat Theology," 11.

36 Joel Slemrod, "Saving and the Fear of Nuclear War," *Journal of Conflict Resolution* 30, no. 3 (September 1986): 403–19.

37 Barker and Bearce, "End-Times Theology," 269.

38 Barker and Bearce, "End-Times Theology," 270.

39 As shown in Bjork-James, "Lifeboat Theology."

FIVE: How to Read the Book of Revelation

1 One other important early Christian apocalypse was also written under the actual name of the author, the Shepherd of Hermas. We don't know a lot about the author, but he was a Roman Christian living in the early part of the second century. His book was unusually popular in the early church; some church leaders considered it part of the New Testament. See my introduction and translation in Bart Ehrman, *The Apostolic Fathers*, vol. 2, Loeb Classical Library (Cambridge, MA: Harvard University Press, 2003), 161–474.

2 For an excellent commentary on Daniel, see John J. Collins, *Daniel* (Minneapolis: Fortress Press, 1993). Collins discusses all the key historical and interpretive issues in the book.

3 As you might have noticed, John of Patmos picks up a good bit of this imagery in the book of Revelation, most obviously a beast of the sea with ten horns who persecutes the saints (see Revelation 13).

4 For the historical context, see Shaye Cohen, *From the Maccabees to the Mishnah*, 3rd ed. (Louisville, KY: Westminster John Knox, 2014). It is important to note that there were strong disagreements over the value of Antiochus's Hellenizing policies among Jews in Israel. Many believed they were a cultural advance; others thought they were an affront to traditional practices and the true worship of God. The conflicts and the resulting uprising are narrated in the book of 1 Maccabees.

5 See Collins, *Daniel*, 274–324.

6   For a full analysis of the linguistic evidence for the dating of Daniel, see Collins, *Daniel*, 17, who argues that the Aramaic used suggests that it was written no earlier than the end of the fourth century BCE. On other grounds he concludes that it was written during the reign of Antiochus Epiphanes, as I explain here.

7   See the classic study of Adele Yarbro Collins, *The Combat Myth in the Book of Revelation* (Missoula, MT: Scholars Press, 1976).

8   As it still is even today, despite the massive reference resources we have. How many of us can say who the president was in 1891?

9   For a full discussion, see Collins, *Daniel*, 304–10.

10 See the groundbreaking work of John Collins, ed., *Apocalypse: The Morphology of a Genre*, *Semeia 14* (Missoula, MT: Society of Biblical Literature, 1979).

11 See Craig Koester, *Revelation*, Anchor Yale Bible Commentaries (New Haven, CT: Yale University Press, 2015) as a prime example. Other historically based commentaries for nonacademic audiences include Gerhard A. Krodel, *The Augsburg Commentary on the New Testament: Revelation* (Minneapolis: Augsburg, 1989), and Leonard L. Thompson, *Revelation*, Abingdon New Testament Commentaries (Nashville: Abingdon, 1998). See also, among many other works, the discussions of Elisabeth Schüssler-Fiorenza, *The Book of Revelation: Justice and Judgment* 2nd ed. (Minneapolis: Fortress, 1998), and Adele Yarbro Collins, *Crisis and Catharsis: The Power of the Apocalypse* (Philadelphia: Westminster Press, 1984).

12 As an example out of a multitude: Peter Jensen, *Apocalypse 2027: Antichrist Unmasked* (Coppell, TX: Quanonical Books, 2018), 10–11.

13 They also represent seven kings, five who had ruled, one said to be ruling at the time John was writing, and one yet to come. Interpreters have had a field day with the passage, trying to use it to work out exactly when Revelation was written. The problem is that there are about 666 proposals, depending on several

factors, including which "king" of Rome one starts with (Julius Caesar? Augustus?) and whether all rulers are to be counted or only some: What, for example, of the single year 69 CE, when there were four emperors in quick succession? Do we just skip the first three, since they were knocked off by competitors in short order? (See table 1 in Koester, *Revelation* [Anchor Yale Bible], 72–73.) It is almost certainly best to see the number "seven" in this case not as a literal enumeration of kings but as another diabolic mirror image of the divine number.

14 For a brief survey, see Bernard McGinn, *Antichrist: Two Thousand Years of the Human Fascination with Evil*, 2nd ed. (New York: Columbia University Press, 2000), 260.

15 See pp. 55–56. It helps to consider the explicit connections of the angel's explanation with what we find in chapter 17. The author says here that the puzzle of the name "calls for wisdom" (13:18). He says nearly the same thing when he explains the Whore of Babylon as Rome (17:9). Moreover, the beast of chapter 17 has seven heads and ten horns, as does this one. Finally, this beast, like the later one, persecutes Christians, corrupts the earth, and exerts massive economic control over its world (13:5–7, 16–17; see also the condemnation of "Babylon," the fallen city, in 18:1–24).

16 See Tacitus, *Histories* 2.8, 9; Suetonius, *Life of Nero*, 57.

17 Sibylline Oracles 4.119–24; 5.137–49; 5.361–85; found in John Collins, "The Sybilline Oracles," in James H. Charlesworth, ed., *The Old Testament Pseudepigrapha*, vol. 1 (Garden City, NY: Doubleday, 1983), 318–472.

18 See my discussion in Bart Ehrman, *How Jesus Became God: The Exaltation of a Jewish Preacher from Galilee* (San Francisco: HarperOne, 2014), 27–28.

19 See James Rives, *Religion in the Roman Empire* (Oxford, UK: Blackwell, 2007), 148–56.

SIX: The Lamb Becomes a Lion:
Violence in the Book of Revelation

1 The only survivors are Rahab, the prostitute who protected Joshua's spies when they originally scouted out the land, and her family.

2 These are sayings scattered throughout the Gospels; the most famous concentration of Jesus's teachings can be found in the Sermon on the Mount, Matthew 5–7; see especially, for example, the Antitheses of Matthew 5:21–48.

3 For an overview and discussion, see Bart D. Ehrman, *The Bible: A Historical and Literary Introduction*, 2nd ed. (New York: Oxford University Press, 2018), 90–106.

4 See the discussions in Ehrman, *The Bible*, 123–51, 163–79.

5 John Dominic Crossan, "Divine Violence in the Christian Bible," in Robert Jewett, Wayne Alloway, and John Lacey, eds., *The Bible and the American Future* (Eugene, OR: Wipf and Stock, 2010), 227–28.

6 As Pieter G. R. de Villiers puts it, the text supports a "divine hegemony with a coercive nature: it will ultimately assert itself completely over those who differ from or oppose it. The book is clear that those who are not part of the author's community and adhere to his prophecy, are enemies who deserve to be annihilated." See his article, "The Violence of Nonviolence in the Revelation of John," *Open Theology* 1, no. 1 (January 2015): 194. For fuller treatments of violence in Revelation, see Greg Carey, *Elusive Apocalypse: Reading Authority in the Revelation of John* (Macon, GA: Mercer, 1999) and Christopher A. Frilingos, *Spectacles of Empire: Monsters, Martyrs, and the Book of Revelation* (Philadelphia: University of Pennsylvania Press, 2004).

7 See Carey, *Elusive Apocalypse*, 162, who points out, with respect to the torments of locusts, that the passage shows that, for John, "'the inhabitants' [of earth] are less than human. John shows less regard for them than he does for plants and animals. It is not

surprising that . . . heavenly orders tell the locusts to spare even the *plants* and afflict only *humans*" (9:4.)

8   The book's glorious and triumphalist rhetoric leads many to overlook this emphasis on divine wrath leading to horrific violence. As explained in a penetrating analysis by Christopher Frilingos: "The poetical force of the book is unquestionable, great enough to obscure for many readers the details of its disturbing plot, in which the earth and its inhabitants are systematically destroyed to make room for a universe of Christian 'conquerors.'" Frilingos, *Spectacles of Empire*, 1.

9   This view is argued at length in Loren L. Johns, *The Lamb Christology of the Apocalypse of John* (Tübingen, Germany: Mohr Siebeck, 2003), and D. J. Neville, *Peaceable Hope: Contesting Violent Eschatology in New Testament Narratives* (Grand Rapids, MI: Baker Academic, 2013). An unusually effective rebuttal, which shows that such sanguine claims about the book are just not true, can be found in Jan Willem van Henten, "Violence in Revelation," in *New Perspectives on the Book of Revelation*, ed. Adela Yarbro Collins (Leuven, Belgium: Peeters, 2017), 49–77.

10   It is not clear from the context whether the martyrs are calling out to God or Christ as "the holy and true Master." The literal translation of the Greek is "Despot."

11   Recall the sequence of suffering in chapters 6–16 (this is not a complete list!): heaven-sent war; economic collapse and the death of one-fourth of the human population; a third of all vegetation burned to a crisp; a third of the sea turned to blood; a third of all sea creatures killed; a third of all ships on earth destroyed; a third of springs and rivers turned to poison; torturous locusts; another third of the human race killed; horrible sores; the death of all sea creatures; all rivers and streams turned to blood; solar heating beyond what humans can endure; the blackening of the sun; massive hail; and on it goes.

12   See Greg Carey, *Elusive Apocalypse: Reading Authority in the Revelation of John* (Macon, GA: Mercer, 1999), 136: "From John's

perspective there are no other perspectives. All voices who might utter a contrary word must be silenced. That they may be relatively close to John's own point of view or diametrically opposed is of no consequence; John rejects such distinctions. Only a few have their names in the book of life (13:8; 17:8; 21:27); the rest of the world faces destruction."

13   See pp. 35–36.

14   That certainly is what some of the authors of the Dead Sea Scrolls thought, as did John the Baptist before Jesus and the apostle Paul after.

15   See his article "The Violence of Nonviolence in the Revelation of John," 194. This much is clear not only from the relatively recent example of the Branch Davidians but from a very long history of apocalyptic violence. See, for example, Norman Cohn, *The Pursuit of the Millennium: Revolutionary Millenarians and Mystical Anarchists of the Middle Ages*, 2nd ed. (New York: Oxford University Press, 1970).

16   See Carey, *Elusive Apocalypse,* 162: The eschatological worship of God is "the acknowledgment of God's greatness, given the fact of God's judgment. That the inhabitants' worship is motivated primarily by fear simply confirms Revelation's morbid fascination with vengeance. It is the worship of an imperial conqueror by a vanquished people."

SEVEN: The Ideology of Dominance: Wealth and Power in Revelation

1   D. H. Lawrence, *Apocalypse* (1931; New York: Viking Press, 1960).

2   Most useful is Lawrence's autobiographical sketch in *Apocalypse*, 3–14. For an intriguing discussion of Lawrence's personal religion—he considered himself highly religious, but in a thoroughly nontraditional way—see Luke Ferretter, *The Glyph and the Gramophone: D. H. Lawrence's Religion* (London:

Bloomsbury, 2013). In the most recent biography, Francis Wilson's magisterial *Burning Man: The Trials of D. H. Lawrence* (New York: Farrar, Straus and Giroux, 2021), only two sentences (in 488 pages) are given over to *Apocalypse*.

3 Ferretter (*The Glyph and the Gramophone*, 141–47) provides a nice evaluation of *Apocalypse* in relation to Lawrence's general views and helpfully shows how his technical discussion of the book of Revelation relates to biblical scholarship of his time.

4 For a full analysis, see Robert M. Royalty Jr., *Streets of Heaven: The Ideology of Wealth in the Apocalypse of John* (Macon, GA: Mercer University Press, 1997). For an interpretation that brings in a good deal of social history—what wealth was like in Rome in those days—see Richard Bauckham, "The Economic Critique of Rome in Revelation 18," in *Images of Empire*, eds. Loveday Alexander and Steven McKenzie (London: Bloomsbury, 2009), 47–90.

5 *Apocalypse*, p. 17 (emphasis his).

6 *Apocalypse*, pp. 187–89 (emphasis his).

7 *Apocalypse*, p. 197.

8 Christopher A. Frilingos, *Spectacles of Empire: Monsters, Martyrs, and the Book of Revelation* (Philadelphia: University of Pennsylvania Press, 2004), 1. Frilingos points out that scholarly interpreters typically (and correctly) identify Rome as the enemy in Revelation. But they also assume that John wants to present an alternative to the Roman ideology of domination by embracing an alternative ideology. The thesis of his book is that, in fact, John models his descriptions of the coming catastrophes on Roman "spectacles," where crowds gather in the arena to observe gladiators, animal hunts, and public executions. The crowds are excited by the spectacle of such brutalities and feel safe and satisfied because they are on the side of the authorities inflicting them. Readers of Revelation are spectators in the arena of the world, watching the slaughter and reveling in it. John, then, does not propose an alternative to Roman ideologies of violence

and dominance. He celebrates them, using them as a model for portraying the coming apocalypse.

9 I am not the only biblical scholar to see this as the message of Revelation (see the preceding note). In an important book on the problem with wealth in Revelation, for example, Robert Royalty points out that "the Apocalypse of John describes a wealthy God, a golden clad Messiah, and their angelic forces destroying an opulent trading city and rewarding their true and loyal followers with a city of gold and jewels." Royalty goes on to summarize the reality that "opposition to the dominant culture in the Apocalypse is not an attempt to redeem that culture but rather an attempt to replace it with a Christianized version of the same thing." In short, Revelation does not embrace distinctively Christian values but standard Roman values. Royalty, *The Streets of Heaven*, 29, 246. See also Frilingos, *Spectacles of Empire*, 2: "Far from being thoroughly critiqued and excluded, the values and institutions of ancient Rome left an indelible imprint upon the visions of the Apocalypse."

10 The widespread Christian idea that those who are heaven-bound will be given a "mansion" for all eternity makes a good deal of sense given the translation of John 14:1 in the King James Version: "In my Father's house there are many mansions." It should be obvious, though, that the word "mansion" does not mean the same thing now as it did for the 1611 translators. Just look at the English carefully: How can a *house* have many *mansions* inside it? The Greek word literally means something like "a place to stay." In a house, that would be a "bedroom"—even if it is large, spacious, and well decorated.

11 The one passage in the Gospels that explicitly indicates how Jesus and the disciples received funds to support themselves is Luke 8:1–3, where they are helped by three wealthy women: Johanna, Susanna, and Mary Magdalene. I am not at all certain, however, that the passage is historically accurate, since it suits so well Luke's interests to stress Jesus's close connection with

women followers. For what it's worth, it is also the only passage in the Gospels connected with Jesus's public ministry (that is, before the Passion narrative) that mentions Mary Magdalene.

12 For an authoritative discussion of the passage that takes the term "camel" seriously, see the magisterial commentary of Joel Marcus, *Mark 8–16*, Anchor Yale Bible (New Haven: Yale University Press, 2009), 730–40.

13 A translation can be found in Alexander Roberts and James Donaldson, eds., *Ante-Nicene Fathers*, vol. 2., revised by A. Cleveland Coxe (Peabody, MA: Hendrickson, 2004), 589–604.

14 Among other key passages, see also Luke 6:20–21, 24–25 (where Jesus praises the impoverished and hungry and condemns the wealthy and sated), and 16:19–21 (the parable of Lazarus and the rich man).

15 See my discussion of Mark's understanding of Jesus as the Messiah in Bart Ehrman, *The New Testament: A Historical Introduction to the Early Christian Writings*, 7th ed. (New York: Oxford University Press, 2020), 103–19.

16 There are a number of superb studies on this topic. See, for example, the classics by master scholars of late antiquity, such as Paul Veyne, *Bread and Circuses: Historical Sociology and Political Pluralism* (1976; London: Allen Lane, 1990), and Peter Brown, *Through the Eye of a Needle: Wealth, the Fall of Rome, and the Making of Christianity in the West, 350–550 AD* (Princeton, NJ: Princeton University Press, 2012). I have a shorter discussion, with a bibliography of other important books and articles, in Bart Ehrman, *Journeys to Heaven and Hell in the Early Christian Tradition* (New Haven, CT: Yale University Press, 2022), 99–124.

17 So, too, as we have seen, in ancient Israel. Remember the battle of Jericho and the slaughter and enslavement of the Midianites. See pp. 147–49.

18 It appears that most people lived in small towns and rural areas—some 80 percent of the population—and as a rule lived

in poverty. In the cities, only about 2 to 3 percent of the population had relative abundance. Another 5 to 10 percent or so enjoyed a moderate surplus above subsistence levels (merchants, traders, artisans, and others who made more than they had to spend to survive). Probably another 20 percent or so were fairly stable, without daily fear of want. See Steven Friesen, "Poverty in Pauline Studies: Beyond the So-Called New Consensus," *Journal for the Study of the New Testament* 26 (2004): 323–61.

19 See my discussion in *Journeys to Heaven and Hell* (pp. 99–124) and the bibliography I mention there. A particularly helpful article-length treatment is Peter Lampe, "Social Welfare in the Greco-Roman World as a Background for Early Christian Practice," *Acta Theologica* 23 (October 17, 2016): 1–28. Even the distribution of grain to the poor ("bread and circuses") was not out of a desire to provide assistance to those in need per se; it was to prevent riots and the disruption of the system.

20 As I explain in *Journeys to the Afterlife*, pp. 118–20.

21 See my discussion in Bart Ehrman, *The Triumph of Christianity* (New York: Simon & Schuster, 2018), 250–71.

EIGHT: The Apocalypse of John and the Gospel of Jesus

1 For a brief discussion of the formation of the canon, see my book *Lost Christianities: The Battles for Scripture and the Faiths We Never Knew* (New York: Oxford University Press, 2003), 229–46. For a fuller account, see Harry Gamble, *The New Testament Canon: Its Making and Meaning* (Philadelphia: Fortress, 1985).

2 My quotations of Eusebius come from the translation of G. A. Williamson, revised by Andrew Louth, *Eusebius: The History of the Church from Christ to Constantine* (New York: Penguin Books, 1989).

3 According to Eusebius, *Church History*, 3.28.1–4. See Craig Koester, *Revelation*, Anchor Yale Bible Commentaries (New Haven, CT: Yale University Press, 2015), 30–32.

4 The book was explicitly named as canonical in smaller venues, including the local Synod of Carthage in 396 CE. But the decision of the synod was not binding on anyone else.

5 On Jesus's view of annihilation, rather than eternal torture, see my discussion in Bart Ehrman, *Journeys to Heaven and Hell in the Early Christian Tradition* (New Haven, CT: Yale University Press, 2022), 147–68. In that discussion I deal with the one obvious exception of the parable of the rich man and Lazarus (Luke 16) and explain why it almost certainly was not spoken by Jesus himself.

6 Albert Schweitzer, *The Quest of the Historical Jesus*, ed. John Bowden (1906; Minneapolis: Fortress Press, 2001).

Index

Page numbers beginning with 209 refer to notes.

abomination, 43, 46, 129, 191–92, 194

Abraham, 59–60, 69, 70, 97, 98, 102, 112, 144

Acts of the Apostles, 17

Adam, 56, 69, 97

Adventists (Millerites), 76–83

Against Heresies (Irenaeus), 18, 52

Alaric I, King of the Visigoths, 56

A La Ronde, 63–64

Alexander I, Emperor of Russia, 65

Alexander the Great, 77, 116

America, as nation favored by God, 66–67

amillennialism, 218

Ammonites, 149

Amos, 149, 151

Amos, book of, 149, 152–53

Anabaptists, 222

angels, 30, 38, 44, 119, 121, 128, 162
  as intermediaries and explainers, 26, 27, 31, 43, 78, 114, 117, 118, 121, 135, 227
  as pouring out bowls of God's wrath, 41, 42, 161

Annals of Rome (Tacitus), 131

Antichrist, 2, 7, 13, 14, 24, 54, 59, 101–2, 136
  beast of the sea as, 41–42, 123, 181
  economy controlled by, 181

Antiochus Epiphanes, King of Syria, 115–19, 121, 225, 226

Apocalypse (Lawrence), 169–72

Apocalypse of Adam, 112

Apocalypse of John, *see* Revelation, book of

Apocalypse of Paul, 111

Apocalypse of Peter, 111

apocalypses (books), xviii, 27, 111–41, 225
  intermediaries in, 27, 120–21
  key features of, 119–20
  Shepherd of Hermas, 111, 225
  two forms of, 122
  written pseudonymously, 112, 120

apostles, 25, 29, 37, 51, 167, 196

Apostles' Creed, 211

Aquinas, Thomas, 9

Arab nations, 7

Aramaic, 115–16, 226

Ark of the Covenant, 54

Armageddon:
  Battle of, xvii, xix, 42–44, 71,
    101, 161, 163
  dates set for, 53, 54
  mountains of Megiddo as site
    of, 42
Arnold, Phillip, 86–87, 89
Artaxerxes, King of Persia, 78
asceticism, 57
Ashdod, 149
Ashkelon, 149
Ashley, Lord, 92–93
Asia Minor, 28
Assyrians, 97, 98, 151
Augustine, 9, 49–50, 56–58,
  65–66
Augustus, Emperor of Rome, 130,
  137, 180

Baal of Peor, 147–48
Babylon:
  Babylonian empire, 77–78, 97,
    99, 111, 112, 116, 129, 151,
    210–11
  fall of, 42–45, 56, 117, 158,
    171, 182
  FBI as, 89–90
  Rome as, 55, 140
Bainbridge, William Sims, 82–83
Balfour, Arthur, 93–94
Balfour Declaration, 94, 97–98
Barker, David, 106, 107
Barnabas, Epistle of, 53–54
Baruch, book of, 111
Baxter, Michael, 212
Bearce, David, 106, 107
beast, 24, 44, 101, 132–39, 161
  mark of, 41–42, 44, 99, 133,
    137, 181
  Nero as, 55
  number of, *see* 666

beast of the earth (second beast),
  137–40
beast of the sea (beast with seven
  heads; first beast), 41–43,
  61–62, 121, 123, 128–30,
  132–36, 181, 215, 225
  economy controlled by, 181
  as Rome, 131–33, 163, 166, 227
Begin, Menachem, 94
"Beginning and End of the
  Universe" conference, 106
Beginning of the End (Hagee), 95
Belshazzar, King of Babylon,
  113–19
Berthier, Louis-Alexandre, 62
Bible, xvii, 199
  evidence for rapture in, 3–4
  inerrancy of, xviii, 7–9, 73,
    209–10, 211
  King James, 24, 68–69, 129, 220
  literal interpretation of, 67, 73,
    128, 209–10
  ways to read, 16–18
  as written for its own time, 124
Bible Belt, 1
birds, feasting on flesh, 43,
  161–62, 163
Bjork-James, Sophie, 106
Book of Life, 44, 46, 191, 230
bottomless pit, 44, 56, 58
Boutelle, Luther, 80
bowls of wrath, seven, 41–42, 128,
  161, 162
Branch Davidians, 83–91, 230
bread and circuses, 234
Brown, Capability, 63
Bureau of Alcohol, Tobacco and
  Firearms, 86

Cage, Nicholas, 14
calendar, modern, 218

Caligula, Emperor of Rome, 137
Calvin, John, 9
Calvinism, 66, 222
camel, passing through the eye of a
needle, 176, 233
Camping, Harold, 20–21, 213
catastrophes, xix, 22, 39–42, 56,
71, 141, 159, 162, 229
Catholic Church, 24
Cerinthus, 197
charity, 188–90, 202–3, 205
chiliasts, 50–51, 57, 60–61
China, 7
Christ, 27, 89, 121, 170, 215,
216
as alpha and omega, 161
children killed by, 35–36,
165–66, 201
crucifixion of, 10, 97, 156,
209
divine nature of, 198
enemies destroyed by, xvii, xix,
10–11, 160–65
as first and last, 30, 33
genealogy of, 59–60
Jesus as one of several, 87–88
John's vision of, 30–31
judgment by, 3–4, 10–11, 123,
160–61, 168
as the Lamb, 38–39, 41, 45–46,
55, 83, 87–88, 99, 129, 159,
165, 206, 216
letters to churches in Asia as
"written" by, 33
as lion, 38, 160, 162
loving nature of, 167, 175, 206
marriage supper of, 163
as messiah, 184–86
miracles of, 184, 205
resurrection of, 33, 133, 185,
209

as ruling during the millennium,
56–58
as salvation, 70, 156, 167, 176,
200–201, 209
second coming of, *see* second
coming of Christ
as slave to all, 186–87
as the Son of Man, 3–4, 30, 42,
114, 118, 119, 160–62
teachings of, *see* Jesus, teachings
of
third coming of, 71–72
two-edged sword of, 30, 161,
163
viewed through ideological
preferences, 205–6
violence committed by, 35–36,
143–68
as Word of God, 161
wrath of, 159–62, 165–68, 206–7
Christianity:
as defined by fundamentalists,
211
dual nature of, 171
Christians:
born again, 5, 28, 209–10
charity and, 188–90, 202–3, 205
envy of, 170
fundamentalist, 2, 4, 8–9, 10,
12, 14, 25, 63, 68, 69, 134,
209–10, 211, 220–21
Old Testament and, 143–44
opinions on second coming, 105,
209
Pentecostal, 104
persecuted by Romans, 32–33,
40–41, 122–23, 131, 139,
172, 216
Protestant, 61
punished by God, xix
strong vs. weak, 171

Christians, evangelical, 1, 66,
  209–10
  and conversion of Jews to
    Christianity, 65
  dispensation premillennialism
    and, 73
  futuristic reading of Revelation
    by, xvii, xix, 99
  Netanyahu and, 94–95
  rapture and, 2, 14
  Zionism supported by, 92, 94–96
Christian Zionism, 62–65, 92–96,
  223
Chronicles, book of, 18
church, as bride of the Lamb, 43,
  163
churches in Asia, seven, 28, 30,
  31, 50
  letters written to, 31–36,
    121–22, 164, 214
  threatened by Christ, 34
Church History (Eusebius), 52, 196
circumcision, 116, 139
City of God, The (Augustine),
  56–58
Clement of Alexandria, 177
climate change, 21
  evangelical indifference to,
    102–6, 223–24
Codex Sinaiticus, 217
cognitive dissonance, 82, 221–22
Cohn, Norman, 20
Cold War, 74, 107
Confessions, The (Augustine), 56
context, literary and historical,
  xviii, 110, 123, 128, 140, 214
  in interpretation of scripture,
    10–13, 19, 25, 48, 152, 153
  Jesus in, 205–7
  of Revelation, xviii, 25, 27–28,
    50, 55, 109–41, 214

Corinthians, Paul's letters to, 11,
  34–35, 36, 215
Crossan, John Dominic, 155
Cyrus, King of Persia, 85, 87

Dallas Theological Seminary, 5–6
Damascus, 149
Daniel, book of, 3, 17, 23, 54,
  76–79, 111–19, 122, 210–11,
  215, 225, 226
  apocalyptic vision of Daniel 7,
    112–19, 160–61
  four beasts of, 113–15, 117, 118,
    119, 132, 133
  interpretation of, 115–19
  "little horn" in, 77, 79, 113–15,
    121
  retroactive prediction in, 118
  Revelation influenced by, 111
  Son of Man in, 30, 114, 132
Darby, John Nelson, 9, 67–72,
  77
Darwin, Charles, 219
Darwinism, 73
David, King of Israel, 38, 84, 85,
  87, 88, 98, 119
Davidian Seventh Day Adventists,
  84, 222
dead, rising up to heaven, 10, 13,
  44–45, 56–57
Dead Sea Scrolls, 230
Death, 30, 39, 44–45, 191
demons, 35, 42, 204, 215
Deuteronomistic History, 150–51
Deuteronomy, book of, 18, 146,
  150–51
Devil, *see* Satan
de Villiers, Pieter, 167
Dionysius, bishop of Alexandria,
  196–98
disasters, *see* catastophes

dispensational premillennialism, 65–71, 77, 220

dispensations, seven, 68–71, 220

Dome of the Rock, 6–7, 100–101, 102

domination, xx, 166, 170, 172, 206

in Revelation, 190–93, 199–200, 231–32

in Roman Empire, 187–90, 231–32

teachings of Jesus on, 183–87

Domitian, 32, 136

dragon, 133, 216

Du Mez, Kristin Kobes, 210

Dylan, Bob, 28

earth, age of, 53–55, 73

economic exploitation, 152

economy, as controlled by the beast/antichrist, 181

Eden, 69

Edom, Edomites, 147, 149

Edwards, Jonathan, 8, 66

Egypt, 70, 98, 116, 137, 147

Ehrman, Bart D. (author), religious background and education of, xviii–xix, 1, 5, 68

88 Reasons Why the Rapture Is in 1988 (Whisenant), 3–4

elders, 29, 37, 38, 180

11:59 . . . And Counting! (Van Impe), 213

Elijah, 112, 184

Elisha, 145–46

Enlightenment, 205

Enoch, 111, 112

Environmental Protection Agency, 103

Ephesus, church in, 28

Episcopalians, 5

eschatology, 18, 61, 64, 65, 82–83, 105, 230

ethics, 156, 188

European Commonwealth, 7

European Union, 136

Eusebius, 51, 52, 196

Eve, 69

Exodus, book of, 54, 147

expectations, frustrated, 81–83

Expositions of the Sayings of the Lord (Papias), 51

Ezekiel, book of, 17, 37, 98–99, 100, 151, 215

Ezra, book of, 78, 111

false predictions, of second coming, 1–22, 55, 60, 61–62, 75–84, 210–13

False Prophet, 41, 44, 121, 139, 163

false teachings, 32, 34–35

Falwell, Jerry, 94–95

FBI, 83–91

as Babylon, 89–90

feet, washing of, 186–87

Festinger, Leon, 81–82

fig tree:

parable of, 3–4, 6

as symbol of Israel, 4

Final Battle, *see* Armageddon, Battle of

final judgment, xix, 2, 55–56, 70–71, 123, 191, 200, 201, 230

flood narrative, 13, 69, 73, 97

Foreign Office, British, 65

foreign policy, 21, 62–65

fornication, *see* sexual immorality, sexual imagery

forth-tellers, foretellers, 151–52

Franciscan monks, 60

French Revolution, 61, 64
Frilingos, Christopher, 172
Frykholm, Amy Johnson, 14, 212
futuristic reading of Revelation,
    xvii, xix, 1–8, 15, 50, 55–57,
    61–74, 75–108, 122–28,
    211
  environment and, 102–6
  fatal flaw in, 124–28
  French Revolution and, 61
  Israel and, 91–102
  political effects of, 6, 75–108,
    212
  rise of, 61–74
  violent effects of, 83–91, 167,
    222, 230

Gabriel, angel, 78
Gandhi, Mahatma, 162
Gaza, 149
gematria, 135
Genesis, book of, 38, 96–97, 105,
    144–45, 217
gentiles, 85, 131
George III, King of England, 65
Germany, 93–94
  "historical criticism" of Bible in,
    73
Gnostics, 18
God, 27, 121
  as "Ancient One" or "Ancient of
    Days," 114–15
  blessing of Israelites by, 150–51
  children killed by, 145–46, 149,
    150
  contemplation of, 59–60
  destruction of enemies by, 40,
    120, 122, 123, 146, 149,
    160–65, 229–30
  jealousy of, 147
  love demanded by, 146, 179

  loving nature of, xix, 144, 146,
    155, 167–68, 179
  mercy of, 36, 106, 140, 141,
    168
  in Old vs. New Testaments,
    145–46, 155
  "proof" of existence of, 157
  punishing of Israelites by,
    148–55
  seal of, 99, 100, 126
  throne room of, 37, 160, 179–81
  violence encouraged by, 158–59
  worshipped by all creation, 37,
    39, 45
  wrath of, 21–22, 36, 41, 42,
    141, 144, 146–55, 161,
    165–68, 229
gods, 56, 123, 149, 153–54, 215
golden lampstands, 30–31, 33
Good Samaritan, 202–3
Gorbachev, Mikhail, 134
Gospel of Climate Skepticism, The
    (Veldman), 223–24
Graham, Billy, 174
Great Awakening (1740s), 66
Great Depression, 74
Great Disappointment, 76–80
Greece, ancient:
  culture and religion of, 115–16
  empire of, 77, 117
Greek language, 26–27, 133–35,
    197–98, 214, 216
greenhouse gases, 105

Hades, 30, 39, 44–45, 191
Hagee, John, 95
Hale, Ezekiel Jr., 80
heaven, apocalypses and visions of,
    40, 111–14, 120, 122
Hebrew language, 26, 42, 115–16,
    134–35, 146

Hebrews, book of, 26, 30, 199, 213
Hechler, William, 93
helicopters, 126–27
Hellenization, 116, 117, 121, 122, 225
Heretics, 146, 196–97
Herod the Great, King of Israel, 218
Herzl, Theodore, 93
Hippolytus of Rome, 52–55, 195
"Historical Roots of Our Ecological Crisis, The" (White), 104–5
history, three ages of, 59–60
Holocaust, 95
horsemen of the Apocalypse, 39
Hosea, book of, 151, 153–54, 164
House of Representatives, US, Interior and Insular Affairs Committee of, 104
Houteff, Florence, 84, 222
Houteff, Victor, 84
Howell, Vernon, *see* Koresh, David
human sacrifice, 148
humility, 183–84
Hussein, Saddam, 134

Interior Department, US, 103
intertemporal choice, 107
Irenaeus, 9, 18, 51, 52, 195
Isaiah, book of, 18, 38, 84, 98, 151, 152
Islam, 100–101
Israel, 7, 64, 77, 97–98, 102, 116, 118, 119, 216, 225
  destroyed by Assyrians, 151
  in Epistle of Barnabas, 53
  Promised Land of, 92, 98–99, 100, 144, 147, 150
  punished by God, 97, 152–53
  reestablished as sovereign state, 4, 64–65, 92, 97–98, 100
  second century destruction of, 4, 92
  sojourn in the Wilderness, 147
  temple destroyed in, 43, 77–78, 92, 97, 99, 130, 210
  temple to be rebuilt in, 7, 78, 92, 99, 100, 102
  twelve patriarchs of, 29, 37
  US policy on, 91–102

Jacob, 98
James, book of, 199, 213
Jeffress, Robert, 95
Jehovah's Witnesses, 83
Jenkins, Jerry B., 14
Jeremiah, book of, 64, 117, 151, 152
Jericho, Battle of, 144, 155, 233
Jerusalem, 6–7, 43, 45, 78, 92, 97, 100–102, 130
  new, 45, 71, 140, 171, 180–81, 191–92, 194, 222
  US embassy moved to, 95
Jesus:
  in historical context, 158, 205–7
  see also Christ
Jesus, teachings of:
  compared with those of John of Patmos, xix–xx, 166–68, 193–94, 199–207
  on fate of sinners, 203–4
  on love, xx, 141, 201, 202–3, 205, 245
  on "lukewarm" Christians, 32, 36, 157
  Sermon on the Mount, 144, 173, 228
  on taxes, 178–79
  on wealth, 173–79, 233

Jesus and John Wayne (Du Mez), 210

Jewish State, The, 93

Jews, 33, 36, 40, 53, 59–60, 63, 97, 122, 131, 144–45, 146, 163–64, 178–79, 190, 202, 225
  Babylonian Captivity of, 115–16
  Christian missionaries' attempted conversion of, 65
  exodus of, 70
  God's covenant with, 97–100, 222
  and Imperial Cults, 138–39
  persecuted by Antiochus Epiphanes, 115–18
  return to Holy Land by, 64–65, 78, 92–96, 99
  salvation of, 144

Jezebel, 35–36, 164–65

jigsaw puzzle approach to scripture, 17–19, 25, 128

Joachim of Fiore, 58–61, 68

Joel, 151

Joel, book of, 17

Johanna, 232–33

John, apostle, 29, 51–52, 195–97, 199, 200, 214

John, Gospel of, 186–87, 200, 214, 216

John of Patmos, xvii, xix–xx, 28–32, 111, 159, 170, 215, 225, 226, 230
  teachings compared with those of Jesus, xix–xx, 166–68, 193–94, 199–207
  tribulation of, 29
  use of pseudonym rejected by, 112
  visions of, 28, 30–31, 37, 121, 125, 160–61, 179–81
  writing style of, 26–27, 196–98, 214

John Paul, Pope, 134

John the Baptist, 184, 230

Jordan River, 147

Joshua, 144, 145, 147, 228

Joshua, book of, 145, 150–51, 155

Judah, 38, 43, 97, 98, 99, 111, 130, 151, 160, 210
  destroyed by Romans, 98

Judaism, charity and, 189

Jude, book of, 199, 213

Judea, *see* Judah

judgment, by Christ, 3–4, 10–11, 123, 160–61, 168

Judges, book of, 42

Julius Caesar, 137

King, Martin Luther, Jr., 162

King James Bible, 24, 68–69, 129, 220

Kings, book of, 35, 42, 145–46, 150–51

Koresh, David, 83–91
  as "sinful messiah," 88

kosher food laws, 139

LaHaye, Timothy, 14, 102

lake of burning fire, xix, 22, 33, 44, 46, 57, 156, 157, 165, 171, 181, 191

lampstands, seven, 31, 33

Laodicea, church in, 28

Late Great Planet Earth, The (Lindsey), 5–8, 124

"lawless one," 101

Law of Moses, 53

Lawrence, D. H., 169–72

Lazarus, 233, 235

Lee, Robert E., 68

Leeds Mercury, 63

Left Behind series (LaHaye and Jenkins), 14, 63
Letters (Pliny), 139
Leviticus, book of, 17, 146, 147, 210–11
Life of the Divine Augustus (Suetonius), 130, 180
Lindsey, Hal, 5–8, 17–18, 20, 102, 124–28
locusts, 124–27, 153, 157, 228, 229
    attack helicopters as, 126–27
London Society for Promoting Christianity among the Jews, 65, 92
Lord's supper, 36
love:
    of Christ for humankind, 167, 175, 206
    demanded by God, 146, 179
    of God for his people, xix, 144, 146, 155, 167–68, 179
    Jesus's teachings on, xx, 141, 201, 202–3, 205, 245
Luke, Gospel of, 17, 26, 201, 203, 218, 232–33
    Good Samaritan in, 202–3
Luther, Martin, 9, 24, 61, 199, 213

MacArthur, John, 106
Maccabees, books of, 116, 118–19, 225
Marcion, 145
Marcus Aurelius, 188
Mark, Gospel of, 175–79, 184–86, 200–201, 203
    camel passing through a needle's eye in, 176, 233
martyrs, 33, 39, 40–41, 44, 56–57, 131, 140, 165, 191, 216, 229

Mary Magdalene, 232–33
masculine values, 210
mass murder, 147–49
materialism, 51–52, 57, 166, 170–72, 173–79, 189, 195, 197–200, 206, 231–32
Matthew, Gospel of, 3, 12, 17, 59–60, 72, 135, 173, 186, 201, 204, 218
    on materialism, 173–75, 183
    parable of fig tree in, 3–4, 6
    parable of sheep and goats in, 201–2, 203
    Sermon on the Mount in, 144, 173, 228
Medes, 77, 117
Mediterranean Sea, 113
Megiddo, 42
Melanchthon, Philip, 9
messiah, 38, 85, 119, 151, 184–86
    David Koresh as "sinful messiah," 88
    see also Christ
metaphors, mixed, 38
Michael, angel, 119
Middle Ages, 9, 20, 91, 190, 218
Middle East, peace in, 7
Midianites, 147–48, 155, 233
millennium, 44, 52, 54, 56–58, 66, 198–99
Miller, William, 76–80
Millerites, or Adventists, 76–83
miracles, 37, 41, 167, 184, 205
missionaries, 29, 65, 167
Moab, Moabites, 147, 149
modernism, 219
Moody, Dwight Lyman, 68
Moody Bible Institute, 5, 68
Moody Church, 68
morality, 156–58
"Moral Majority," 94

Moses, 54, 70, 147–49
  laws of, 53, 70, 116
Mount Sinai, 147
multivalence, of symbols, 132, 135
Mussolini, Benito, 134

Nahum, book of, 18
Napoleon I, Emperor of the French, 62, 64
narcissism, 91
nationalism, 206, 210
Nebuchadnezzar II, King of Babylon, 210
Nero, 32, 131, 216
  666 and, 135–36
"Nero redivivus," 136
New Testament, 144–46, 155, 175, 225
  Revelation accepted into, xvii, 121, 155–56, 195–99
Nicene Creed, 211
Noah, 69, 97
nonviolent resistance, 38–39, 159, 161, 167, 206
Norman, Larry, 13
North Carolina University at Chapel Hill, 1, 26, 134
nuclear war, 2, 7, 74, 107, 125
number of the beast, *see* 666
Numbers, book of, 36, 147–51, 155

Octavius, *see* Augustus, Emperor of Rome
Old Testament, 143–51
  John of Patmos's allusions to, 215
  seven seals and, 55–56
Origen, 9
Oxford University Press, 68

pagan idols, food offered to, 34–36, 164–65, 215
pagans, paganism, 33, 34–36, 85, 121, 138, 163–65, 190, 215
Palestine, 64, 93–94, 96, 97, 102
Pantokrator, 192–93
Papias, 51–52
Paris Agreement, 105
Parminter, Jane and Mary, 64
Patmos, 28–29
  see also John of Patmos
Paul, apostle, 9–13, 34–35, 101, 170, 215, 230
peace on earth, thousand year period of, 2, 50–51, 57, 198
Pergamum, church in, 28
persecution, 32–33, 40–41, 115–18, 122, 131, 139, 172, 216
Persians, 77–78, 116, 117
Peter:
  apostle, 177–78, 184–85
  book of, 53, 76
Philadelphia, church in, 28, 87, 124
Philistines, 149
Phinehas, 148
Pius VI, Pope, 62
plagues, 147–48
Pliny the Younger, 139
Plutarch, 188
Plymouth Brethren, 67–68, 72
polytheistic religions, 138
pope, as beast of the sea, 24, 61–62
pork, 53, 116
postmillennialism, 66, 73, 218
power, *see* domination
predictions:
  retroactive, 118
  of second coming, 1–22, 55, 60, 61–62, 75–83, 212–13

see also futuristic reading of
  Revelation
premillennialism, 67–71, 218
proof-texting, 18
Prosperity Gospel, 182–83
Protestant Reformation, 24, 199
Protestants, 61, 65–66, 209–10
Psalms, book of, 53, 88–89,
  192–93

Quest of the Historical Jesus, The
  (Schweitzer), 205

Rahab, 228
rape, 165
rapture, 2, 20–21
  1830s origins of, 9
  of 1988, 3–4
  Christians taken in, 7
  commercial success of, 13–14
  invented by Darby, 71–72, 77
  popular belief in, 2–3, 72–73
  "secret," 72
  and text of Bible, 9–13
Rapture Culture (Frykholm), 212
rationalism, 205
Reagan, Ronald, 6, 103, 109
resurrections:
  first, 44
  of martyrs of Christ, 44, 57,
    185
  spiritual vs. physical, 57–58
retribution, 40, 159, 160
Revelation, book of:
  accepted into New Testament,
    xvii, 121, 155–56, 195–99
  author of, *see* John of Patmos
  curse to prevent alterations in,
    46
  cyclical nature of, 162
  domination in, 190–93

early interpretations of, 50–56
futuristic reading of, *see* futuristic
  reading of Revelation
Greek writing style of, 26–27,
  196–98, 214, 216
intermediaries in, 27, 120–21
jigsaw puzzle approach to,
  17–19, 25, 128
Koresh's interpretation of,
  83–91
literal reading of, xviii–xix,
  50–52, 57, 103, 128
Luther and, 24–25, 199
as metaphor, xvii–xviii, 166–68
rapture and, 9
scribes and, 23–24
2 Thessalonians and, 101–2
social and cultural effects of, 21,
  75–108
spiritualized reading of, 49–50,
  56–58, 65–66, 198–99
as story of hope, xvii–xviii, xix,
  xx, 61, 74, 166, 172
summary of, 26–47
symbols in, 23, 31, 50, 121–23,
  132–34, 166–68, 217, 225
viewed as forgery, 195–97
viewed as metaphor, 49–50
violence in, 21–22, 143–68, 172,
  199–200, 228–29
wealth in, 179–83
wrath and vengeance in, xix–xx,
  40, 159, 160–62, 165, 166,
  168, 170, 172, 204, 229,
  230
Riecken, Henry W., 81–82
rock music, Christian, 13
Roden, Benjamin, 84, 87
Roden, Lois, 84
Romans, Paul's letters to, 3, 17, 34,
  100, 215

Rome, Roman Empire, 62, 97,
99, 121, 122–23, 130–32,
140, 178–79, 180–81, 183,
200–201, 226–27
as beast, 131–33, 163, 166
bread and circuses in, 234
dominance and, 187–90,
231–32
envied by Christians, 170, 172
fall of, 56
false gods of, 56, 123
great fire of, 131
Imperial Cults in, 137–39
as new Babylon, 130, 159
"spectacles" in, 231–32
Romulus, 137
Roots of Fundamentalism, The
(Sandeen), 212
Rosh Hashanah, 2
Rothschild, Lionel Walter, 94
Russia, 7, 109
Rutgers University, 1

Sabbath, observation of, 53–54,
83–84
saints, 44, 46, 50–52, 54, 61, 99,
133, 166, 171, 180, 182, 183,
192, 198, 225
blood of, 43, 129, 131
salvation:
behavior vs. belief and, 201–5
through Christ, 70, 156, 167,
176, 200–201, 209
Samaria, 153
Samuel, book of, 150–51
Sandeen, Ernest R., 61, 212
Sardis, church in, 28
Satan, 33, 36, 44, 56–58, 133,
140, 159, 181, 185
as dragon, 133, 216
Synagogue of, 163–64

Schachter, Stanley, 81–82
Schweitzer, Albert, 205
Scofield, Cyrus I., 68–69
Scofield Reference Bible, 68–71,
219
scorpions, 126, 156
scrolls, 37–39, 83, 160
sea, symbolism of, 117
seals, seven, 38, 39–42, 55–56, 83,
159, 160, 216
Koresh and, 87–90
second coming of Christ, 66, 96,
102, 105–8, 123
American beliefs about, 14–15,
209
day and hour of, as
unpredictable, 21, 72, 74, 79
false predictions of, 1–22, 55,
60, 61–62, 75–84, 210–13
as perpetually imminent, 47–48,
56, 60, 61–62, 75–80, 103–8
second death, for humans, 44
Seneca, 188
Sermon on the Mount, 144, 173,
228
Sermons (Augustine), 56
service, xx, 32, 184–90, 193, 201
washing of feet and, 186–87
seven, significance of, in the Bible,
41, 227
Seventh-day Adventists, 83–84
sexual immorality, sexual imagery,
34, 35, 43, 128, 130, 147,
152–54, 164, 181–82
Shema, 146
Shepherd of Hermas, 111, 225
Sibylline Oracles, 136
sickle, carried by Christ, 162–63
Sierra Club, 103
Signs of the Times (Van Impe),
212–13

"Sinners in the Hands of an Angry God" (Edwards), 8, 66
666, 24, 41, 132–36, 226–27
slavery, 149, 150, 152, 184, 186–87, 188, 189
slaves, of God, xix, 27–28, 46, 99, 157, 162, 168, 180, 181, 183, 192
Slemrod, Joel, 107
Smyrna, church in, 28
Son of Man:
    as angel, 119
    Christ as, 3–4, 30, 42, 114, 118, 119, 160–62
Soviet Union, 7
Stark, Rodney, 82–83
stars, seven, 30, 31, 33
Suetonius, 130, 180
suffering, explanation of, 120, 122, 186
Sunday, as the Lord's day, 29–30
Susanna, 232–33
sword, two-edged, of Christ, 30, 161, 163, 201
symbolism, 4, 23, 31, 50, 117, 121–23, 132–34, 166–68
    multivalence of, 132, 135
Synagogue, of Satan, 163–64
Syria, 115–16, 117, 118, 122, 149

Tabor, James, 86–87, 89, 222
Tacitus, 131
taxes, Jesus on, 178–79
Temple Mount, 6, 92, 100–101, 102
ten, significance of, in apocalyptic texts, 117
Ten Commandments, 54
Tertullian, 9
Thessalonians, Paul's letters to, 9–13, 100–102

Thief in the Night, A, 13, 14
Thompson, Frank Charles, 220
Thompson Reference Bible, 220
three, significance of, in the Bible, 41
Thyatira, church in, 28, 35, 164, 192
Tiberius, Emperor of Rome, 137
torture, xix, 116, 125–27, 156, 157, 159, 165, 166, 167, 203–4, 206, 229
    destruction vs., for sinners, 203–4, 235
Trajan, Emperor of Rome, 139
tree of life, 46
Trinity, 59, 84
triumphalism, xviii, 27, 38–39, 120, 122, 141, 166, 171–72, 229
Trump, Donald, 134
Trump administration, 95
trumpets, 10, 41, 42, 125, 145, 162
Turkey, 28, 51
Tyre, 149

UFO cults, 81–82
Ussher, James, 217–18
utopian kingdom for the saved, 2, 50, 51–52, 59, 200

Van Impe, Jack, 17–18, 102, 212
Vatican, 62
Veldman, Robin Globus, 103–4, 223–24
vengeance, xx, 40, 159, 160–62, 165, 166, 168, 170, 172, 204, 206, 229, 230
Victorinus of Pettau, 40, 55–56, 123, 134, 195
Vietnam war, 127

Vigilius, Pope, 62
violence, xx, 21–22, 42, 83–91,
    143–68, 172, 190, 199–200,
    222
virgins, 149
Visigoths, 56, 62

Waco, Tex., 83–91
war, xix, 22, 42, 159, 161, 229
Watt, James, 103–4
Way, John, 63
Way, Lewis, 63–65, 92
wealth:
    divine vs. demonic, 181
    in Revelation, 179–83
    teachings of Jesus on, 173–79,
        233
Weaver, James, 104
Weinberger, Caspar, 6
Weizmann, Chaim, 93
"What Rich Man Can Be Saved?"
    (Clement of Alexandria), 177
When Prophecy Fails (Festinger,
    Riecken, and Schachter),
    81–82

Whisenant, Edgar, 2–3, 6, 17,
    19–20, 77, 210–11
White, Ellen G., 83
White, Lynn, 104–5
Whore of Babylon, 43–44, 121,
    128–32, 181–82, 216, 227
    as caricature of Rome, 132
wine press, for the wrath of God,
    42, 161–63
world, age of, 54, 217–18
World War I, 73–74, 93
World War II, 74
worship:
    of God, 37, 39, 45, 168, 183
    of other gods, 56, 123, 149,
        153–54, 215

Y2K, 217
"You've Been Left Behind," 13

Zacchaeus, 203
Zechariah, book of, 3, 17, 84
Zionism, *see* Christian Zionism
Zionist Congress, First (1897),
    93

About the Author

BART D. EHRMAN is the *New York Times* bestselling author or editor of more than thirty books, including *Misquoting Jesus*, *How Jesus Became God*, *The Triumph of Christianity*, and *Heaven and Hell*. A professor of religious studies at the University of North Carolina, Chapel Hill, and a leading authority on the New Testament and the history of early Christianity, he has been featured in *Time*, the *New Yorker*, and the *Washington Post*, and has appeared on NBC, CNN, *The Daily Show with Jon Stewart*, the History channel, the National Geographic channel, BBC, major NPR shows, and other top print and broadcast media outlets.